Inseparable

Desire Between Women in Literature

EMMA DONOGHUE

PICADOR

First published 2010 as a Borzoi Book by Alfred A. Knopf,
a division of Random House, Inc., New York,
and in Canada by Random House of Canada Limited, Toronto

First published in Great Britain in paperback 2013 by Picador
an imprint of Pan Macmillan, a divsion of Macmillan Publishers Limited
Pan Macmillan, 20 New Wharf Road, London N1 9RR
Basingstoke and Oxford
Associated companies throughout the world
www.panmacmillan.com

ISBN 978-1-4472-4817-0

1 3 5 7 9 8 6 4 2

A CIP catalogue record for this book is available from the British Library.

Printed and bound by CPI Group (UK) Ltd, Croydon, CR0 4YY

Visit **www.picador.com** to read more about all our books
and to buy them. You will also find features, author interviews and
news of any author events, and you can sign up for e-newsletters
so that you're always first to hear about our new releases.

Inseparable

Born in 1969, Emma Donoghue is an Irish writer who spent eight years in England before moving to Canada. Her fiction includes *Slammerkin*, *Life Mask*, *Touchy Subjects*, *The Sealed Letter* and the international bestseller *Room* (shortlisted for the Man Booker and Orange prizes).

For more information, go to www.emmadonoghue.com.

ALSO BY EMMA DONOGHUE

Astray

Room

The Sealed Letter

Landing

Touchy Subjects

Life Mask

The Woman Who Gave Birth to Rabbits

Slammerkin

Kissing the Witch: Old Tales in New Skins

Hood

Stir-fry

Dedicated to my remarkable mother,

Frances Donoghue,

who has never asked me to put down a book

and do something useful.

Contents

ILLUSTRATIONS

Inseparable

Introduction

WHEN I WAS A SMALL CHILD I read fairy tales. I carried straining plastic bags of them home from the library every Saturday: Grimm, Perrault, Hans Christian Andersen, *Arabian Nights*, Br'er Rabbit, Celtic myths, Polish folktales, Italian ones, Japanese, Greek . . . Soon I started spotting repetitions. It thrilled me to detect the same basic shape (for instance, the motif of the *selkie*, or wife from the sea) under many different, exotic costumes. When I announced my discovery to my father, he broke it to me gently that others had got there first: a Russian called Vladimir Propp, and before him a Finn called Antti Aarne, who published his system of classifying folk motifs back in 1910. Ah well. This disappointment taught me, even more than the fairy tales had, that there is nothing new under the sun.

I remained a greedy reader, and when I found myself falling for a girl, at fourteen, I began seeking out stories of desire between women. The first such title I spent my hoarded pocket money on was a truly grim Dutch novel first published in 1975, Harry Mulisch's *Twee Vrouwen* (in English, *Two Women*). Sylvia leaves Laura for Laura's ex-husband, Alfred—but, it turns out, only to get pregnant. The two women are blissfully reunited for a single evening of planning the nursery decor before Alfred turns up and shoots Sylvia dead, leaving Laura to jump out a window. Shaken but not dissuaded, I read on, for the next twenty years and counting. You would be forgiven for thinking that my book list must have been rather short. But the paradox is that writers in English and other Western languages have been speaking about this so-called unspeakable subject for the best part of a millennium.

What I am offering now in *Inseparable* is a sort of map. It charts a territory of literature that, like all undiscovered countries, has been there all along. This territory is made up of a bewildering variety of landscapes, but I will be following half a dozen distinct paths through it. Despite a suggestion in the *New York Times* in 1941 that the subject of desire between women should be classified as "a minor subsidiary of tragedy," in fact it turns up across the whole range of genres. Reading my way from medieval romance to Restoration comedy to the modern novel, mostly in English (but often in French, and sometimes in translations from Latin, Italian, Spanish, or German), I uncover the most perennially popular plot motifs of attraction between women. Here they are, in a nutshell.

TRAVESTIES: Cross-dressing (whether by a woman or a man) causes the "accident" of same-sex desire.

INSEPARABLES: Two passionate friends defy the forces trying to part them.

RIVALS: A man and a woman compete for a woman's heart.

MONSTERS: A wicked woman tries to seduce and destroy an innocent one.

DETECTION: The discovery of a crime turns out to be the discovery of same-sex desire.

OUT: A woman's life is changed by the realization that she loves her own sex.

At this point you may wonder, are the women in these plays, poems, and fictions lesbians? Not necessarily, is how I would begin to answer. But perhaps we are better off postponing that question until we have asked more interesting ones. In the first five of my six chapters, I will be

Anne-Louis Girodet de Roussy-Trioson (better known as Girodet-Trioson), "Songe de Sapho"
[Sappho's Dream], engraved by Henri-Guillaume Châtillon, in Sappho, Bion, Moschus.
Receuil de compositions dessinées par Girodet *[1827] (1829).*
    This is the third of the French Romantic painter's designs in the "antique vase" style to
accompany his translations from Sappho. They were published three years after Girodet's
death by his student, friend, and executor, Marie-Philippe Coupin de la Couperie, who
claimed that this image showed Sappho in the arms of the goddess Venus, dreaming of her
ideal husband.

looking at relations between women, rather than the more historically
recent issue of self-conscious sexual orientation. Although I occasionally say *lesbian* as shorthand, the twenty-first-century use of that word as
a handy identity label does not begin to do justice to the variety of
women's bonds in literature from the 1100s to the 2000s. The past is a
wild party; check your preconceptions at the door.

It is customary to lament the fact that desire between women, before
the twentieth century, was one long silence. After all, everyone has
heard the story about Queen Victoria, whose ministers wanted to make
lesbian sex illegal in 1885 but could not bring themselves to explain to
her that it was even possible . . . Except that it turns out that never happened. (Dating from 1977, the Victoria story is a popular urban myth

that allows us to feel more knowledgeable and daring than our nineteenth-century ancestors.) On the contrary, literary researchers over the past few decades have unearthed a very long history of what Terry Castle calls "the lesbian idea"; her eleven-hundred-page anthology *The Literature of Lesbianism* (2003)—by far the best available—can only sample the riches.

In writing *Inseparable*, I have had to be very selective. A hint or a glimpse does not constitute a plot motif: I include only texts in which the attraction between women is undeniably there. It must also be more than a moment; it must have consequences for the story. The emotion can range from playful flirtation to serious heartbreak, from the exaltedly platonic to the sadistically lewd, but in every case it has to make things happen.

Take, for instance, "The Man of Law's Tale," the fifth of the *Canterbury Tales* (1400) by courtier and diplomat Geoffrey Chaucer. It tells how Custance, daughter of a Christian Roman emperor and bride of the sultan of Syria, is cast adrift in a boat through her mother-in-law's machinations. Shipwrecked on the Northumberland coast, Custance immediately arouses the protective passion of Dame Hermengyld, the constable's wife: "Hermengyld loved hire as hir lyf." Over months of prayers and tears, Custance wins Hermengyld from paganism to Christianity, and Hermengyld manages to cure a blind man in the name of Jesus—which prompts her husband to convert too. But a knight whom Custance has rejected is jealous of the women's closeness; he sneaks into the room where they are sleeping together and slits Hermengyld's throat, leaving the bloody knife beside Custance to frame her for murder. The people are not fooled by this circumstantial evidence, since they have witnessed the women's relationship with their own eyes: "For they han seyn hir evere so vertuous, / And lovyng Hermengyld right as hir lyf." (For they have seen Custance be virtuous all the time, and love Hermengyld as her life.) The people's suspicion is confirmed by divine intervention: as the knight tells his lies in court, his eyeballs suddenly drop out of his head. This is an excellent example, perhaps the earliest in English, of how a mutual passion between two women can be not just an ornamental extra, but what moves the story along.

Because of the time frame I have chosen, most of the texts discussed in *Inseparable* are by British or French men. For the purposes of this book, I do not much care who wrote them, nor why. What interests me is the stories themselves, and the ways they connect. Though love between women can be found in some medieval romances, it was in the sixteenth century that it really moved into the spotlight, and from that point on it has taken up more and more space, growing from a mere theme into a literary tradition of its own.

But as traditions go, it is a peculiar one. One reason is that—if I may state the obvious—lesbian storylines begin with two or more *women,* rather than a man and a woman. This means that gender roles are up for grabs. Those who write about love between the sexes, from the book of Genesis on, have relied on a certain consensus about the differences between husband and wife, say, or lover and mistress, or rake and ingénue. Even if they bend those hallowed cultural rules, they are playing a familiar game. And those who write about love between men—although the subject is fraught with danger—have the classical past to draw on, and especially the Platonic ideal of the older male lover/mentor and the beautiful young beloved/protégé. Those who write about love between women have no such agreed starting point.

Here, for instance, is the moment in Mary McCarthy's *The Group* (1963) when Lakey's old college friends fret over the fact that she has come home with a female lover.

> On the one hand, there were Lakey-and-Maria, as you might say Polly-and-Jim, a contented married pair; on the other, there was an exquisite captive of a fierce robber woman, locked up in a Castle Perilous, and woe to the knight who came to release her from the enchantment. But it was possible to see it the other way around. Supposing it were Lakey, the inscrutable, intelligent Lakey, who had made poor Maria, who was not very bright, her slave? The fact that it was possible to reverse the relation like an hourglass was what the girls found so troubling.

If this easily flipped "hourglass" was still a puzzle in the 1960s, how much more so in the 1100s. Perhaps this is one reason the theme has aroused the interest of so many writers, who, like Lakey's friends, find the notion of desire between women a lasting source of wonder and fantasy, as well as anxiety.

Another oddity of this literary tradition is that it includes as much denial or coyness as assertion. I picture this literature as an archipelago: thousands of stories, but scattered like islands in little pools of silence. Interestingly, you might expect that the earlier texts would be veiled, and the later ones explicit—but I have found that erotic situations between women are sometimes presented frankly in medieval or Renaissance romance, whereas well into the twentieth century many novelists evoke passion with the discreet vocabulary of friendship.

Passion between women has never had a settled status in Western culture, or even a definition with fixed parameters. Right through the hymns of praise to noble love between ladies crash discordant rants against lust between wicked females. In every generation, it seems, writers have asked themselves whether desire between women is un-precedented or omnipresent, holy or evil, heartwarming or ridiculous. No matter how often it is written about, it remains somehow unoffi-cial, lurking below the radar: an unsolvable puzzle, a perpetual nov-elty. Unlike say, flowers, or food, or the weather, this subject could be extremely tricky for writers. Queen Victoria—myths aside—probably knew more or less what could go on between women, but that does not mean that the subject was a safe one in her time, or before, or after. In 1921, twenty years after her death, the House of Lords did defeat an attempt to add lesbianism to the law against male homosex-uality; the peers feared to "advertise" this vice by naming it. Quite a few of the books and plays I discuss in *Inseparable* were censored, sup-pressed, or prosecuted in their day. And even if there were no legal consequences for writers who tackled this subject, there was always the risk of mystifying or outraging part of their audience.

So what did they do, these men (and eventually women) of the scribbling tribe, who were troubled or intrigued by the idea of passion between women, but unsure how to shape it into a story, and wary of how people might take it? They looked over their shoulders. They relied heavily on their reading (either of their contemporaries or of ancient sources), whether by copying without scruple, self-consciously echoing a name or a speech from a previous work, borrowing aspects of several different storylines to make something new, confirming or countering or defying previous literary models.

Being a novelist and playwright by trade, I say this by experience as much as observation: writers like old plots because they work, and for all our claims of originality, we do a lot of recycling. If all writing is intertextual, writing about desire between women—because of its controversial status—has been particularly so.

So *Inseparable* could also be called a family tree, because it lays out certain motifs that have been repeated over the centuries, hybridizing and mutating in every generation. Or you could think of it as a field guide to the flora and fauna of lesbian-themed literature. It calls attention to what is there, but generally goes unnoticed, and reveals how the rare is related to the common-or-garden variety.

Which begs the question, if literature has been full of the theme of women in love for so many centuries, then why has it so often gone unnoticed? Why is desire between women still generally presumed to be a late-twentieth-century theme?

Some of the texts I look at here have been forgotten because they did not reach many readers in the first place, or because, although popular in their day, they have long since dropped out of circulation. But given that this tradition includes such canonical authors as Chaucer, Shakespeare, Sidney, Richardson, Rousseau, Johnson, Diderot, Dickens, Balzac, Charlotte Brontë, Wilkie Collins, Maupassant, Hardy, James, and Lawrence—given that, as Terry Castle puts it, "virtually every author of note since the Renaissance has written something, somewhere, touching on the subject of love between women"—how can we have collectively forgotten it, let it slip out of the history of ideas, or not registered it in the first place?

Writers must bear some of the responsibility. Very often they break a same-sex story up and scatter the pieces across a longer narrative, or limit the story to the subplot where it will attract less attention. Judith Roof argues, of Sigmund Freud's "Three Essays on the Theory of Sexuality" (1905), that

> Freud envisions both story and sexuality as a single strong stream gushing gleefully into the wide sea of human generation. This oceanic finale exalts both healthy heterosexuality and the satisfying story. Any impediments to an unobstructed flow force the current away from its appointed end into tiny, doomed side-streams, their deviance spawning a degenerate or perverted story.

There is a certain logic, then, to the fact that many of the most interesting stories of desire between women lurk in the "side-streams" of novels and plays, not the main orgasmic "flow" of the narrative. Also,
novelists and playwrights often seem to have suffered from a failure of
nerve—beginning a story of passion between women and then veiling
or disavowing it, breaking it off, or hastily bringing on a man to erase
the significance of what is happening between the women. Thomas
Hardy in *Desperate Remedies* (1871) offers what may be a sly commentary
on his novel's evasive presentation of an older woman's attempt to
seduce her maid:

> It was perceived by the servants of the House that some secret
> bond of connection existed between Miss Aldclyffe and her com-
> panion. But they were woman and woman, not woman and man,
> the facts were ethereal and refined, and so they could not be
> worked up into a taking story.

Writers—and not just pre-twentieth-century ones—have sometimes resisted any attempt by a critic to "work up" the lesbian implications of their text into a "taking story" (meaning one that takes the
fancy or seizes the imagination). Shirley Jackson, enraged by Jeannette
Foster's lesbian reading of her horror story *Hangsaman* (1951), wrote to
her biographer to insist, "Damnit, it is about what I say it is about."
(She does have my sympathy: when I publish my fiction, I sometimes
wish I had a veto over interpretations of my work, but as a reader, I am
glad that is not the case.) However, writers' descriptions of the themes
of their work should not always be taken at face value. For instance, it
was during a legal battle that would ultimately shut down their play, at
a huge financial loss, that Dorothy and Howard Baker released the following statement to the press in 1944:

> The booking troubles that *Trio* has run into have started the mis-
> leading and damaging rumour that *Trio* is a drama about Lesbian-
> ism. This report falls short of the truth. We, the authors, would
> have had no interest in dramatizing anything so special, so
> chaotic, so finally uninteresting as Lesbianism, and the attach-
> ment between the two women in our play is a very small part of a
> much larger pattern of psychological domination.

That this explanation is intended to cover the Bakers' backs, legally, is obvious. But it is peculiarly phrased too: how can the dreaded subject be simultaneously too "special" and too "uninteresting" to tackle? How can lesbian relationships be simultaneously "chaotic" and controlling, and besides, why is the "chaotic" bad to write about and "psychological domination" good? To say that the perilously attractive "attachment" between Pauline and Janet (which I will discuss in chapter 3) is only a "small part" of "a much larger pattern" could in fact suggest that this lesbian relationship is peculiarly interesting because it exemplifies an entire society's neurosis. The Bakers' statement seems worded in a way that deliberately calls attention to its contradictions, and may be tongue-in-cheek, since a reader of *Trio* will conclude that there has rarely been a play so clearly about lesbianism.

Not that readers always notice what writers choose to leave implicit, or even what they present calmly, without emphasis. When I was a child, for instance, I read a classic 1906 story by O. Henry called "The Last Leaf." It stuck in my mind as a charming tale of a gravely ill young woman who, convinced she will die when the last leaf falls from the ivy outside her window, is tricked into living by a neighbor who paints a leaf on the wall. Coming across "The Last Leaf" again decades later, I was startled to find that it is a story about a female couple: Sue and the butchly nicknamed Johnsy are starving-artist roommates in New York who dream of painting the Bay of Naples together. When Johnsy is on the verge of death by pneumonia, their slangy dialogue takes on a tenderer tone: " 'Dear, dear!' said Sue, leaning her worn face down to the pillow; 'think of me, if you won't think of yourself. What would I do?' " The obtuse doctor remarks to Sue that her friend will recover only if she has someone to live for, and asks if there is a man in Johnsy's life; Sue reacts with scorn. Something else I had forgotten about this rather magical story is that the neighbor—an old drunken Jewish painter who stays out one wet night, painting the leaf—is the one who dies of pneumonia: he sacrifices himself so the pair of women he is so fond of can survive. Is it stretching a point to wonder whether the unreal (painted) leaf which substitutes so successfully for the real one may be O. Henry's symbol for a same-sex partnership which gives just as much meaning to life as the "real" (heterosexual) kind? Short of calling Sue and Johnsy lovers, he could hardly have spelled it out more clearly. But because he takes their choice of each other for granted, and because the story's spotlight falls on Johnsy's illness, I did not notice the relationship until I read it again, as a lover of women, on the lookout for such stories.

Like the servants in Hardy's *Desperate Remedies*, literary historians— even today—often fail to read a narrative of desire between women as a "taking story." The problem may be simple phallocentrism, that is, the notion that nothing really counts unless it involves a penis or the owner of a penis. Even literary historians who are not phallocentric may define sex in the traditionally clear-cut way, as a matter of genital contact—with the consequence that they interpret all the erotic confusion in Renaissance plays as mere fun, and all the throbbing embraces between the heroines of eighteenth- and nineteenth-century novels as mere sisterliness.

Sometimes critics do notice the theme, but prefer not to comment at length. Their vocabulary often reveals their squeamishness, but generally they hide their distaste behind a show of scruple—fearing, they explain, that to explore desire between women in a beloved classic by, say, Dickens or James, would narrow that work's meaning rather than add to it. Jean-Pierre Jacques, in his 1981 study *Les Malheurs de Sapho*, draws a useful distinction between critics who prudishly avoid mentioning a work's lesbian theme, and those who raise smokescreens around that theme by insisting that the work is really, primarily, about something else.

Often such critics protest that it would be anachronistic for us to find lesbian themes in a text whose writers and first readers would have seen none. But this is a false assumption; as Denise Walen asks after studying more than seventy English plays written between 1570 and 1660 that include eroticism between women, "Why would playwrights construct so many homoerotic scenarios in dramatic form if they had no expectation that their audience would understand them?" If even the nonliterate in the pit were getting the point of these scenes, then there must have been a "tacit, if not fully articulated, public cultural discourse" about desire between women. Walen's argument is supported by the plethora of references to lesbian possibilities in other Renaissance genres such as medical and travel writing and pornography.

Most commonly, nowadays, literary historians use the "not the same thing at all" argument to divide (and therefore conquer) this literary tradition. They sort by costume, for instance, keeping texts in which some of the women wear breeches (see chapter 1) at arm's length from texts in which they all wear skirts.

A critic may acknowledge the theme in the rare fictions which refer to genital sex, such as Denis Diderot's *La Religieuse* (1797; discussed in chapter 4)—but refuse to grant that such stories might benefit from being read alongside more romantic stories of devotion between women such as Samuel Richardson's *Clarissa* (1747–48; see chapter 3) or Jean-Jacques Rousseau's *La Nouvelle Héloïse* (1761; see chapter 2).

Others misuse the theory of romantic friendship (a high-status social institution from the Renaissance to the nineteenth century), as Bonnie Zimmerman puts it, "with an audible sigh of relief, to explain away love between women" as customary and therefore needing no comment.

What I hope to show is not that it is "all the same thing," but that, in studying the full spectrum of passionate relationships between women in literature, it is a pointless exercise to erect a fence down the middle, dividing the lesbians from the just-really-good-friends.

Remember Chaucer's Dame Hermengyld, so pious and so passionate, with a husband as well as a woman she sleeps with and treasures "as hyr lyf": how can we be sure which parts of her story count as erotic? Or listen to one woman speak of herself to another, in a Latin lyric from a century or two before Chaucer, as a "hungry little bird" who "loves you, as you yourself know, / With her soul and body." Like all the great stories of male-female love, this poem assumes that passion can be a matter of "soul and body" at the same time.

The literary tradition of passion between women, then, has many contrasting strands, but they are—to use a word which has often been applied to pairs of women, from the sixteenth century on—*inseparable.* So my chapters focus on different storylines, not different kinds of relationships; we will encounter the lustful and the affectionate, the selfish and the saintly, the shallow and the deep all the way through this book.

Just as I am not interested in dividing this literature of love into "friendship" vs. "lesbianism," so I do not sort it according to its "positive" or "negative" attitude. When I began my career around 1990, those of us in the fledgling discipline of lesbian literary history felt understandably embattled, and we tended to approach the past by way of identity politics, assigning points for "sympathy" or "authenticity" (especially if the author herself just might have been a woman who loved women), taking them away for "stereotyping" or "voyeurism" (especially if—you guessed it—the author was a straight man). These days, it seems high time to let readers of all stripes hear about and enjoy the whole range of literature about desire between women, whether romantic or smutty, thrilling or funny, and with bloody-fanged fiends included too.

Nor do I think it particularly helpful to sort these stories according to whether love between two women is granted a happy ending. Endings are overrated; they are often the point when the writer bows to convention, and there is a lot more to a story than who gets the girl, or who dies. When I write fiction or drama, I know that my liking for a character is shown by my giving her a lot of page time and vivid scenes, however I may dispose of her by the end.

Finally, reader beware: no conclusions about real life should be drawn from all this storytelling. (I recently saw an essay by a literal-minded undergraduate that claimed, "In the nineteenth century, most lesbians were vampires.") The social history of relationships between women is a distinct and fascinating subject that I cannot tackle here. Fiction, poetry, and drama are not reliable guides even to attitudes the people of that era held toward same-sex desire; after all, cross-dressers were adored on the stage of the Globe and stoned in the stocks outside. A society's literature is its dream: immensely suggestive, yes, but not a simple reflection of its daily reality.

Of course there are times when a book or play can only be illuminated by a consideration of when and under what circumstances it was written. But having read scores of studies that attempt to fix the historical moment when something changed in the way women's love was experienced and interpreted, whether in life or literature or both—I remain dubious. There seem to be just two points of consensus.

The first is that it was in the sixteenth century that British authors began to write about such love with increasing interest. Contributing factors may have included the translation of classical texts, the rise in theaters and publishing, and a growth in female literacy.

The second is that in the late nineteenth and early twentieth centuries a new idea spread from medicine into popular culture: the woman-desiring woman as a clearly defined type. (As Peter Cryle comments perceptively of Guy de Maupassant's 1881 story "La Femme de

Paul" [in English, "Paul's Mistress"], in which a riverside crowd deri-
sively greets a boatload of female couples with a roar of *"V'là Lesbos"*
["There's Lesbos"], no crowd before Maupassant's day would have
been able to shout out that or any equivalent phrase with the same
"hearty confidence.") Factors in the spread of this idea may have
included women's admission to universities and entry into the work-
force in numbers, especially in World War One. The debate was
lively—sexologists saw this type of woman as a case of congenital gender inversion; psychoanalysts blamed arrested development—but it
seems clear that by the 1930s, in Europe and the United States, a broad
sense of erotic possibilities between women had given way to the more
stereotyped notion of "the lesbian."

Apart from those two clear changes, "differing depictions of desire
were always more or less acceptable," Denise Walen concludes from her
study of sixteenth- and seventeenth-century drama—and I would go
further and say that inconsistency has always been the norm. Once we
give up what Eve Sedgwick has dubbed "the historical search for a
Great Paradigm Shift," what stands out is an unexpected continuity
over the last millennium. Authors, imaginative but also self-conscious
about the tradition in which they write, have kept on ringing the
changes on the half dozen plots of passion between women which
appeal to readers most.

Over the dozen-odd years I have been working on *Inseparable,* I
have read many good books. Three memories stand out. Spending an
entire fortnight stretched out on my moldy grad-school futon, living—
almost in real time—through the longest novel in the English language,
Richardson's *Clarissa.* Finding in the British Library Rare Books Room,
at the end of a long, sore-eyed day, an utterly obscure and brilliant
short story by Cynthia Asquith, "The Lovely Voice." Scaring myself
stiff as I read Sarah Waters's ghostly *Affinity* cover to cover on the red-
eye from Toronto to London.

I have had moments of boredom, too, huddled over a microfilm
reader in the dark, cranking at speed through yet another dreary three-
volume novel to see if what the female characters felt for each other had
even a flicker of interest to it. And I've felt revulsion, particularly when
suffering through the Marquis de Sade's *Juliette.* But among the bad
books I have found some *great* bad ones—outrageous in their insinua-

tions and eye-popping in their plot twists—and one of the real pleasures of this project has been juxtaposing the best of schlock with
Shakespeare or Brontë such that each illuminates the other, and
together they add up to more than the sum of their parts: a literary tradition the best part of a thousand years long.

CHAPTER ONE

Travesties

W ESTERN LITERATURE IS FULL of characters who disguise
their sex, going *"en travesti"* (a pseudo-French phrase), or playing
a travesty role (as it is called in opera), and effortlessly fooling everyone
they meet. As Marjorie Garber puts it, "transvestite theatre is the *norm*,
not the aberration." Since all the roles on European stages were played
by males until the sixteenth century (England holding out until the
mid-seventeenth), it is hardly a coincidence that so many playwrights
put the spotlight on cross-dressing in their plots too: a boy playing a
woman disguised as a man, or playing a man disguised as a woman,
must have given the audience a wonderfully complex frisson. But interestingly, the same goes for nontheatrical genres: medieval and Renaissance romance (in both verse and prose) and fiction of the eighteenth
and nineteenth centuries constantly resort to gender disguise for the
sake of suspense, entertainment, poignancy, and a surprisingly poly-
morphous eroticism.

Winfried Schleiner finds that such storylines celebrate "an ideal in
which the erotic charge does not derive, as it were, from the genders
being apart or diametrically opposed but from their similarity." Dis-

guise plots have allowed writers to explore, as if between quotation marks or parentheses, all sorts of possibilities. By far the most popular has been the idea of accidental desire between women.

There are two main scenarios. For the heroines of plays and romances, the motives for male disguise are many and varied, as are the consequences. But one thing is sure: girls in breeches turn women's heads. This is often known as the female bridegroom motif, because many authors ratchet up the tension by using an imminent wedding as a ticking time bomb for the cross-dresser, who may experience just as much erotic confusion as she causes in others.

Less commonly, but fairly often in the sixteenth and seventeenth centuries, a male character puts on skirts, winning access to women-only space and, under cover of friendship, wooing a woman—who may fear she is falling for one of her own sex. Since the hero generally chooses the persona of a female knight or Amazon, I call this the male amazon motif. (A helpful mnemonic is to think of the female bridegroom and male amazon motifs, in 1980s film terms, as the *Yentl* and the *Tootsie*.)

The traditional scholarly line is that neither of these scenarios is really about same-sex attraction. The woman who falls for a woman-in-breeches is mistaken, this argument goes, and so not really wanting *her* but the "man" the breeches make her seem to be. On the other hand, the woman who falls for a man-in-skirts is mistaken, and so not really *wanting* "her," just liking "her" very much, or perhaps (without knowing it) desiring the real man behind the skirts. To deny the lesbian implications of these two scenarios, this paradoxical argument has to define desire as conscious but illusory in the first, unconscious but authentic in the second.

Another problem is that such interpretations rely on reading the cross-dresser as just one thing or another—a male or a female, whether defined by clothes or physiology. Marjorie Garber has argued influentially that we should look not *through* but *at* the cross-dresser, whom she calls a third term—a figure who can break the binary code of gender. As I see it, to keep insisting that a cross-dressed character is *really* male or female is to reduce that character's interest and power, and similarly to ask what these works are *really* about is rather beside the point. They celebrate desires fleeting or ambiguous, but no less powerful for that; they are fantasies, games, speculations, outrageous *travesties* of the real and the natural.

So why was desire between *women* the most common result of these storylines? Because in Western literature there is a long tradition of considering such a form of illicit attraction as ultimately harmless— therefore funny, or poignant, or aesthetically pleasing. What Joseph Harris concludes from his study of seventeenth-century cross-dressing romances is just as true of theater:

> Women in seventeenth-century literature are often allowed a degree of lenience in desiring both real men disguised as women, and other women disguised as men. The fact that this is very rarely the case for men suggests that there was a great deal of anxiety about the possibility that male desire could be inadvertently misdirected.

Passionate attraction between women was often described in terms of *amor impossibilis,* impossible love: this did not mean a love that could never happen emotionally, but one that could not be satisfied sexually—whether because there could be no penis-ejaculating-in-vagina, or just no orgasm, is far less clear, but the second event was generally held to depend on the first. In both drama and prose, Western writers repeatedly used images of "fruitless" (meaning nonprocreative, and therefore pointless) desire between women.

The "lenience" Harris mentions has its limits; the understanding is that the woman's erotic interest in someone she either believes to be female or who secretly is female is a mistake, which will be magically corrected by the eventual dropping of the disguise. Often the middle of these stories is more interesting than the ending; as Harris suggests, "Something in cross-dressing frequently seems to resist the general narrative flow," producing episodes of sexual confusion which are secondary or entirely irrelevant to the main plot and undermine its tidy conclusions. The safety net enables the riskiest tricks.

THE FEMALE BRIDEGROOM

In Aelfric's *Lives of Saints* (a sermon-cycle of the 990s), the cross-dressed Saint Eugenia heals a woman who, when the saint rejects her advances, ungratefully accuses "him" of rape. For the last thousand years, then, it

Walter H. Deverell, "Viola and Olivia," in Art and Poetry *(formerly* The Germ*), No. 4 (May 1850).*

In the final issue of the Pre-Raphaelite Brotherhood's magazine, this etching by English painter Walter Deverell (who died at the age of twenty-seven) was published alongside a poem of the same name by John Lucas Tupper, an anatomical draftsman. Tupper mulls over the "natural" attraction between the two Shakespeare heroines, calling them "lovers" and "married souls . . . / having an inward faith that love, called so / In verity, is of the spirit clear / Of earth and dress and sex." Deverell used his sister as a model for Olivia, but for Viola he "discovered" a part-time milliner named Elizabeth Siddal; she would go on to pose for, study with, and finally marry his friend Dante Gabriel Rossetti two years before her own early death.

seems a heroine cannot disguise herself without attracting at least one girl, and often bevies of them. The motif shows up frequently in romances (from the 1200s) and plays (from the 1500s) in Latin, French, Italian, and Spanish. The anonymous Sienese comedy *Gl'Ingannati* (1537) adds a delicious twist which would have a lasting influence: a girl disguised as a page is in love with her master, but he sends her to court his beloved for him, and she accidentally wins the lady's love herself. The female bridegroom entered English romance by the 1580s, and by the 1590s was a stock character on the English stage (in the quick-change costume of hat and long black cloak) who would not leave it for another two centuries.

The earliest and most important source for the motif is the myth of Iphis and Ianthe, told in many classical texts but most memorably by the Roman poet Ovid in his *Metamorphoses* (composed around 8 C.E.). Raised as a boy (to save her from infanticide), Iphis at thirteen is engaged to marry her friend Ianthe. As Ovid tells it, with an audible relish for the contradiction, "Iphis loved a girl whom she despaired of ever being able to enjoy, and this very frustration increased her ardor." He gives her a long soliloquy, the original lesbian lament, which we will hear echoed in many later texts: "What is to be the end of this for me, caught as I am in the snare of a strange and unnatural kind of love, which none has known before?" She must be a monster, Iphis argues, because "cows do not burn with love for cows," mares for mares, ewes for ewes, and so forth. (Without the benefit of modern biology, she has no idea that same-sex goings-on can be observed right across the animal kingdom.) What Iphis sees as distinguishing lesbian desire from other sick whims—such as bestiality—is that it has no hope of consummation, since sex is what happens between males and females. She lectures herself sternly: Ianthe "cannot be yours, nor can you be happy, whatever happens . . . Pull yourself together, Iphis, be firm, and shake off this foolish, useless emotion." But the plot rolls on: she makes no attempt to excuse herself or run away, even though she expects that to play Ianthe's bridegroom will feel like "thirst in the middle of the waters." On the day before the wedding, her despairing mother takes Iphis to plead at the altar of the goddess Io, who was the one who said she should be raised as a boy in the first place. The temple shakes; on the way out, Iphis "walked with a longer stride than usual . . . she who had lately been a woman had become a man." Notice Iphis is still "she," her girl-self lingering like a ghost. Only when recounting the wedding itself does Ovid shift to a male pronoun, to tell us that "the boy Iphis gained his own Ianthe." You could say that the sex change is a daring way of making the girls' illicit passion acceptable—or a cheap trick to reestablish the status quo. I see it as both at the same time: a handy device to wind up the story, which has the side effect of reward-ing same-sex love.

Ovid's *Metamorphoses* enjoyed a great vogue in European literature from the Middle Ages on. The Iphis story was radically reworked in *Yde et Olive,* an anonymous epic poem written in Old French before 1311 as one of the many sequels to *Huon de Bordeaux.* (When Lord Berners translated the whole *Huon* cycle into English around 1534 it became extremely popular, before falling into obscurity in the seventeenth cen-tury.) *Ide and Olive* (as the poem is known in English) is about a princess who runs away in disguise to escape her father's incestuous advances. The emperor of Rome employs the promising young "squire" Ide as ser-vant to his daughter, the Lady Olive, who has refused countless suitors but is immediately won over by Ide's gentle manner. (This is typical of female bridegroom plots: it is almost always the cross-dresser's femi-nine charms that attract other women, rather than any machismo she may display.) Interestingly, three other medieval romances inspired by the Iphis story—Heldris de Cornuälle's *Roman de Silence* (1200s) and the anonymous *Roman de Cassidorus* (c. 1270) and *Tristan de Nanteuil* (c. 1375)—refer to their cross-dressed heroines by masculine (or a mix-ture of masculine and feminine) names and pronouns. But this anony-mous author gives his the gender-neutral name of Ide, and uses feminine pronouns throughout, which keeps reminding us that she is a woman.

> The Damsell [Olive] often times gladly regarded her, and began in her heart sore to love her, and she (who perceived her [Olive]) prayed our Lord God, that he would so deale, that she be not accused neither of man nor woman.

Notice that Ide's first reaction is fear of being "accused" of wooing the emperor's daughter—as an upstart who is breaking the rules of class as much as gender. But the emperor is a meritocrat: grateful for Ide's mili-tary services, diplomacy, and wit, he offers his daughter's hand. "Great dammage it should be to so noble a Damsell," Ide protests, "to be assigned to such a poore man as I am." Poor, that is, in manhood as well as in money. But nobody is going to "assign" Olive anywhere; in fact she begs her father to hurry up the wedding, with such obvious desire that the courtiers burst out laughing. (Joseph Harris shows that in female bridegroom stories, it is almost always the woman-in-skirts who is obliged to take the erotic initiative, stepping into the male position— so the cross-dresser's act of sartorial gender bending sparks off a more deeply scandalous masculinization in the other woman.)

In an intriguing soliloquy, Ide makes up her mind that she would be a "Foole" to reject fate's terrifying gifts of a princess and an empire: "I will wed her, and doe as God will give me grace to do." Unlike Ovid, this author does not bring on a miraculous sex change before the ceremony, and this allows the story to unroll with appalling suspense. On the wedding night, Ide locks the doors for fear of eavesdroppers and lies down with Olive. She makes the traditional claim of impotence, but her tone is yearning and sorrowful: "My right sweete Love, God give you good night, for as for me, I can give you no good, because I feele such a disease, the which greeveth me sore, and therewith she kissed her." Olive is not convinced that her "sweete Lover" lacks the relevant thing that will do Olive "good," since Ide is "the thinge in the world that I most desire, for the bountie and sweetness that I knowe in you." (Notice that instead of calling each other husband and wife, they use the gender-neutral vocabulary of "sweete Love" and "sweete Lover.") In case her bridegroom might think her desperate for consummation, she offers to postpone it for fifteen days. "It sufficeth me to kiss you, & as for the privie love, I am content for this time (since it is your pleasure) to forbeare it." (This suggests that she has guessed that Ide is not sick, but stalling.) So the couple relax, and pass the whole night "clipping [embracing] and kissing." The next morning, when the emperor asks how she is, Olive gives a defiantly upbeat answer: "Sir, (quoth she) even as I desire, for I love Ide my Husband better than I love you." What everyone wants to know is how her "desire" (in a technical sense) has been satisfied; Olive turns the question and tells them about her "love" for her bridegroom instead.

But after a fortnight of kissing, it comes to the crunch: "Then she [Olive] drew neere to her and touched her, and she [Ide] (who knew well what her [Olive's] desire was) turned toward her, and wold hide himselfe no longer from her, but all weeping cryed her mercie." The effect of all these pronouns (eight feminine, one masculine) is a melting of the two women's different feelings into one pool of melancholy eroticism. And Ide's confession that she is female does not split them apart again. Olive reacts with an extraordinary speech:

My right sweete Lover, discomfort not your selfe, for you shall not
be accused by me neither to no man nor woman living, we are
wedded together, and I will be good and true to you, since you
have kept your selfe so truly, with you I will use my time and passe
my destiny since it is thus, for I see that it is the pleasure of our
Lord God.

Just as Ide embarked on this adventure in a spirit of knightly obedience
to "God" and "destiny," so Olive proves herself a fit mate by showing
the same spirit. When she credits Ide with having "kept your selfe so
truly," this could refer to the fact that Ide has been honest with Olive at
last—or that, all along, Ide has maintained some kind of personal
integrity by means of the disguise, a truth within the lie. Or perhaps
"truly" here means faithfully, and what Olive is praising Ide for is for
being a virginal, chaste bridegroom. In any case, it is clear that Olive
still considers herself truly "wedded together" with Ide's "selfe"
(another gender-neutral word), whatever biological sex that self may
happen to be. Their marriage is presented here not as a sham but as a
very private mystery.

   But this is not a modern novel; such a subtle and open ending
would hardly do for the medieval listeners. Exposed by an eavesdropper, the newlyweds are sentenced to burning alive by the weeping
emperor. By making their punishment identical, he is acknowledging
that his daughter is no victim but a true partner in the marriage. Intriguingly, their crime is called buggery in Bourchier's original translation
(c. 1534)—"he wold not suffer such boggery to be used"—but by the
third edition in 1601 the word has been euphemized to "falsehood." In
any event, as the fire rises, God intervenes to announce that Ide is now
transformed into a man, and that the emperor has only eight days to
live. (Clearly a punishment for having tried to execute the misunderstood couple.) Olive's father rushes off to make out his will in their
favor, and she and Ide-the-man go to bed and conceive an heir who will
be a great leader.

   Ide and Olive may have more or less the same ending as the myth,
but it deviates sharply from Ovid by allowing the bride to discover the
truth. It suggests that a same-sex marriage can include everything—
attraction, complementary roles, loyalty, lovemaking—except the
intercourse necessary for reproduction, and that there is nothing evil

about it. *Ide and Olive* may have been shocking to some of its audience, because when it was rewritten later in the fourteenth century in dramatic form as *Miracle de la fille d'un roy* (in English, *Miracle of a King's Daughter*), the ending was changed to marry the cross-dresser and her bride to each other's aged fathers.

So why would this anonymous French author, working in the late thirteenth or early fourteenth century, have fastened on this theme? Not with a view to social commentary, I would argue; his listeners and readers are most unlikely to have interpreted the story as a proof that women did (or should be allowed to) desire each other. Instead, he seems to me to have chosen it, much as Ovid did, to make a point about love in general: its wild unpredictability and power. The tone had changed over the more than millennium that separated the two, of course: on top of the Roman author's concept of Eros, the French medieval author added layers of Christian purity, humility, and faith, as well as melancholic, self-abnegating *amour courtois* (on both sides, interestingly—the bride's as well as the bridegroom's). But his basic impulse seems to have been the same as Ovid's: perhaps it took a romance as unprecedented as Olive and Ide's to prove that classical motto so popular in medieval times, *amor vincit omnia,* or love (even "impossible love") conquers all.

Ovid's *Metamorphoses* remained popular in the Renaissance; an English translation went through five editions in the late sixteenth century. When French playwright Isaac de Benserade dramatized it as *Iphis et Iante* in 1634 (published in 1637), he made the same key choice as the *Ide and Olive* author—to postpone the sex change until after the wedding, so the bride is forced to realize her predicament as a woman with a female husband. As a further turn of the screw, he added a male character, Ergaste, who both knows Iphis's secret and is hopelessly in love with her. Ergaste can be read as a sort of mouthpiece for the male libertines who were Benserade's target audience. In several speeches, with a mixture of amused condescension, excitement, and jealousy, Ergaste broods over the paradoxical nature of his beloved's passion for one of her own sex; the way both women are "too innocent to know how to commit a crime," but that they are planning to do exactly that by fraudulently formalizing what he calls their "clownish love" in the sacrament (and legal bond) of matrimony.

Some have seen this tragicomedy as mere titillation for a male audience, but Benserade's approach stresses fascinating epistemological questions. His Iphis—not thirteen, as in Ovid, but twenty years old—is a strong character who resists her mother's urging to stifle her forbidden passion for Iante. She swings between suicidal impulses and hope that the gods will somehow solve her problem. In many speeches, Iphis simultaneously emphasizes her despair and her desire, her inability to tell Iante what the matter is, and her inability to "do the impossible for her" by consummating the marriage. Kissing her beloved's breast, she groans that this is like "dying of thirst beside a fountain." The frustration seems as much a matter of knowledge as sex: she needs to figure out a way to break through Iante's innocence as well as her maidenhead.

In a startlingly frank speech toward the end of the play, Iphis tells her mother how the wedding night went. "Possessing her thrilled me," she admits:

> I satisfied my love fever with a kiss,
> And my soul was on my lips.
> In the sweet feeling of these excessive delights,
> I was forgetting the thing I aspired to most.
> I embraced her beautiful body, whose pure whiteness
> Excited me to make a place for it in myself.
> I was touching, I was kissing, my heart was content

Here Iphis wavers between what we might call a phallic sexuality (the claiming of kisses and embraces, the thrill of possession) and a much more uncertain, diffusely ecstatic, receptive kind of desire that leads to "forgetting" the "thing" itself, the consummation: where we might expect this bridegroom to focus on the task of deflowering her bride, she confounds our expectations by longing to (symbolically or literally?) "make a place for" Iante's body in herself. Only when her appalled mother asks how Iante reacted does the story turn more conventional. Iphis reports that as soon as she revealed the secret by stripping naked, Iante rejected her embraces and went off weeping, "ashamed to see herself the wife of a girl."

But one oddity of the play's fifth act is that we have *already* heard from Iante, who does not seem ashamed at all. In a soliloquy, two scenes earlier, she hints that the wedding night brought her pleasure as well as disturbing knowledge. "This marriage is sweet, it has charm enough for me, and if only people didn't laugh at it, I wouldn't complain . . ." What embarrasses her is the thought of what others might say about her story (or, specifically, how they might present it onstage; here the play becomes a sort of commentary on itself). She only belatedly considers the moral aspects, adding that if two girls could marry "without offending heaven and natural law," her heart would make no objection.

Her wishful thinking here suggests that Iante means to hold on to the shreds of her naïveté as long as she can, because she does not want to lose Iphis. If audiences or readers might have been outraged by the brazenness of a woman who consciously defies heaven and nature by having sex with another woman, they may have found it much easier to be indulgent to a wide-eyed heroine who made them feel amused and worldly.

Only at this point does Benserade bring on the deus ex machina to turn the two women into an orthodox couple. Interestingly, Iante's reaction to her bridegroom's sex change is extremely muted. *Iphis et Iante* is an odd play, both structurally and tonally; Isaac de Benserade makes fun of his heroines even as he sympathizes with them, presenting their situation as simultaneously romantic and clownish, and casting Iphis as a combination of eunuch and freak and hero.

Four centuries apart, the *Ide and Olive* author and Isaac de Benserade both doubled Iphis's dilemma by forcing the Iante figure to realize that, without taking any active steps across the gender line, she has ended up in a same-sex marriage. English playwright John Lyly doubled it another way in his fantastical comedy *Gallathea* (performed in 1583, published in 1592): his *two* cross-dressed heroines, Gallathea and Phillida, not only fall in love with each other, but also become objects of desire to various of Diana's nymphs. (To add to the strangeness, all these roles were written for small boys in a juvenile theater company.)

Cupid states the play's theme of lesbian love as a cosmic joke: "I will make their paines my pastimes, & so confound their loves in their owne sexe, that they shall dote in their desires, delight in their affections, and practise onely impossibilities." Falling in love with another woman is a "paine," a state of being "confounded" or confused, of dotage (meaning excessive affection, but also feeblemindedness). It also brings "delight," even though all these lovers can "practise" together are "impossibilities." (In this statement of *amor impossibilis*, "practise" means "do," but there may also be a hint that practice makes perfect.) At first each of Lyly's heroines presumes the other is a boy, then they start to suspect otherwise—but remain in a state of romantic uncertainty for much of the play. It is Phillida who takes the initiative, telling Gallathea, "Come let us into the Grove, and make much of one another, that cannot tel what to think one of another." She suggests they copy the dynamic of a male-female relationship: "Seeing that we are both boyes, and both lovers, that our affection may have some showe, and seeme as it were love, let me call thee Mistris." She is suggesting that the roles they may adopt are entirely arbitrary. Later, almost sure that her beloved is as female as herself, she soliloquizes: "Poore *Phillida*, what shouldest thou thinke of thy self, that lovest one that I fear mee, is as thy self is." (Compared with the speech of agonized self-reproach that Ovid gives Iphis, this is a mild reaction.)

The discovery of the truth only complicates the girls' passion; it does nothing to reduce it. In a scene which goes further than anything else in Renaissance literature toward an ethical assessment of lesbian desire as such, the two stand before the gods for judgment. They get a stern lecture from Diana, goddess of chastity—"You must leave these fond affections; nature will have it so, necessitie must." The word "fond" here means "loving" but also "imbecilic." Similarly Neptune calls it "an idle choyce, strange, and foolish, for one Virgine to doate on another; and to imagine a constant faith, where there can be no cause of affection." But Venus sees it very differently.

VENUS   I like well and allowe it, they shall both be possessed of
             their wishes, for never shall it be said that Nature or
             Fortune shall over-throwe Love and Fayth. Is your
             loves unspotted, begunne with trueth, continued with
             constancie, and not to be altered tyll death?

GALLATHEA   Die *Gallathea* if thy love be not so!

PHILLIDA   Accursed be thou *Phillida,* if thy love be not so!

Like the wife in the medieval *Ide and Olive,* Lyly's Venus grants that a love can be "begunne with truth" even if it involves a sartorial trick; she recognizes the sincerity of the girls' mutual love, its "constancie" in prizing the inner self rather than the gender role. This remarkable scene goes on:

DIANA   Suppose all this *Venus,* what then?

VENUS   Then shall it be seene, that I can turne one of them to be a man, and that I will.

DIANA   Is it possible?

VENUS   What is to Love or the Mistrisse of Love unpossible? Was it not *Venus* that did the like to *Iphis* and *Ianthes?* how say ye? are ye agreed? one to be a boy presently?

PHILLIDA   I am content, so I may imbrace *Gallathea.*

GALLATHEA   I wish it, so I may enjoy *Phillida.*

Until this point, it might seem as if Gallathea's doubling of the Iphis situation is less interesting than that found in *Ide and Olive* or Benserade's *Iphis et Iante:* after all, Gallathea and Phillida are going through exactly the same thing. But this mirroring becomes an asset now, because there is no obvious candidate for the miraculous sex change. Both girls are content to leave it up to Venus to decide who will be turned into the husband; all they want is to be married, either way. And Lyly seems to share their indifference: he ends the play with everyone walking offstage to the church door where the transformation will take place, a decision that keeps his heroines in a state of blissful suspension in which their only fixed identity consists of desire for the other. If the *Ide and Olive* version of Ovid's story focuses on the meaning of love, and Benserade's on the meaning of innocence, then what Lyly offers is a playful meditation on selfhood.

But the most common female bridegroom storyline is not that of a mutually devoted pair such as Olive/Ide or Phillida/Gallathea, but a cross-dressed woman who accidentally attracts other women. She may react with embarrassment, amusement, panic, sympathy, guilt, fondness, or a muddy mixture of all these emotions. Sometimes the deceived woman is clearly being punished by means of this unfulfillable desire—perhaps for stupidity or her callous treatment of her male suitors, as in the case of Phebe in *As You Like It* (performed in 1600). Shakespeare allows his cross-dressed Rosalind to rebuff Phebe's hapless desire with merciless satire, but in his *Twelfth Night* (performed in 1601) he treats a similar situation in a much more poignant and romantic spirit. One difference is that the haughty, enamored one in *Twelfth Night* is a lady rather than a shepherdess; another is that her beloved, Viola (cross-dressed as the page "Cesario"), is a much gentler character than Rosalind. Sent by Orsino to court the heiress Olivia on his behalf, Viola displays an anxious tenderness in a famous speech about how "he" would court Olivia if "he" were his master:

> Make me a willow cabin at your gate,
> And call upon my soul within the house;
> Write loyal cantons of contemned love,
> And sing them loud even in the dead of night;
> Holla your name to the reverberate hills,
> And make the babbling gossip of the air
> Cry out, "Olivia!" O! you should not rest,
> Between the elements of air and earth,
> But you should pity me.

This is a declaration full of action, but frozen in the conditional tense. Olivia, overwhelmed, murmurs, "you might do much," already losing her heart to the eloquent page.

Viola is no cynical role-player; she is expressing a kind of hypothetical desire, an if-only-I-could yearning that is common among female bridegrooms. This note is audible in several subplots of *Amadis de Gaule,* a French chivalrous romance cycle published in twenty-four volumes between roughly 1540 and 1595 (an expansion of an equally famous Spanish source, *Amadis de Gaula*), which has been called the most influential prose work of the sixteenth century. Oronce, a woman disguised as a man, is just as entranced with the lady Lucence as vice versa: "The virtuous Oronce found her so beautiful and congenial that she could not avert her eyes from her, taking in all her royal countenance and saying to herself, 'If I were a knight and my heart was free, I would not want to have any lady but her.' "

In *Twelfth Night,* Shakespeare keeps the emphasis, according to stage custom, on the fruitlessness of attraction between women, but puts it in financial rather than botanical terms: realizing that the Lady Olivia is falling for her, Viola laments, "What thriftless sighs shall poor Olivia breathe!" This is typical of Renaissance texts that describe a woman who desires a woman as sighing—not just wistful, but frustratedly aroused. Here "thriftless" means spendthrift or unprofitable; it is a pointless outlay of affection for Olivia to desire "Cesario," because her investment will fail to pay off.

Amor impossibilis was the official version, then: the punch line of the joke. But we should not assume that authors, readers, and audiences all actually believed that it was impossible for women to give each other pleasure. In fact, many of Shakespeare's predecessors, peers, and successors were less cautious on the topic than he was. One example of a play that alludes to *amor impossibilis* in a playful, tongue-in-cheek way is Abraham Cowley's lastingly popular *Love's Riddle* (1638). The cross-dressed Callidora enjoys the kisses of two rival women, Hylace and Bellula, and tells them:

> I pitty both of you, for you have sow'd
> Upon unthankful sand, whose dry'd up wombe
> Nature denies to blesse with fruitfulnesse
> ‘
> . . .
>
> And I protest I love you both. Yet cannot,
> Yet must not enjoy either.

"Cannot" or "must not"? Physical impossibility or just cultural taboo? Cowley's play is a pastoral comedy; in the more worldly seventeeth-century genre of city comedy we hear occasional heavy hints (in plays by Brome, Middleton, and Webster) that a female bridegroom and another woman might be able to "enjoy" each other after all. But it remains the convention, in plays, poems, and novels about cross-dressing, to keep these thrilling possibilities hovering *outside* the story.

Most playwrights and romance writers place great emphasis on the moment of revelation, when the cross-dresser drops the disguise, whether willingly or otherwise, verbally or sartorially. (Or even physically: in the fifth act of Jean de Rotrou's *Célimène* [1633], the stage direction instructs the actress to bare her breast.) As Joseph Harris points out, the revelation is usually a conservative moment, in which the baroque elements of deception and disorder are cleared away to expose a bedrock of reality.

In the case of female bridegroom plots, typically the other woman recoils in embarrassment, anger, or grief. "If sight and shape be true,"

Shakespeare's Phebe laments in *As You Like It*, looking at Rosalind-in-skirts, "why then, my love adieu!" Since the beloved's female "shape" is "true," then the desire must have been untrue, so Phebe says "adieu" to it. Or perhaps "my love adieu" means that she is obliged to say good-bye to "Ganymede"/Rosalind, whom she still loves but now has no hope of marrying? Cannot or must not, again: this ambiguity is a common one in female bridegroom plays.

This moment of recoil, or adjustment to the news that the beloved is a fellow female, is generally a quick tying-up of loose ends, a return to the status quo. But there are interesting exceptions. In the twentieth volume of the *Amadis de Gaule* cycle, for instance, the Infanta Licinie is so traumatized by the discovery of the sex of her beloved Chevalier that she cannot trust her next suitor in case he too is a woman. In some plays, such as John Ford's *The Lover's Melancholy* (1629), the deceived woman expresses a deep sexual shame.

And it may go further than this, leading to protracted ambiguities on both sides. In the twenty-first volume of *Amadis de Gaule*, for instance, when La Belle Sauvage has been revealed as female, she softens the blow by telling the enamoured Lucence,

> "Madame, you should know that your beauty and good grace so much pleased me that in my deepest being I became fond of it. And therefore I found it to be true what the queen has said, namely that often a lady is so fond of the beauty of another lady that she falls in love with her. I always want to be known to love you." The gracious lady [Lucence] answered smiling, "Although you are a young lady, I will not stop loving you, for I will remain content only to contemplate your beauty. Nonetheless, I ask that you allow me always to stay with you."

As Winfried Schleiner comments, "Surely this dialogue is a profession of love, but just as surely it is a renunciation, or, from Lucence's point of view, a redefinition." Both parties insist that, although no heterosexual relationship can exist, the homosocial one can be just as passionate and important.

Lucence manages to smile, but this conversion of desire into friendship can be a painfully difficult one, as in Robert Greene's history play *James the Fourth* (1598). Lady Anderson struggles to tame her desire for the "squire" who she has just learned is really the "deceitful beauty" Queen Dorothea.

LADY ANDERSON *(to herself)*
> Blush, greeve and die in thine insaciat lust!

DOROTHEA
> Nay, live and joy that thou hast won a friend
> That loves thee as his life by good desert.

LADY ANDERSON
> I joy, my Lord, more than my tongue can tell,
> Allthough not as I desir'd, I love you well:
> But Modestie that never blusht before
> Discover my false heart. I say no more.

Lady Anderson's transition is so sudden that her claim of "joy" rings false; her jerky "tongue" is having difficulty catching up with reality, as shown by the fact that she is still addressing Dorothea as "my Lord" (just as Dorothea is still using male pronouns such as "his"). Lady Anderson will force herself to make do with a nonerotic form of "love," but with gritted teeth: was her heart "false" when it tricked her into insatiable "lust" for a woman, or is it being "false" in its performance of mere affection now? "Say no more," indeed. The desire sparked by a pair of breeches smolders on after the breeches are packed away; illusory emotions prove to have a lingering half-life.

Sometimes the flame cannot be extinguished by any means. Ludovico Ariosto's epic *Orlando Furioso* (published in Italian in 1516–32 and translated into English beginning in 1591) was an instant and lasting hit with readers, but it troubled many critics with its admixture of the romantic and the lyric, its jumble of high and low characters, its broken narrative threads and parodic undercutting of its own chivalric material. One of its most startling episodes is that of the Princess Fiordispina—a mature, confident woman at the point where the man she has fallen for owns up to being an Amazon warrior called Bradamante. This much is borrowed from an early epic, Matteo Maria Boiardo's *Orlando Innamorato* (1483–94), but Ariosto pushes through the apparent narrative impasse. When the Amazon tries to talk her out of her passion, Ariosto's Fiordispina resists: her "fansie" may be "uncouth," she admits, but it is "firmely fixt." She asks Bradamante to change into women's clothes, to see if that will put out the fire—but no. In Ovid's story of

Iphis and Ianthe, it is the cross-dresser who feels that her desire for another woman makes her a freak, but here it is Fiordispina—the feminine one—who echoes that famous speech of Iphis's (though without acknowledging she has ever heard of Ovid's story), crying out to Cupid and Nature about her dilemma:

> In passed times I think there hath beene none,
> In time to come it will not be believed,
> That love should make by such a strong infection
> One woman beare another such affection.
> . . .
> I sole am found in earth, aire, sea, or fire,
> In whom so strange a wonder thou hast donne.
> On me thou showst the power of thine ire
> And what a mighty conquest thou hast wonne . . .
> No *Dedalus* could not remedie my bale,
> Nor art can frame nor sence imagin how:
> This knot dame nature hath so firmly knit
> It cannot be dissolv'd by any wit.

It is interesting that Fiordispina describes the "knot" of lesbian desire as being tied by Nature, rather than (as Iphis saw it) being against Nature. Bradamante rushes to contradict her on this point, insisting that Nature is not to blame for Fiordispina's fault of "will":

> And wisht her this unbridled will to tame,
> Sith nature could not suffer it prevaile,
> And that she would let that desire be daunted
> Which possiblie by no meanes could be graunted.

But Fiordispina will not "let that desire be daunted," even though, unlike her sophisticated author, she seems ignorant of any way of satisfying it. Ariosto has her describe her longing with the highly erotic image of an open wound: "Nought could salve that sore nor swage her woes." What she lacks in information she makes up for in determination. Unlike Iphis in the myth, Fiordispina seems almost to glory in her fate; despite being repeatedly told that she is in despair, we hear in her speeches more than a hint of perverse pride that nothing can "remedie" her "infection." The only solution she considers, during a long night tossing and turning in bed beside Bradamante, is Ovid's:

> That little sleepe straung dreames and fansies bred:
> She thought the gods and heav'n would so assist her
> Into a better sex to chaung my sister.

The narrator here is Bradamante's identical brother, Ricciardetto. Ariosto can achieve the traditional resolution only by another disguise: Ricciardetto will disguise himself as his sister to get into bed with Fiordispina, then announce that by means of a miraculous sex change, courtesy of a river nymph, "she" is now male and can "asswage your care," i.e., satisfy the overheated princess. The age of miracles is over; this is the sixteenth-century Italian author's sly, secular homage to the pagan or Christian deus ex machina that resolves earlier versions of the female bridegroom story. The episode is handled playfully, which is not to say unseriously; while Fiordispina's position as the butt of Ricciardetto's joke might seem a humiliating one, the length, eloquence, and courage of her speeches express her passion for the Amazon with memorable force. More than any other heroine in her position in Renaissance literature, she insists on the undeniability of her desire for another woman.

The substitute-brother ending of the Fiordispina episode in *Orlando Furioso* was perhaps its most influential aspect. Often, as in the case of the anonymous Sienese play *Gl'Ingannati* (1537), it is the sister rather than the brother who arranges the swap. In fact, at times the brother has all the agency of a dildo: "I lov'd you well, though I could never ease you, / When I fetch'd in my brother thus to please you," Kate tells Lady Goldenfleece fondly in Thomas Middleton's *No Wit, No Help Like a Woman's* (performed c. 1611).

These substitute-brother endings are about winding up the story, rather than psychological realism. This causes a jarring gear change in such works as Shakespeare's *Twelfth Night* (performed 1601), in which Olivia falls deeply in love with "Cesario" (Viola) over the course of several long, intimate têtes-à-têtes—but, discovering she has been tricked into marriage to Viola's identical twin, Sebastian, raises not the slightest objection. The comic convention strains to accommodate Shakespeare's subtle characterization, like the proverbial new wine in old skins. "A sister!" Olivia cries, which might seem like an unconvincing expression of banal friendship. But Denise Walen argues that Olivia's immediate declaration that she will host Viola's wedding to Orsino can be read as her way of holding on to the girl she still loves, by means of a sort of permanent, four-person union.

The motif of the female bridegroom remained popular on the stage until the late 1700s. What really changed was not the storyline but the tone; we can register an overall shift from the freshness of Elizabethan cross-dressing comedies to a more glum or hostile tone by the Jacobean and Caroline periods, and a formulaic use of the motif in the eighteenth century.

But as far back as *As You Like It* (staged in 1600), we can detect in the cocky speeches of a character such as Rosalind a certain relish for the piquant situation in which she finds herself; without having intended to make women fall in love with them, these cross-dressers often seem flattered, titillated, and downright triumphant. In Jean de Rotrou's *Célimène* (1633), Florante marvels at how easy women are to seduce. More unsettlingly, the heroine of Rotrou's *Cléagénor et Doristée* (1634), despite having put on breeches to escape the men who keep trying to rape her, laughs about how one of the women fawning over her "would love to be forced a little."

A novelty in Jacobean treatments of the female bridegroom is that the secret of her sex is often kept from the audience until quite late in the play; this allows the audience (or readers) to take the desire seriously before realizing it is a same-sex one. Less often noticed is a more important Jacobean innovation: the cross-dresser who *deliberately* woos another woman. Her hidden motive is usually a nasty one, but that does nothing to reduce the sexiness of the scenario.

Rivalry over a man is the most common reason: in the tight triangle of two women and the man they both want, cross-dressing often turns the link between the two rivals into something highly charged. In Margaret Cavendish's *Matrimonial Trouble* (an understated title for a sort of Restoration *Fatal Attraction*), the sinister Mistress Forsaken crashes her ex-lover's wedding in breeches, to dance with and win the heart of his new wife. Similarly, in Antoine Jacob Montfleury's box-office smash *La Femme, juge, et partie* (performed 1669—in English, *The Wife, Judge, and Accuser*), a cast-off wife returns in male disguise to seduce her husband's new fiancée; the scene in which she kisses and gropes her caused such a scandal that Montfleury wrote a play-about-the-play to defend it.

Equally, it can be the woman-in-skirts who takes the initiative and seduces her rival. In James Shirley's *The Doubtful Heir* (performed c. 1638, published 1652), for instance, the beautiful, domineering Queen Olivia (her name clearly borrowed from *Twelfth Night*) decides to make her husband, Ferdinand, jealous by seducing his page "Tiberio," really his mistress, Rosania. Ferdinand encourages Rosania to go through with the late-night bedroom assignation, to keep the sexually frustrated queen at least temporarily happy, but Rosania is understandably nervous:

> But shall I not expose
> Myself to danger if her love pursue
> Immodest ends, since you advise I should
> Apply myself to her desires?

Sure enough, the ensuing scene hovers on the brink of rape. As Olivia plays with the hair of "Tiberio" and caresses "his" cheek, the stage direction is wonderfully vague: *"The Queen is pleasant with Ros."* Although Olivia does not know the page's secret, Shirley maximizes the titillation for the audience by having her play outrageously with gender.

OLIVIA   I suppose you a Lady all this while,
          And I the man, our lips must meet again,
          Will this instruct thee nothing?

ROSANIA   Gracious Madam.

OLIVIA   And yet this recreation comes short, Dear Lady, of
          what love might well allow us.

The next minute, it is a class boundary she is breaching: "Admit you are a Queen . . . I am become your servant." Then she demands they swap clothes, for extra excitement:

> Come, we'l in
> And change our Sexes; Thou shalt wear my clothes,
> And I will put on these, help on with thine,
> And I will dress thee handsomely, and then
> We'll act again.

"Not for the world dear Madam," gasps the panic-stricken Rosania.

This pattern of rivalry-turned-to-seduction could be treated romantically rather than lecherously, as in Sir John Suckling's *Brennoralt* (1646). Francelia and the cross-dressed Iphigene enter after spending the night together, in a scene reminiscent of *Romeo and Juliet:* "Look, the day breakes," says Iphigene. She asks for a picture to keep, but Francelia goes one better by giving her beloved "this virgin-bracelet of my haire" instead. Enter the jealous Almerin, who stabs them both. Iphigene confesses that she is a woman who courted Francelia to keep her away from the man she loves, Almerin. But instead of reacting with the expected rage and shame, Francelia insists she adores Iphigene as much as ever. (As for her original love object, Almerin, she rather snappishly sends him off to fetch a surgeon.) Iphigene marvels:

> Have you
> So perfectly forgiv'n already, as to
> Consider me a losse? I doubt which Sexe
> I shall be happier in. Climates of Friendship
> Are not lesse pleasant, 'cause they are lesse scortching,
> Then those of Love; and under them wee'l live;
> Such pretious links of that wee'l tye our souls
> Together with, that the chaines of the other
> Shall be grosse fetters to it.

The vocabulary of friendship as cooler and loftier than love is conventional; the situation, in which two women pledge themselves to each other forever as they lie bleeding in each other's arms, is anything but. It is the woman in skirts, not the one in breeches, who insists on the passionate nature of their bond; Francelia, aware she is not going to survive, refuses to tone down her language. "Oh would you / Had never un-deceiv'd me, for I had dy'd with / Pleasure, beleeving I had been your Martyr." In Suckling's remarkable tragedy, the death of both women does not function as a punishment, but a pedestal: they are lifted above any possible disapproval or disgust their passion for each other might arouse in the audience.

The heyday of the female bridegroom motif, in fiction, was the eighteenth century, when she did not need to have any motive loftier than liberty. The storyline spread contagiously across prose genres; we find women in breeches making conquests of other women in biographies or pseudo-memoirs of female rogues as well as in novels. My favorite female bridegroom story is the anonymous *Travels and Adventures of Mademoiselle de Richelieu* (1744), a brilliant if haphazard rake's progress which was completely forgotten until Professor Carolyn Woodward rediscovered it in the early 1990s. Its heroine, Alithea de Richelieu, describes herself as an unwomanly eccentric who roams around Europe, mostly in male disguise as the "Chevalier Radpont." The majority of her conquests of women are narrated in the predictable style, with gleeful arrogance and a last-minute withdrawal, but she strays into new territory when she finds herself becoming deeply attached to a young widow called Arabella de Montferan.

Feeling guilty about deceiving her, Alithea literally bares all—and at the sight of her breasts, far from recoiling, Arabella cries out in relief.

> How happy do you make me by this Discovery, which I hope will unite us in Bands of Friendship more solid and more noble than that of Love; and if your sentiments correspond with mine, nothing but Death shall separate us.

The context of cross-dressing and nakedness gives the "Bands of Friendship" a heightened tone which makes this speech sound very like a proposal. But how are these two women to share their lives, given that Alithea is not ready to go back into skirts, and a wedding ceremony, they agree, would put them at risk of prosecution for fraud? Arabella comes up with an imaginative solution: "If I cannot persuade you, continued she smiling, to give over your travelling project, I will take Breeches too, and we will set out together upon our Adventures." Alithea lets her readers know that she was just as ready to make the concession:

> I never in my Life felt so much Joy at her consenting to go along with me, and I expressed my Satisfaction in terms more proper for a Lover than a Friend; for to speak the truth, I found my Heart so rapt up in this lovely Woman, that had she stood out [held out], I certainly should have come into petticoats again.

Rather like the two heroines of Lyly's *Gallathea*, these women care only about being together, whichever role each ends up playing. Their vocabulary is diverse and relaxed: each refers to the other as her "Partner," and when they are briefly parted, Arabella writes to Alithea, "every Minute is an Age till I have the Pleasure of embracing my dear *Alithea,* who is Husband, Lover and Friend to Arabella." On the road, the two women in breeches break the hearts of many deceived girls; each is titillated by the other's successes, and only occasionally jealous of the other's closeness to other women. After being kidnapped by a female lecher, they escape and—tired at last, but still flexible in their "Friendship and Freedom"—decide to spend every winter on Arabella's estate in the south, and every summer on Alithea's estate in Paris. Though they make no promises of lifelong commitment, after several years Alithea observes that they are "without the least Thoughts of altering our Scheme 'till Death parts us" (her language echoing the Anglican wedding ceremony). Perhaps the most surprising text in the whole female bridegroom tradition, *The Travels and Adventures of Mademoiselle de Richelieu* takes advantage of a narrative convention so well-worn (by the mid-eighteenth century) that it raised no eyebrows. Starting out with the most formulaic cross-dressing plot, it ends up with a female marriage that—in its equality and flexibility on everything from houses to monogamy to roles—looks entirely modern.

The Male Amazon

Stories of disguised *women* are not the only ones that have lesbian repercussions. When a man puts on skirts, his motive is very often to court or seduce a woman under cover of female bonding, and just as much interesting havoc ensues. This literary tradition derives from various legends about men and gods (Achilles, Hercules, Theseus, Vertumnus) donning skirts. But by far the most interesting source, found in Hesiod, Apollodorus, Hyginus, Euripides, and Pausanias, is the tale of Diana and Callisto.

Goddess of hunting and the moon, Diana (a Roman version of the Greek goddess Artemis) is beautiful, wild, terrifying, and the original man-hater: in one legend, she punishes a man who spies on her by making his own dogs hunt him down and tear him apart. Her band of warrior nymphs—variously portrayed as her friends, servants, or worshippers—form a permanent community, passionately loyal to the goddess and their way of life. The Callisto story is told most fully and eloquently by Ovid in his *Metamorphoses* (circa 8 c.e.). "None of the nymphs . . . was dearer than she to the goddess of the Crossways: but a favourite is never a favourite for long," Ovid warns. When Jove, father of the gods, tries to seduce Callisto, the nymph resists his overtures so fiercely that he has to resort to a magic trick, changing his appearance so that he looks like Diana. Thinking she sees her beloved, Callisto lets her guard down.

> "Greetings, divine mistress," she cried, "greater in my sight than Jove himself—I care not if he hears me!" Jove laughed to hear her words. Delighted to be preferred to himself, he kissed her—not with the restraint becoming to a maiden's kisses. And as she began to tell of her hunting exploits in the forest, he prevented her by his embrace, and betrayed his real self by a shameful action.

Notice that Callisto is not put off by unrestrained kisses and embraces from the faux Diana. Only when these erotic overtures reach the "shameful action" of rape does she recognize that this must be a man.

Pieter van der Borcht, "Jupiter Seizes Callisto," in P. Ovidii Nasonis Metamorphoses *(1591).*
The rape of Callisto—or rather, the moment just before the rape, when the nymph believes she is being embraced by the goddess Diana—inspired many paintings as well as a great number of illustrations in editions of Ovid's Metamorphoses *from the fifteenth century to the eighteenth, such as this one by a painter of the Flemish school at Antwerp.*

Fallen and (inevitably) pregnant, the warrior girl lurks on the margins of her old world: "She scarcely raised her eyes from the ground, and did not stay close by the goddess as she usually did, nor did she take her place in the forefront of them all." But when Diana invites all her nymphs to bathe with her, and Callisto has to bare her swollen body, the merciless goddess neither asks nor cares whether it was rape or seduction: either way, the punishment for losing virginity is banishment. Poor Callisto finally ends up getting turned into a bear by Jove's furious wife.

The lesbian implications of the story were not lost on the many painters (including Titian and Boucher) who took it as their subject. What Jove does, disguised as Diana, has the paradoxical effect of gesturing toward a prior erotic connection among Diana and her nymphs: among any women who live secluded from men, in fact. A good example is *The Golden Age* (1611), in which Jacobean playwright Thomas Heywood specifies that Diana's nymphs sleep two by two, "coupled / And twinn'd in love," and take the following vow:

> You never shall with hated man atone,
> But lie with woman, or else lodge alone . . .
> With ladies only you shall sport and play,
> And in their fellowship spend night and day . . .
>
> Consort with them at board and bed,
> And swear no man shall have your maidenhead

Jupiter, disguised as a new applicant, promises jokily, "If e'er I lose't, a woman shall have mine!"—an answer Diana seems to like. When she orders the nymphs to "hand each other and acquaint yourselves," this literally means "go hand in hand and get to know each other," but Heywood's audience would have heard a suggestion of mutual handling, and a pun ("quaint," meaning "cunt") that dates back to Chaucer. The brief Callisto episode in William Warner's epic poem *Albion's England* (1586) is even more explicit:

> He feeleth oft her Ivorie breasts, nor maketh coy to kisse;
> Yet all was well, a Maiden to a Maiden might doe this.
> Then ticks he up her tucked Frocke, nor did *Calisto* blush,
> Or thinke abuse; he tickles too, no blab she thinks the Bush.

The last two lines can be roughly modernized as "then he touched her under her nightgown, and she did not blush or take offense; he tickled her too, and she did not take Diana's bush (i.e., vulva) for a bubble or swelling (i.e., penis)." All of which suggests that the serpent was already in this garden of all-girl intimacy. The man-in-skirts motif is not just about men's desperate desire for women, then, but also about the less definable eroticism among women that such a trick can bring to light.

Clearly influenced by the Callisto myth, the male amazon shows up in literature as early as the twelfth century, in Latin, French, Italian, Spanish, German, and English, becoming quite common in the sixteenth and seventeenth centuries. The disguised man was a familiar visual image: Giovanni Battista Guarini's 1590 play *Il Pastor Fido* (in English, *The Faithful Shepherd*), for instance, was not only translated into many languages but illustrated in scores of different paintings, prints, tapestries, and wall hangings across Europe. What may surprise readers familiar with the uneasy tittering caused by cross-dressed men in the movies today is that the skirt-wearing hero of these romances and plays is presented as young, gorgeous, virile, and clever—playful, without being laughable.

In many texts, his disguise causes no erotic confusion, because as soon as he gets a moment alone with his beloved, he declares himself as a man. But in some interesting romances and plays, he keeps up the act and courts her undercover. The earliest example of this may be Guillaume de Blois's extremely popular *Alda*, written in Latin around 1170. Pyrrhus disguises himself as his twin sister to reach and seduce his secluded beloved; "she" convinces Alda that "her" penis is an instrument "she" bought in the marketplace, and Alda suggests "she" should have bought a bigger one! After a week in bed, this prototypical gullible heroine is left pregnant, without any idea that her lover was not a woman.

When Robert de Blois took up the *Alda* plot for his thirteenth-century romance *Floris et Lyriopé,* he changed it to emphasize psychological interest over bawdry. Disguised as his twin sister, Florie (companion to the duke's daughter Lyriopé), Floris lies kissing Lyriopé in an orchard, reads her the story of *Piramus et Tisbé,* and sighs that if "she" were a man, "she" would love Lyriopé as much as Piramus did his Tisbé. Significantly, this desire is presented as a matter of cross-gender identification and borrowed roles; it is by reading and fantasizing that the faux Florie learns to express desire for "her" own sex. As for Lyriopé,

> "I don't know," she said, "what could I say.
> Loving too much seems madness to me.
> Sure we have to love each other,
> but love makes me sigh,
> it sends me to my bed, it makes me yawn and suffer.
> I do not wish to experience such things.
> I do not know if it is love
> that has made me sigh so frequently.
> I am falling apart, I sob,
> I love you much more than I should,
> And I know I should not, anyway, let myself go in such a way.
> At the same time, I know that you love me very much.
> I have not heard anywhere of
> Two young women loving each other in such a way.
> But I don't think I would love
> any man as much as I do you,
> nor would I have so much pleasure, I think,
> In the act of kissing, if a man were to kiss me."

Her speech is reminiscent of the one Iphis makes in Ovid's story. But where Iphis clearly identifies her desire for a girl as a problem with no precedent in nature or culture, Lyriopé mulls over the difficulty of knowing exactly what constitutes girls "loving too much," and she weighs its various pains and pleasures. Her conscience is troubled; such love is something she seems to think she should be able to rein in somewhat, but then again, on both Florie's side and hers, it seems too strong to resist. Lyriopé even goes beyond Iphis in seeing this as a permanent preference, because she doubts any man could move her as much. It is only at this point in the romance that Robert de Blois, having put his heroine through the wringer, has his hero unmask and prove her wrong by bedding her, to their great mutual satisfaction.

Though never as popular as the female bridegroom, the male amazon would linger for six centuries. He is utterly seductive; interestingly, although the amazon or female knight persona lets him show off his muscles, physical courage, and gallantry, it is usually his womanly qualities (such as beauty and gentleness) that clinch the deal. The male amazon often appears alongside the female bridegroom—or back to back, rather, as we saw in Ariosto's *Orlando Furioso* (1516–32), in which Ricciardetto cross-dresses to get into bed with the woman who loves his cross-dressing sister. The title of Walter Hawkesworth's Latin play of 1603, *Labyrinthus,* neatly describes the kind of erotic tangle that can ensue.

Just as we saw in adaptations of the Callisto story, women characters in satirical fiction can be amazingly relaxed about undefined physicality with their female friends. In a chaster way, heroines in the much loftier genre of romance—for instance, Emanuel Ford's very popular *Ornatus and Artesia* (1607)—generally take it in their stride when they find themselves (as they think) kissed and caressed by another woman. The great example of a heroine embarking on what she believes is a same-sex relationship is Honoré D'Urfé's vast, and vastly influential, pastoral romance *L'Astrée* (1607–27). Set outside Lyons in the fifth century C.E., it features hundreds of characters, a dozen of them in gender disguise; the *Amadis de Gaule* cycle was a key source. Joseph Harris points out the irony of the fact that D'Urfé, like other seventeenth-century romance writers, features cross-dressing so regularly as to render it banal, but always insists on calling it unprecedented; Harris describes this as the "constitutive amnesia" of cross-dressing plots.

D'Urfé must have been particularly fascinated by the situation of a man in skirts, because his main hero, Céladon, appears in three different female personae right through thousands of pages of *L'Astrée,* and in fact is shown dressed as a man in only a couple of scenes. (This constant skirt-wearing did not stop Céladon's name from becoming a byword for amorousness by the eighteenth century.) Having been banished by his beloved Astrée, Céladon approaches her as a Druidic priestess called "Alexis" and instantly wins her devotion, partly because "she" looks so like Céladon, whom Astrée believes drowned. Céladon has the bittersweet pleasure of being "cherished and caressed" as a beloved woman friend by the naïve heroine—and unable to reveal himself to her without losing all he has gained. Bed-sharing is agonizing enough, but one day, seeing Astrée half naked as she changes her clothes, "Alexis" cannot help seizing her

> and pressing her against her breast, and feeling her almost stark naked, it was just as well then that the shepherdess [Astrée] had little suspicion of her or she would have realized that these caresses

were a little tighter than those that girls customarily share; but she who thought nothing of it, freely gave her kisses, just as she received them, maybe not as if to Alexis but as if to the living portrait of Céladon.

But to analyze their relationship as if it is a private one would be misleading, because everything happens within Astrée's circle of intimate female companions—so intimate, in fact, that they all seem to embrace each other frequently, flirtatiously, and jealously.

We get the impression that the invisible masculinity of "Alexis" has somehow turned up the temperature in the group, even if the women do not understand why. Other texts that support this reading include a 1635 play by Jean de Rotrou, *Agésilan de Colchos* (based on *Amadis de Gaule*), in the third act of which Diane and Ardénie compete in a titillating "duel of kisses" for the affection of "Daraïde," a man in female disguise.

But in *L'Astrée*, the grand passion between the heroine and her new friend "Alexis" distinguishes itself sharply from the general mass of female intimacy. Astrée is in love, and proud of it; it does not occur to her that anything could be wrong with such a lofty, platonic form of passion. There is a key moment in the fourth volume, when she has been with her beloved "Alexis" for five years. "Alexis" (clearly hoping to play the same trick as in *Orlando Furioso*) asks if Astrée would love "her" if the gods changed "her" into a man. Astrée hates the idea, because she is sure she could never love another man after Céladon, and she would be losing the woman she adores: "From then on I would say farewell to all forms of pleasure and contentment." Weeping at the thought of ever losing "Alexis," Astrée makes a formal vow of eternal fidelity.

> Nothing—not parental pressure, financial crisis, nor any other consideration whatsoever that can be imagined, will ever separate me from my dear mistress, whom I embrace now—she said, flinging her arms around Alexis's neck—and who I'll never loose from the chains of my embrace until she has made this promise, unless she wants me to drop dead of sorrow!

"Alexis" matches this marital-style vow, swearing on what "she" calls the holiest place in the world, Astrée's bosom. Interestingly, when they hear people coming in the door, the two jump apart "so as not to be seen." This suggests a new awareness that their embraces, if not a cause for shame, at least require privacy. But Astrée will not admit that her choice of life-mate is in any way peculiar.

As Joseph Harris argues, Céladon's taste for cross-dressing verges on transvestism in the modern sense of a fetish; at one point "Alexis" even swaps costumes with "her" beloved, and sings a madrigal to express jealousy of Astrée's clothes. So this most famous of cross-dressing romances actually breaks the rules of the genre by refusing narrative closure: Céladon's disguise, although initially adopted for a good heterosexual reason, stalls the flow for a thousand pages. His female persona, "Alexis," starts to take over from him; the narrator increasingly uses "her" name and feminine pronouns to refer to Céladon, and the frontispieces to the third and fourth volumes feature "her." Our hero, clinging to a fantasy of spending the rest of his life as "Alexis" in blissful union with Astrée in an all-female Druidic temple, is frozen, unable to act. Perhaps unsurprisingly, D'Urfé left this vast saga unfinished at his death. When his secretary Baltazar Baro published a fifth volume, he let a Druid scold the hero: "My plan, said the Druid, was to help you marry Astrée, not this costume." In Baro's ending, it requires a direct order from the Druid to make Céladon take the risk of revealing himself to Astrée—who, as she predicted, is robbed of all "contentment." Mortified that others will think she was complicit in the trick all along, she rages at "her" (still using the name Alexis): "Perfidious and deceitful Alexis, die for the expiation of your crime." Even when Astrée is finally brought to accept Céladon as her husband, she expresses no regrets about the long years she spent (as she thought) loving a woman.

But perhaps the most interesting moments in *L'Astrée* are when characters become self-conscious about the idea of romantic love between women. Just as the men enjoy the novelty of trying on femininity, so they seem to relish making eloquent speeches to prove that, when it comes to loving women, women just do it better. (The game is temporary, after all, and so perfectly safe.) Notably, Filande—disguised as his married sister "Callirée"—makes a declaration of love to Diane that takes up Iphis's famous complaint from Ovid's *Metamorphoses* but manages to make a virtue of impossibility.

Are you astonished that, being Callirée, I speak to you with such affection? Remember that none of the impotence of my condition could ever diminish it in me; far from it, rather, it will preserve my love and make it more violent and more eternal, because nothing diminishes the ardour of desire so much as the enjoyment of what one desires, and that being impossible between us, until I am in my coffin you will be always loved, and I always the lover.

He alludes to the possibility of a divine sex change—not Iphis's (perhaps because it will already be in the readers' minds), but that of Tiresias.

And besides, if Tiresias having been a girl became a man, why may I not hope that the gods might favour me equally, if you are agreeable? Believe me, my lovely Diane, because the gods never do anything in vain, it does not seem that they have instilled in me such a perfect love, to let me struggle vainly with it, and if nature has caused me to be born a girl, my extreme love might well make it so that it has not been done pointlessly.

"Callirée" seems to be leaving it open as to whether the gods might turn "her" into a man, or simply let "her" and Diane discover some way to express their "extreme love" that will not be "in vain." Perhaps the strangest thing about this speech, for modern readers, is that the men who hear it are described as being left in ecstasies. One suitor irritates "Callirée" by exclaiming that the exquisite pathos of this love between women makes him love "her" all the more. "She" tells him coldly that he offends "her" honor as a married woman—whereas "her" own passion for Diane is so pure it does not threaten Diane's *honesteté* (chastity).

But in other works both before and after Honoré D'Urfé's *L'Astrée*, women do become confused and troubled when they find themselves falling for their friends. *Amadis de Gaule* (published from 1540 on) features several male amazons. In the eleventh volume, "Daraïde" (really Agesilan)—aware of being the object of infatuation of a woman called Lardenie—offers a new spin on *amor impossibilis*: "For a girl to love a girl, alas, what is that except to be in love with the moon and try to take it between your teeth?" But when courting another woman called Diane, "Daraïde" turns more optimistic, claiming Sappho as a glorious precedent for lesbian love. (His friend Arlanges, disguised as "Garaye," claims that they come from the land of Amazons, where women both fight like and love like men.) The Amazon's kisses, "sucking the honey from her purpled mouth," throw Diane into confusion; she cannot "understand such violent love from one girl to another." But she cannot resist it either, and she carries on allowing "Daraïde" all the privileges of friendship, including nude bathing. And when Agesilan finally reveals that he is a man, Diane's fury and refusal to speak to him except through an intermediary suggest that her sense of self has been badly shaken by the episode.

By far the most psychologically probing treatment of a woman's response to a male amazon is found in Sir Philip Sidney's tragicomic pastoral romance, the *Arcadia* (1593)—a work of such lasting popularity that Charles I is said to have quoted it as he mounted the scaffold. Its male amazon subplot is hinted at before it is told: an oracle warns the prince and princess of Arcadia that their daughter Philoclea and her sister are going to fall prey to "strange loves," so they hide them away. But young Prince Pyrocles invades their sanctum in the persona of an Amazon, "Zelmane"; with his golden helmet and velvet buskins, Pyrocles may well be the most gaudy hero in English literature. Interestingly, the narrator refers to him as "Zelmane" and "she" throughout, even when the prince is talking to his friend Musidorus, who knows about the disguise—so the feminine names and pronouns act as a sort of prose costume, letting readers forget that the Amazon is really a man.

"Zelmane" displays such a glamorous combination of feminine and masculine traits—being witty, singing love songs, killing a lion that scares Philoclea, kissing her hands with "more than womanly ardency"—that not only Philoclea but both her parents are attracted. Her mother is shrewd enough to guess the visitor's secret, but for the innocent Philoclea, these "burning kisses" have troubling implications. She gradually becomes aware that her friendship with the Amazon is "full of impatient desire, having more than ordinary limits." First she finds herself wishing that they were sisters, or that "they two might live all their lives together like two of Diana's nymphs" (which indirectly reminds readers of what happened to Callisto when she mistook a man for a woman)—but then she realizes that she could not bear to share with the other nymphs "who also would have their part in Zelmane." No, what she wants is an exclusive love, and here again Sidney gestures to a classical source (Ovid's legend of Iphis and Ianthe) without naming it.

Then, grown bolder, she would wish either herself or Zelmane a man, that there might succeed a blessed marriage betwixt them—but when that wish had once displayed his ensign in her mind, then followed whole squadrons of longings that so it might be, with a main battle of mislikings and repinings against their creation that so it was not.

Notice that the moment Philoclea realizes that her love is erotic, the language becomes military: an internal war. Dreams of her friend by night "did make her know herself the better" by day, and Philoclea starts to panic. This desire has crept up on her like a "disease" which is "impossible to be cured," or "like a river, no rampires being built against it till already it have overflowed." Sidney's dazzling succession of metaphors culminates with an image of Eros which hints at the Amazon's true nature: "for now indeed love pulled off his mask, and showed his face unto her, and told her plainly that she was his prisoner." This unmasking of desire—stripping off the guise of friendship—comes long before Prince Pyrocles's unmasking as a man.

Angst-ridden, Philoclea alternates between "paleness" and "extraordinary blushing," Sidney says, "desiring she knew not what, nor how, if she knew what." Kept by her jealous mother from talking to "Zelmane" alone, she walks in the moonlit wood and delivers a long soliloquy which recalls that of Iphis but is far more analytical. The sight of a marble stone on which Philoclea once wrote a vow of virginity shames her now; a cloud passing across the face of the moon (symbol of Diana) stands for the "outrageous folly" blotting her chastity. She asks the stars to judge: did she choose to catch this "plague," did she leave herself open to this "sin" and "shame" by lustful daydreams—or did it just happen to her with "unresistable violence"? Though she calls herself an "unfortunate wretch," Philoclea proves surprisingly tough-minded. However it may have happened, the important question is: what next? "It is the impossibility that doth torment me," she admits. "Alas, then, O love, why doost thou in thy beautiful sampler set such a work for my desire to take out?" The plague/sin/shame has become a piece of art, embroidery too intricate to unpick. Philoclea is not only coming to terms with her desire, but questioning whether it really is the *amor impossibilis* that tradition calls it. After all, her own mother is clearly panting for the Amazon. "Either she sees a possibility in that which I think impossible, or else impossible loves need not misbecome me." Sidney shows a wonderful comic touch here in having Philoclea play the dutiful daughter, following her mother in everything, even lesbian lust. At this point she goes beyond the wide-eyed heroine of Isaac de Benserade's *Iphis et Iante* (1637), who merely, vaguely wished that she could marry a woman without offending natural law. In the whispered but defiant conclusion of Philoclea's speech, she seems to conclude that natural law does not matter:

> "Away, then, all vain examinations of why and how. Thou lovest me, excellent Zelmane, and I love thee!" And with that embracing the very ground whereon she lay, she said to herself (for even to herself she was ashamed to speak it out in words), "O my Zelmane! Govern and direct me, for I am wholly given over unto thee."

Sidney puts the lovers through many more complications and embarrassments (including the obligatory bathing scene) before "Zelmane" finally reveals his sex. Philoclea's shock gradually gives way to relief— but, interestingly, she is not ready to deny the same-sex desire that led her to this point. In fact, she harps on it.

> Though the pureness of my virgin mind be stained, let me keep the true simplicity of my word. True it is (alas, too true it is), O Zelmane (for so I love to call thee, since in that name my love first began, and in the shade of that name my love shall best lie hidden), that even while so thou wert—what eye bewitched me, I know not—my passions were fitter to desire than to be desired.

It is as if she is almost nostalgic for the old "stain," the time when she was the active desirer rather than the passive desired, and is not yet ready to let go of the imaginary "Zelmane" who first won her love.

One of Sidney's sources was Jorge de Montemayor's pastoral romance *Diana* (1559), an influential bestseller not only in Spanish but in French, Dutch, German, and English translation, which includes a remarkable twist on the male amazon plot. At a party of shepherdesses, Selvagia finds herself "suddenly enamoured" with a visitor whose face—except for her beautiful eyes—is veiled.

But she seeing me sitting in this perplexitie, pulled out the fairest, and most dainty hand, that ever I did see, and taking mine into it, did with a sweete and amorous eie a little while behold me: whereupon being now so striken in love, as toong cannot expresse, I said unto her. It is not onely this hand, most faire and gracious Shepherdesse, that is always ready to serve thee, but also her hart and thoughts, to whom it appertaineth.

This is a spontaneous passion in one woman for another, not prompted by cross-dressing. But the crafty Ismenia immediately "complotted in her minde to mocke" Selvagia, as one of her "fonde prankes," we are told: Ismenia assures her she returns her feelings. What amazes Selvagia is not that her beloved is a woman, but her own luck in winning a woman of whom she is so unworthy: "How can it be, gentle Shepherdesse, that thy selfe being so passing faire, shouldest fall in love with her, who wants it so much," i.e., who lacks that beauty. After the usual vows of eternal love, "our mutual embracings were so many" that the two are completely distracted from the singing and dancing. When Selvagia pleads to see behind the veil, Ismenia reveals a "somewhat manlike" but beautiful face, and makes a startling declaration:

> And because thou maist knowe (faire Shepherdesse) the summe of this paine which thy beautie hath made me feele, and that the words which have passed betweene us but in sport, are true, knowe, that I am a man, and not a woman.

Selvagia "then was so far besides my selfe, that I knew not what to answere her"—possibly because she had not been thinking of their wooing as "sport" at all. Notice that she cannot help still using feminine pronouns for her beloved: "I felt my selfe so intangled in her love." She issues only a gentle rebuke:

> Faire Shepherdesse, that hast (to make me live without libertie, or for some other respect, which fortune best knows) taken upon thee the habit [costume] of her, who for thy love hath entirely vowed her affections to thee, thine owne hath sufficed to overcome me, without making me yeelde with mine own weapons.

The male amazon trick is here described oddly as a matter of overpowering a woman with her own weapons—taking advantage of her natural appreciation for the beauties of her own sex. But of course, the real trick is that Ismenia is only pretending to be a man in disguise; she is conquering Selvagia with the borrowed weapon of (putative) manhood. Once again, it seems as if the motif of the male amazon has the primary purpose of revealing the erotic potential in women's friendship.

The sheer length of Renaissance prose romance, and its accommodating structure, derived from Greek fiction as well as chivalric sources; the intertwining of different plots, and the nesting of distinct episodes within the text, could be said to make it an obvious home for a subject that required some explanation, such as desire between women. Philosophically, too, it was the right form; it is in works with a Neoplatonic emphasis on lofty emotions, including *Amadis de Gaule, L'Astrée,* the *Arcadia,* and *Diana,* that we find extended dialogues and monologues devoted to a heroine's awareness of her growing involvement with (as she thinks) another woman.

But what theater lacks in leisurely analysis, it can make up in excitement. John Fletcher's gripping tragicomedy *The Loyal Subject* (written 1618, published 1647), for instance, hinges on a lady's tormented attraction to her maid. Olympia falls for the "handsome wench," "Alinda," so hard and fast that she cannot convince herself it is merely friendship, especially since it involves breaching age and class boundaries. She reacts with fierce jealousy when her own brother, the duke, starts making up to "Alinda." The context of war heightens everything, and intensifies the play's theme of loyalty under fire: as an enemy army approaches, "Alinda" vows to defend "her" mistress to the death, and Olympia hovers on the verge of acknowledging her feelings as sexual: "O my Jewell, / How much I am bound to love thee: by this hand wench / If thou wert a man—" She cannot finish her sentence, but she and "Alinda," take the pseudomarital step of exchanging rings. When a misunderstanding over the duke parts them, the maid's "too much loving Mistris" is thrown into into what is described significantly as a "monstrous melancholy." The inappropriateness of this relationship borders on the monstrous, and certainly on the insane: "Sure she was mad of this wench," comments one woman. Enter a man called Archas, claiming to be the identical brother of "Alinda," and announcing her death. Olympia's devastated, guilty speech uses curiously gender-neutral pronouns for the maid who was her "best companion":

> I saw all this, I knew all this, I lov'd it,
> I doated on it too, and yet I kil'd it:
> O what have I forsaken? what have I lost?

It is as if she cannot dare to say, "I loved *her*, I killed *her*." Only at this point are any anxieties the audience may be feeling about this same-sex passion relieved by the revelation that this is a man-in-skirts plot after all. Like Shakespeare in *Twelfth Night*, Fletcher winds up his daring story-line with a jarringly pat transition; Archas admits to Olympia that he was "Alinda" all along, and she accepts the news—and Archas—with a readiness that in no way matches the turbulent complexity of her feelings for his "sister." Denise Walen makes the interesting suggestion that the last-minute introduction of the brother-who-was-only-pretending-to-be-the-sister does not nullify the women's love, but acts as an Ovidian sex change, turning an officially impossible relationship into a marital one.

That argument helps explain the reader's experience of Margaret Cavendish's drama *The Convent of Pleasure* (1668), which was never performed in her lifetime and languished in obscurity for centuries but is attracting great attention today. Lady Happy and her rich friends have withdrawn from the world to give themselves over to the pleasures of the senses in an all-female community. Their friendship becomes erotically heightened when some of them dress up in men's clothes to "act Lovers-parts" in private theatricals. Then comes a visitor, a "Princess" whose "Masculine Presence" makes her particularly good at wearing breeches and wooing Lady Happy. Like Diane in *Amadis de Gaule*, Lady Happy confronts her dilemma head-on: she fears her desire is against "Nature"—but then starts wondering, "why may not I love a Woman with the same affection I could a Man?" This kind of explicit analysis is more commonly found in romance (*Orlando Furioso, Arcadia, Amadis de Gaule, L'Astrée*) than in drama. The persuasive "Princess" assures Lady Happy that love between women is innocent. (An eavesdropper who watches them kiss, Madam Mediator, mutters that "Womens Kisses are unnatural.") The blissful couple exchange vows to "Join as one Body and Soul," with the whole community dancing in celebration. Only then, after this same-sex wedding, is the "Princess" revealed as a prince in disguise. By keeping the disguise a secret from the audience/readers, as Fletcher did in *The Loyal Subject* but with more open eroticism, Margaret Cavendish effectively creates a play about passion between women, with an Ovidian transformation ending.

If the delayed revelation of a female bridegroom's true sex, in seventeenth-century drama, has the effect of allowing audiences to take a courtship seriously because they believe it to be a heterosexual one, then the postponed unmasking of a male amazon has the opposite effect: it forces watchers or readers to confront the idea of same-sex desire for quite a while before soothing them with a last-minute transformation. But Joseph Harris makes the interesting point that both motifs stress "the contiguity of female desire and friendship," whether by "de-sexualising inter-female desire" in female bridegroom stories (presenting it as jokey, platonic, or easy to tone down into friendship) or by "eroticizing inter-female affection" in male amazon ones (letting the hero discover a discreet world of flirtatious kisses and caresses between women friends). Once again, we must conclude that it is impossible to completely separate the cultural history of desire between women from friendship; not that it is "all the same thing," but that it is in the vast territory where they overlap that the most interesting works are written.

The male amazon motif seems to have peaked in the seventeenth century. It lingered for a while: a popular example is the legend of Deidamia competing with her own father for the love of "Artamene" (Achilles in female disguise), which was the subject of more than thirty operas performed between 1663 and 1785. But it effectively died out of Western literature during the eighteenth century, probably because its feminizing of the hero and the scenes of self-conscious same-sex eroticism it provoked became more troubling to audiences and readers.

The female bridegroom, too, began to arouse some unease in the eighteenth century, at least on the public stage. (It was still thriving in fiction.) It is hard to date this shift, but according to playwright Nicolas Boindin, the Princesse Palatine banned his comedy *Le Bal d'Auteuil* (1702) purely because of a scene in which two mutually duped female bridegrooms made advances to each other. Laurence Senelick, in his study of cross-dressing and theater, quotes an English review of 1750 complaining about a scene in which Peg Woffington, in one of her famous "breeches parts,"

> makes love; but there is no one in the audience ever saw her without disgust; it is insipid, or it is worse; it conveys no ideas at all, or very hateful ones; and either the insensibility, or the disgust we conceive, quite break in upon the delusion.

This does not signal the end of female bridegroom roles, only a new uncertainty about whether such scenes were merely unrealistic or actually perverted. Lasting in highly conventionalized forms (think of the Principal Boy, hero of the traditional British pantomime, always played by a woman), this kind of cross-dressing has never been entirely banished from the stage.

In English fiction, nineteenth-century authors did not quite give up on the female bridegroom, but those few who did write about her felt obliged to provide her with armor against her critics. In Elizabeth Gaskell's Gothic story "The Grey Woman" (published by Dickens in *All the Year Round* in 1861), Lillie Devereux Blake's *Fettered for Life* (1874), and Dorothy Blomfield's "The Reputation of Mademoiselle Claude" (*Temple Bar,* July 1885), for instance, the cross-dressed woman must have an altruistic motive for her disguise, to make her intense romance with another woman acceptable, and at least one of the two must die.

A notable French exception is Théophile Gautier's philosophical novel *Mademoiselle de Maupin* (1835). (Gautier is said to have been inspired by his friend George Sand, by the seventeenth-century actress Madeleine de Maupin, and also by Henri de Latouche's influential novel of 1829 about a hermaphrodite, *Fragoletta.*) Critics have focused on the book's interest in aestheticism and androgyny, but what they often fail to point out is how central the theme of same-sex desire is. Mlle de Maupin, finding herself liberated by male disguise as "Théodore," is strongly attracted to both the Chevalier d'Albert and his lover, Rosette, and she befriends and flirts with them both. In a graceful nod to the female bridegroom tradition, Gautier has them act out *As You Like It,* with Maupin playing Rosalind to d'Albert's Orlando and Rosette's Phebe. Neither is sure whether Maupin is a man or a woman, and both have to face the likelihood that their desires are same-sex ones. Maupin claims to have no idea how she might satisfy Rosette, but in a nice irony, it is heterosexual initiation that enlightens her about the whole range of possible techniques: once d'Albert has bedded Maupin, "Théodore" goes into Rosette's room. Here follows a paragraph of tongue-in-cheek circumlocution, beginning with "What she said or did there I have never been able to ascertain, though I have done the most conscientious research." The narrator claims to have grilled the chambermaid, who not only described the way Rosette's sheets were "rumpled and untidy and carried the imprint of two bodies," but produced two pearls (just like the ones "Théodore" was wearing onstage) she found in the bed.

> I pass this piece of information on to my wise readers and leave them to make of it what they will. As for myself, I have made a thousand conjectures on the subject, each more preposterous than the one before, and so outrageous that I really don't dare to set them down on paper, even in the most respectable, euphemistic words.

The negative space of the mark left by two bodies; the clitoral symbolism of two pearls: that is all Gautier sets against the seven pages of joyous lovemaking he has given us between Maupin and d'Albert.

Patricia Duncker points out that Gautier could have written an erotic scene between the women here if he had wanted to; by 1835 French readers had encountered such things before, in literature as well as pornography (see chapter 4), and earlier in *Mademoiselle de Maupin* we have been treated to elaborate descriptions of nipple-stiffening embraces between Rosette and "Théodore." She argues that Gautier is able to show us d'Albert in bed with Maupin-as-a-woman, but not what happens in Rosette's room, because s/he who finally satisfies Rosette is "the cross-dressed lover, the woman who is also a man," the third term, which cannot be "made visible" but lives in the reader's mind. Duncker's reading accounts for the tantalizing oddity of the scene, but we should also remember that Gautier, for all his iconoclasm, was writing within a literary tradition. A tradition in which, for at least three centuries, *amor* between women, whether cross-dressed or not—

perhaps *impossibilis,* or perhaps not—had been routinely called (to borrow Gautier's words) "strange," "preposterous," and "outrageous," and veiled by language coy, "euphemistic," and downright deceptive.

Even so, Maupin could be called the last great female bridegroom. Unlike most of her predecessors, she refuses to settle in the end for the pleasures of one gender role or one sexual preference.

> I am of a third, separate sex which does not yet have a name . . . My dream, a chimera, would be to have both sexes in turn, to satisfy this dual nature. Man today, woman tomorrow, I should reserve for my lovers my loving tenderness, my submissive and devoted attentions, my softest caresses, my sad little sighs, everything which belongs to my feline, feminine nature. Then with my mistresses I should be enterprising, bold, passionate, dominant, with my hat pulled down over my ear, with the demeanour of a captain and an adventurer.

Although the phrase "third sex" would be borrowed, in the second half of the nineteenth century, to describe "inverts" as male minds trapped in women's bodies (or vice versa), its original meaning here is much less tragic. Maupin seems to have no objection to her female body, she just does not want to have to pick one sartorial, behavioral, and sexual style. Or, God forbid, one lover. Unlike in *Fragoletta* (1829), or later works in the same line, such as Rachilde's *Madame Adonis* (1888), this promiscuous androgyne does not die. Gautier lets Maupin ride confidently off into the dawn, writing to d'Albert and Rosette (with, as Duncker points out, a blasphemous echo of Christ's words in the Mass) that they should "love one another in remembrance of me."

In the preface, Gautier declares, "The only things that are really beautiful are those which have no use," which is applicable both to his artistic credo and his heroine's playfully nonreproductive sexuality. Though *Mademoiselle de Maupin* invokes the spirit of Shakespearean comedy, its readers found it breathtakingly modern. It would become the bible of decadent literature half a century after publication, and influence many other novels—including Virginia Woolf's *Orlando* (1928), in which the title character gets to literally fulfill Maupin's dream of living as a man and a woman in turn.

In the twentieth century, lesbian writers began to rework the female bridegroom motif self-consciously. Jeanette Winterson's postmodern fantasia of Napoleonic Venice, *The Passion* (1987), is an excellent example of a text that can be illuminated by an awareness of the long tradition in which it sits. Winterson may have had all sorts of reasons for centering her story on a girl dressed as a boy (to work as a croupier), but what is undeniable is that this erudite author was also giving her own spin to the ancient motif of the female bridegroom. Having won the love of a married woman, our heroine-in-breeches decides to risk being honest with her by means of a classic gesture.

> I went back to her house and banged on the door. She opened it a little. She looked surprised. "I'm a woman," I said, lifting up my shirt and risking the catarrh.
> She smiled. "I know."
> I didn't go home. I stayed.

What is new is not the smile—we saw that in some eighteenth-century novels such as *Mademoiselle de Richelieu*—but the "I know," which demolishes the cliché of the naïve bride. *The Passion* simultaneously takes part in the old game of gender-bending, and takes it apart.

CHAPTER TWO

Inseparables

From a twenty-first-century perspective it is easy to see why women dressing as men would trigger desire in other women, because *opposites attract:* it is one of our culture's most beloved truisms. So why is it that in most of the texts we have been looking at, it is the female bridegroom's beauty, sweetness, delicacy, politeness, and compassion—more or rather than her borrowed masculinity—that other women find so irresistible? And why, if it is opposites that attract, would female characters be equally drawn to men (gentle, polite, beautiful men) disguised as women?

The fact is, in Renaissance literature, love was very often thought to be based not on contrast but on similarity; the classical model was the romantic bond between two men. Like calls to like; birds of a feather flock together. There is an intriguing exchange in Honoré D'Urfé's *L'Astrée* (1607–27), when a jealous man called Hylas asks sneeringly if "Alexis" (a man disguised as a priestess) finds shepherdesses more appealing than shepherds, and "she" answers proudly, "Have no doubt about it, and blame no one but nature, who wants everyone to love his own kind." When Leonard Willan dramatized D'Urfé's saga as *Astraea*

(1651), he included a debate between a woman and a man, to be judged by their mutual object of desire, Diana. Phillis argues that same-sex passion is strongest because love grows from "Equality and Sympathy"; Sylvander counters that mating requires difference.

> You plead th'advantage of yoor Sexe, as bent
> To love semblable were natures Intent;
> In Beasts see where her motives simple be,
> Their preservations shall t'each contrarie.

Impressed by both arguments, Diana declares a draw between her two lovers. More than two centuries before the invention of sexual-identity words such as "heterosexual" or "homosexual," this obscure English playwright recognized distinctions between the love of the same sex and the love of the opposite sex, but presented both as valid, in the dialectical form of a civilized debate.

In this chapter, then, I explore the second storyline of love between women: based on likeness, it springs up spontaneously, with no need for gender disguise as a trigger. Let us begin with this plot's earliest source, a famous declaration of love that has been read at a million weddings.

> Intreat me not to leave thee, or to return from following after thee: for whither thou goest, I will go; and where thou lodgest, I will lodge: thy people shall be my people, and thy God my God: Where thou diest, will I die, and there will I be buried: the LORD do so to me, and more also, if ought but death part thee and me.

The odd thing is that Ruth is making this promise not to her bridegroom, but to her former mother-in-law, Naomi. The story of this unlikely pair is told in the Old Testament book of Ruth, an anonymous Hebrew tale written down probably before the Babylonian Exile of 586 B.C.E. Since the death of Naomi's son—Ruth's husband—the two women have no legal relationship, and nothing obvious in common: not age, nor tribe, nor religion (Ruth is Moabite, Naomi Israelite). Yet "Ruth clave under her," we are told, and the verb (*dabaq,* to cling, cleave, or hold fast to something), is used four times in two chapters to emphasize the seriousness of the younger woman's purpose. For modern readers it is hard to grasp the enormity of Ruth's plan to go with Naomi into Israel: think of a one-way trip to the moon. "Where thou lodgest, I will lodge" refers not to the location but to the quality of shelter: Ruth means that she is willing to be a vagrant and beggar. Her generosity even extends beyond this life, since she is giving up all hope of being buried with her ancestors. The vow at the end formally places Ruth in Naomi's bondage and asks to be—in the more explicit original—struck with afflictions if she lets anything but death divide her from Naomi. By the end of this peculiar story, Naomi has helped Ruth elicit protection, and then a proposal of marriage, from one of Naomi's kinsmen. But its climax is when Ruth puts her newborn son into Naomi's arms. The women neighbors remark that Naomi has a son once more, "for thy daughter in law, which loveth thee, which is better to thee than seven sons, hath born him."

So what is this bond between two women which can surpass the love of seven sons? It has generally been glossed as daughterly affection—but it is quite different, because it is voluntary, not based on the duties of blood, law, or tradition. Over the centuries, many readers have seen the book of Ruth as a scriptural proof of the potential for a same-sex love that is as holy as it is romantic. One of them, in a Scottish poem written before 1586, offers Ruth and Naomi as a shining example to set against the more famous male-female and male-male couples that the poet lists. It is more than a little ironic that a story about two women reduced to begging for food became the touchstone for the ideal of love between leisured, literate ladies.

Perhaps what writers liked about this kind of bond was that it seemed so *un*like the one between men and women as codified in marriage. They imagined it as pure emotion, soaring above the worldly concerns of law, economics, and reproduction. Sharon Marcus says of Victorian women that

> as an ideal, friendship was defined by altruism, generosity, mutual indebtedness, and a perfect balance of power. In a capitalist society deeply ambivalent about competition, female friendship offered a vision of perfect reciprocity for those who could afford not to worry about daily survival.

So was this kind of love thought to be sexual? Well, that all depends. If sex is about penises in vaginas, then no, obviously. If sex is about the touching of genitals, then no, probably not, in most cases.

The writers I look at in this chapter seem to share a working assumption that is subtly different from *amor impossibilis*. Not that *women cannot have sex with each other,* but that *women* (upper- and middle-class women, at least—educated and virtuous women) *would not dream of such a thing.* Whatever private views some authors may have held, this was the official line.

But (as we have already seen with cross-dressing plots) a safety net allows for free movement: if everything heroines felt for their friends was technically nonsexual, then it was acceptable to represent it as important, intense (whether idyllic or stormy), and expressed by passionate caresses as well as words. Sharon Marcus sums it up neatly: "Precisely because Victorians saw lesbian sex almost nowhere, they could embrace erotic desire between women almost everywhere." Nowadays we tend to define sex much more broadly, which is why I will be reading certain passages about particularly ecstatic, private embraces as, effectively, sex scenes. Bear in mind, however, that in the world of these plays and fictions, the embraces are neither shocking nor the focus: it is the love they express that really matters to the story.

In French and English literature from the sixteenth to the nineteenth centuries, such love goes by many names, from "romantic" or "tender" friendship to "amity," "*amitié,*" or simply "love." Typically, playwrights and novelists borrow the feelings of Ruth and Naomi, but not their situation: they are more interested in the charming scenario of a pair of girls whose bond emerges naturally from their similarity and mutual familiarity. The girls are either shown as growing up together or as being "kindred spirits" who fall in love at first meeting. Because of their likeness in age and background, they can act as mirrors to each other, although events will often reveal their characters as contrasting. Because of their youth, their bond can represent freedom and innocence on the brink of being lost in adulthood. The fervor of the girls' love is often further justified—especially in Victorian fiction, with its cult of family—by their being cousins or sisters (full, step, half, or foster). In many eighteenth- and nineteenth-century novels, two women passionately drawn to each other on sight will turn out to be—surprise!—sisters; as in the case of the male amazon disguise, we are supposed to assume that their unconscious recognition of each other prompted the attraction.

The shorthand I use for such love is *inseparability,* not only because *inseparable* was a common term for female pairs by the late sixteenth century, but because the word foreshadows the plot this kind of love tends to produce: a threat of separation, whether of the literal or emotional kind. Just as, in the scripture, we hear nothing of Ruth's feelings until the moment Naomi tells her to go home, so in Western literature from the sixteenth to the nineteenth centuries, love between two inseparables rarely moves into the spotlight until the moment someone tries to pry them apart.

Shall We Be Sunder'd?

William Shakespeare's comedy *As You Like It* (staged in 1600, published in 1623) is still the most famous portrayal of female friendship in the literary canon, and the prototypical inseparability plot. Rosalind and her cousin Celia have grown up together at the ducal court of Celia's father (who has banished his brother, Rosalind's father, as a traitor), and they delight everyone with their witty, warm sparring; "never two ladies loved as they do," comments one man. When Duke Ferdinand, jealous of the niece who outshines his daughter, strips Rosalind of her fortune and sends her into exile, Celia stands up to him and insists that the two must be judged as one:

> I know her. If she be a traitor,
> Why so am I: we still have slept together,
> Rose at an instant, learn'd, play'd, eat together;
> And wheresoe'er we went, like Juno's swans,
> Still we went coupled and inseparable.

Celia is insisting that what makes their bond unbreakable is not law, not blood (even though they are kin), but intimacy. "Shall we be sunder'd? Shall we part, sweet girl?" she asks Rosalind. "No; let my father seek another heir." So they run away together in disguise, Rosalind (crossing gender lines) as a man and Celia (crossing class ones) as a shepherdess. Shakespeare borrowed his plot from Thomas Lodge's *Rosalynde* (1590), which has origins both classical (Lodge describes the girls, in an ancient phrase that has been attributed to Aristotle, as having "two bodies, and one soule") and Christian (since her cousin's vow to be Rosalynde's "faithful copartner" and "felow mate" through all trials audibly echoes the book of Ruth). But Shakespeare added some interesting ambiguities. For all the heroic setup, the friendship has the flippant rhythms of a music-hall act. From her first few lines, Celia often (and only semi-teasingly) implies that their passion is lopsided: "I see thou lov'st me not with the full weight that I love thee," she complains, and a few scenes later, "Rosalind lacks, then, the love / Which teacheth thee that thou and I am one." Celia bears the weight of this friendship, does all the work. Again in that opening scene, she warns Rosalind to "love no man in good earnest," and when her cousin does fall for the handsome Orlando, Celia's teasing has a persistently dark edge ("his kisses are Judas's own children") that suggests her resentment of any suitor daring to encroach on their joint adventure. In the sketchy way that Shakespeare often winds up his subplots, he produces a brother of Orlando's at the end who—offstage, with no warning—proposes to Celia. This ensures that the two friends will not be "sunder'd," at least. But something has been lost; Rosalind and Celia could hardly be described as "coupled and inseparable" anymore, and Celia is given not a word to say in the fifth act. As a love story, theirs is anticlimactic. But the sparkling repartee and credible warmth of their rapport—and, of course, their adventuring in butch/femme disguise—make them an unforgettable duo, with an immense influence on later plays and fiction about love between women.

In her groundbreaking study *The Renaissance of Lesbianism in Early Modern England*, Valerie Traub argues that love between girls in plays such as *As You Like It* is only allowed to amount to a charming phase, a brief delay in the plot's thrust toward a marital resolution. Certainly, in George Chapman's *Monsieur D'Olive* (1606) and in *The Two Noble Kinsmen* (performed in 1613, published in 1634, probably a collaboration between Shakespeare and John Fletcher), one girl is already dead when the action begins, so the onus is on the survivor to get over her grief and grow up. Emilia in *The Two Noble Kinsmen* not only feels a commitment to her dead friend but a strong "persuasion" toward women, what Hippolyta criticizes as a "sickly appetite"; Emilia insists that she will never "love any that's call'd man," and argues "That the true love 'tween maid and maid may be / More than in sex dividual" (meaning "between opposite sexes"). In both plays the relationship has already been curtailed by death, but is still described in terms serious and erotic enough to disturb observers. Certainly this kind of love does not prevent marriage—since both characters will finally be persuaded to break the vows of virginity they made to their lost beloveds—but it has a lingering force.

Along the same lines as *As You Like It,* but often without humor to leaven the heroics, there are many plays and fictions in which young women go to extraordinary lengths for each other's sake. Leading the field is William Davenant's *Love and Honor* (written about 1634, published in 1649), about the "fond excess of love" between two kidnapped princesses. In a climax that verges on the ludicrous, when Evandra is under sentence of death Melora ties her up, borrows her clothes, and presents herself for execution in Evandra's place "with / As liberall joy, as to the marriage priest"; the simile suggests that this is an ecstatic consummation of friendship.

Occasionally the friends are not a pair of similar young ladies but mistress and maid, their intense fondness based on sworn service but transcending it: examples include Chrétien de Troyes's romance *Yvain* (1100s), adapted into the anonymous English *Ywain and Gawain* (1300s); Lodowick Carlell's play *The Deserving Favourite* (1630); Jane Wiseman's play *Antiochus the Great* (1702); and Samuel Johnson's *The History of Rasselas* (1759)—a short philosophical bestseller, composed in a week to pay for his mother's funeral. John Fletcher's play *The Pilgrim* (1622) gives a maid the startling declaration, "My Mistresse is my husband, with her I'le dwell still." This kind of loyalty becomes pathological in Daniel Defoe's novel *Roxana* (1724): the heroine both damages and is damaged by her fiercely protective maid, Amy, who ends up murdering Roxana's long-lost daughter.

But perhaps the most extraordinary take on mistress-maid inseparability is Jane Barker's brusque story "The Unaccountable Wife" (part of her patchwork-style fiction of 1723, *A Patchwork Screen for the Ladies*). Here a bond formed within the traditional family ends up destroying it. Because the (unnamed) wife is barren, the (unnamed) maid swaps roles with her and gives birth to the husband's babies; the wife pampers her and does the housework, and all three share the marital bed. This arrangement, shocking though it is to the neighbors (mostly for its violation of class boundaries), lasts until the husband, feeling financially burdened by all these children, kicks them and their mother out. The

Hubert François Gravelot, "Le premier baiser de l'amour" ["Love's first kiss"] (1760), engraved by N. Le Mire, in Jean-Jacques Rousseau, Julie, ou la nouvelle Heloïse *(1761).*
    A student under Boucher, a friend to Hogarth, and a teacher to Gainsborough during a thirteen-year sojourn in England, Gravelot was known for his illustrations to luxury editions of novels. Although his title refers to the famous first kiss between Julie and St. Preux in the little grove, arranged by Claire in complicity with Julie, what Gravelot actually shows is the moment just before it, when the man seems to be aspiring to share (or break?) the intimacy of the female couple.

joke is that the deal he thought was for his convenience turns out to have nothing to do with him: the wife makes the "unaccountable" choice to go with the woman she describes as her only friend in the world, and ends up begging on the street to support her and the children. This enigmatic tale has none of the gushy rhetoric of a play such as Davenant's *Love and Honor,* but they sit side by side in a long tradition of women's inseparability put to the test.

    In the novel as it had developed in England and France by the middle of the eighteenth century, such "unaccountable" devotions were to be fully accounted for in terms that may sound gushy to modern ears, but are no less burningly sincere for that. French philosopher Jean-Jacques Rousseau's *Julie, ou la Nouvelle Héloïse* (1761), probably the best-

selling work of fiction of the century, sent many of its readers into fren-
zies of emotion; one of them wrote to tell Rousseau that it had worked
so powerfully on him that it cured his cold. *La Nouvelle Héloïse* is one of
the most famous treatments of a lasting passion between two women;
plot summaries, which always focus on the men in Julie's life, fail to
capture the importance for Rousseau of love between women as an
expression of pure, unworldly sensibility. Claire is our heroine's "inseparable Cousin," and, like Celia in *As You Like It,* the one who feels most.
But as Janet Todd argues, despite her name there is nothing clear about
her love for Julie: it is complicated throughout the novel by her urge
to manipulate and dominate her beloved. Claire insists on being the
intermediary in Julie's courtship by their tutor St. Preux, for instance,
and is outraged to hear that the couple thought of eloping without
her: "To intend to abandon your friend! To plan to run away without
me!" Through correspondence she keeps a close hold on Julie through
the subsequent crises (pregnancy, miscarriage, renunciation, and an
arranged marriage to Wolmar).

"As a woman I am a sort of monster," Claire warns D'Orbe before
their own wedding ceremony, "and by I know not what quirk of nature
friendship for me takes precedence over love. When I tell you that my
Julie is dearer to me than you, you merely laugh, and yet nothing is
more true." D'Orbe may laugh, but he does nothing to interfere with
his wife's prior commitment. Julie's lover St. Preux, on the other hand,
adores watching the young ladies together.

> Ye gods! What a ravishing spectacle or rather what ecstasy, to
> behold two such moving Beauties tenderly embracing, the one's
> face resting on the other's breast, their sweet tears flowing
> together . . . I was jealous of such a tender friendship.

But this is jealousy without a sting, and years later he tells Claire that
"my heart knows no difference between you, nor feels the least inclina-
tion to separate the Inseparables." Although St. Preux's titillated
"voluptuous empathy" with the women's love might seem to have
nothing in common with D'Orbe's laughter, the two men have come
by different routes to the same conclusion: that this overwhelming passion between women need not get in the way of men's claims on them.
Widowed, Claire arrives to finally live with her beloved and Wolmar

and raise their children together—but instead, Julie dies in her arms. Claire

> threw herself upon her body, warmed it with hers, endeavoured to revive it, pressed it, clung to it in a sort of rage, called it loudly by a thousand passionate names, and sated her despair with all these pointless efforts [...] rolling around on the floor wringing her hands and biting the legs of the chairs, murmuring some extravagant words in a muted voice, then at long intervals uttering piercing cries [...] the convulsions with which she was seized were something frightening.

Eighteenth-century readers, no less than twenty-first-century ones, would have registered the pornographic overtones of this passage; in 1959 Hans Wolpe commented nervously that "the ambiguity is preserved only by one fact: we are dealing with a *dead* body." In this vast novel's last letter the "inseparable Cousin" writes of her death wish: Julie's coffin "awaits the rest of its prey . . . it will not wait for long." Rousseau presents Claire's lifelong refusal to be parted from her beloved as peculiar, in some ways destructive to both, and yet gloriously romantic.

Writing about the ways Rousseau's and other eighteenth-century novels reconcile marriage and same-sex love, Susan Lanser calls the women's friendships "consolatory adjuncts that enable the heterosexual plot." But Sharon Marcus's book on Victorian literature rethinks this enabling role: she comes to the conclusion that there is nothing subordinate about relationships between women in courtship novels. The friend is beloved, confidante, matchmaker, and permanent beloved family member rolled into one: "Marriage plots unite not only a man and a woman but two social institutions, friendship and marriage, which begin as separate but are finally united in a kind of Moebius strip or feedback loop." Perhaps the most fascinating of Marcus's examples is Anthony Trollope's *Can You Forgive Her?* (1864–65), in which spinster Kate is not merely happy at the prospect of her brother George marrying her friend Alice, so they can all live together, but does the wooing for him, including the traditional proposal on bended knee: " 'Oh, Alice, may I hope? Alice, my own Alice, my darling, my friend! Say that it shall be so!' And Kate knelt at her friend's feet upon the heather, and looked up into her face with eyes full of tears."

But it is a rather different plot I am interested in here, the story of friends threatened with separation—a story which sometimes includes marriage, but sometimes keeps it at bay. Despite the friends typically being described in terms of likeness, the narrative pattern was an asymmetrical one from the start: in *As You Like It,* it is Celia who sacrifices her family and fortune for Rosalind, who is not sacrificing anything in return. By the eighteenth century, in novels such as *La Nouvelle Héloïse,* a clear distinction has developed between the vulnerable heroine and her gallant friend. It seems there is nothing these protectors will not do for the sake of the beloved: risk their own reputation, even marry men they cannot stand.

Interestingly, nineteenth-century novels often feature a bond between a virginal woman and a fallen one—whether a deflowered innocent or a longtime prostitute. The friendship is redemptive and uplifts both of them in different ways. Sometimes these novels are strongly feminist, highlighting solidarity between women across the social chasm. Often a Christian context allows for the description of the relationship in erotically overwrought terms, for instance in *Joanna Traill, Spinster* (1894)—the novel that made the name of Annie E. Holdsworth, a missionary's daughter from Jamaica—in which Joanna takes in a penitent whore called Christine. It is no accident that many of these characters are named after Christ or Mary—Marion in Elizabeth Barrett Browning's verse novel *Aurora Leigh* (1856), for instance, or the title character in Rosa Mulholland's *The Tragedy of Chris* (1903). Mulholland's novel begins as an idyll, with two Irish flower sellers managing to rent a room together and foster a baby while the mother is in jail. It segues into the "tragedy" of the title when Chris is kidnapped. The tireless Sheelia tracks her for three years through the urban wilderness of London—only to find her "darling" trapped in white slavery (the Victorian euphemism for prostitution). "I'm goin' to save you now," Sheelia insists valiantly. "We'll go away somewhere, home to our own country, some place where nobody will ever know what happened." But you can't go home again, as the saying has it, because while Ireland is only a boat ride away, the country of innocence, of prelapsarian girlhood romance, is beyond reach. The reunion is only temporary; Chris must die in that unspecified depressed/poxed/consumptive way that white slaves do, freeing Sheelia to start a new life with a good man. By English literary convention, extramarital sex is fatal for women.

Work, an 1873 novel by Louisa May Alcott—more famous for the *Little Women* series—is one of the few exceptions to the rule that death must ultimately separate the fallen woman and her virginal protector. The seamstress Christie—yet another of those Christlike names—and the fallen Rachel, having endured painful tests of loyalty and years apart, are finally rewarded with a shared life in a women's household. But then, Alcott intones fatalistically:

> Only one summer allowed for the blossoming of the friendship
> that budded so slowly in the spring; then the frost came and killed
> the flowers, but the root lived long enough underneath the snows
> of suffering, doubt and absence.

This botanical parable makes love between women seem natural—but it also naturalizes its persecution. It is no enemy in particular that attacks the plucky little plant, simply "the frost." Even an author as feminist as Alcott, writing a story with a happy ending, cannot see female inseparability outside the traditional framework of endurance.

Sometimes, instead of producing dramatic events, love between women merely survives them: the inseparables, despite their name, consent to separation. For instance, in *Euphemia* (1790), by Charlotte Lennox, the heroine is married off to a lout who insists on taking her into the wilds of America, so she and her beloved Maria have to maintain their love by thoughts and letters for more than a decade before being rewarded by reunion. Here inseparability is sublimated into pure suffering. (Lennox, incidentally, walked out on her own bad marriage.) We are left wondering whether, over the gap of two centuries, Shakespeare's Celia would recognize this pious, passive way of being "coupled and inseparable."

JEALOUSIES

"It is not absence which severs friends, but changes in heart, and mind, and position," warns *Woman's Friendship* (1851) by Anglo-Spanish/ Jewish novelist Grace Aguilar. Often what threatens inseparables is not literal parting but alienation from each other. What would it take, many writers wondered, to break such a bond? How would it fare in a tug-of-

C. Carleton [attributed], "Love felt her soft lips on her cheek," in Mary E. Wilkins Freeman, The Love of Parson Lord and Other Stories (1900).
   In this story the motherless heroine Love is greeted by her patron and "first love," the squire's lady, whose grandson waits impatiently to be introduced. The book's illustrations were credited to "C. Carleton and Another."

war with other virtues such as honor, patriotism, or filial feeling? Or—perhaps most interestingly—the attraction between the sexes?

As Janet Todd puts it succinctly in *Women's Friendship in Literature*, "female friendship is rarely allowed to exist in a pair." Though, as we have seen, it can coexist harmoniously with the relationship one of them has with a man, in other texts the two bonds are set against each other in a tense triangle, when a man is introduced as a wedge between the inseparables. This motif of women friends turned rivals—a variation on the ancient triangle in which men friends fight over a woman—is played out in many dramas and fictions from the seventeenth to the nineteenth century. A typical example is Henry Wadsworth Long-fellow's novel *Kavanagh* (1849), which presents the love between Cecilia and Alice as a mere trial run, "a rehearsal in girlhood of the great drama of woman's life." When they both fall for a man, the metaphors become downright ejaculatory:

> The old fountain of friendship, that hitherto had kept the lowland landscape of [Alice's] life so green, but now being flooded by more affection, was not to cease, but only to disappear in the greater tide, and flow unseen beneath it.

That is, Alice's feeling for Cecilia must "disappear," and Cecilia must conveniently drop dead.

Oddly enough, only one of the women needs to actually want the man for the ritual of sexual competition to be set in motion. For instance, the problem in Shakespeare's *A Midsummer Night's Dream* (staged around 1595, published 1600) is that Helena loves Demetrius, who has abandoned her to court her friend Hermia. Despite the fact that Hermia rejects him in favor of Lysander, Helena becomes insanely jealous. Puck's reversal of the situation with a magical flower only makes it worse, because both men now pursue Helena, who is convinced she is being mocked and makes a famous lament for lost intimacy.

> We, Hermia, like two artificial gods,
> Have with our needles created both one flower,
> Both on one sampler, sitting on one cushion,
> Both warbling of one song, both in one key;
> As if our hands, our sides, voices, and minds,
> Had been incorporate. So we grew together,
> Like to a double cherry, seeming parted,
> But yet an union in partition,
> Two lovely berries moulded on one stem;
> So, with two seeming bodies, but one heart;
> Two of the first, like coats in heraldry,
> Due but to one, and crowned with one crest.
> And will you rent our ancient love asunder,
> To join with men in scorning your poor friend?

Notice that Shakespeare ascribes to love between girls a pseudodivine power, a spiritually fertile quality. Like "gods" the two "create" a flower with their needles, and the "double cherry" is a literally fruitful image (as well as a symbol of virginity). The fact that their "union" is compared to a symmetrical "crest" suggests that their love is like the marital bond recorded in heraldry.

Whereas Celia in *As You Like It* asked, "shall we be sunder'd" by harsh circumstances, Helena's is a more psychological question—"And will you rent our ancient love asunder?"—which clearly echoes the Anglican marriage ceremony, with its "Those whom God hath joined together, let no man put asunder." She is not accusing Hermia here of taking her man, but of something rather more subtle: letting men into the secret garden of girls' love. The irony is that it is Helena herself who, by falling so hard for Demetrius and becoming possessed by the demons of jealousy, could be said to have "rent our ancient love asunder." At the end of *A Midsummer Night's Dream* both women do "join with men" (each marrying the one she wants), and though they are all officially friends again, it is significant that Shakespeare does not show Hermia and Helena speaking another line to each other.

A much darker version of this rivalry powers Nicholas Rowe's *The Tragedy of Jane Shore* (1714), one of the most frequently produced plays in eighteenth-century England. When Jane's affair with King Edward leads to disaster, she runs to her childhood friend Alice in search of an emotional haven, volunteering to "give up Mankind" and be her loving "Partner." Here friendship joins forces with a fervent proto-feminism— a subject that Rowe helped to introduce to the early-eighteenth-century stage. Alice seems to welcome Jane as her "other self," and makes a vow in the tradition of the book of Ruth.

> Be witness of this Truth, the holy Friendship,
> Which here to this my other self I vow.
> If I not hold her nearer to my Soul,
> Than ev'ry other Joy the World can give,
> Let Poverty, Deformity and Shame,
> Distraction and Despair seize me on Earth.

But in fact the garden has already been desecrated: Alice, jealous of her male lover's interest in the unwitting Jane, means to destroy her. When

Jane finally comes to Alice's door as a starving beggar, Alice rejects her in language that reveals a desire turned inside out:

> See where she comes! Once my Heart's dearest Blessing,
> Now my chang'd Eyes are blasted with her Beauty;
> Loath that known Face, and sicken to behold her.

It is interesting that in both *A Midsummer Night's Dream* and *The Tragedy of Jane Shore,* a storyline of bitter alienation evokes (whether nostalgically or perversely) a lost world of female eroticism.

Often, however, at least one of the friends will rise above jealousy, saving the inseparables from being alienated. Catharine Trotter—a prodigy who published her first novel at fourteen—centered her eloquent tragedy *Agnes de Castro* (1696) on a passionate friendship between two women. The remarkable Princess Constantia insists that her husband and her lifelong friend Agnes

> share my divided Heart
> So equally, I cannot tell myself
> To which I have given most . . .
> For you are both so equal dear to me,
> So closely wove by Fate to my fond breast,
> That neither can be sever'd from my love,
> Without unravelling this Web of Life.

Constantia describes her divided loyalties in surprisingly positive terms as a "Web of Life." By contrast, the equally strong Agnes is a one-woman woman, who adores Constantia and feels only friendship for the Prince. He, a more helpless character, is beginning to fall in love with her. Shaken to learn it, Princess Constantia nonetheless resists the predictability of a resentful response.

> My Reason must approve the Prince's choice,
> For I my self, prefer her to my self,
> And love her too, as tenderly as he.

She insists that the triangle formed by the Prince's and Agnes's love of Constantia is only reinforced by the new triangle superimposed on it:

the Prince's and Constantia's love of Agnes. Since sexual competition
is not enough to break up the threesome, Trotter has to bring in an outside factor to begin the tragic "unravelling" of the "Web": a conspiracy
of enemies who are jealous of the women's intimacy. And the plotters'
victory is a Pyrrhic one, because when both our heroines have been
fatally stabbed, Agnes has a vision of the other side, where no hearts
need be divided:

> I shall meet my Princess where I go,
> And our unspotted Souls, in Bliss above,
> Will know each other, and again will love.

Over the eighteenth and nineteenth centuries, it became a cliché
for one or both heroines to make a noble withdrawal from the battlefield, sacrificing a man's love for the sake of the adored woman. Sharon
Marcus finds throughout Victorian fiction "an altruistic exchange econ-
omy in which women do not compete for men but instead give them to
each other." Often the bewildered fellow is not even consulted, but
thrown around like a hot potato.

One of the only authors to allow her characters self-consciousness
about the jealousy plot is Charlotte Brontë in *Shirley* (1849)—her most
political, peculiar, and unpopular novel, an indictment of the different
oppressions of women and workers in mid-nineteenth-century England. Shirley, a whistling Yorkshire landowner who boasts of having "a
touch of manhood," forms an intense, flirtatious friendship with the
thoughtful, impoverished Caroline; she lays a bouquet in her friend's
lap, for instance, with "the aspect of a grave but gallant little cavalier."
(Shirley is an exception to the rule that says inseparables must be feminine. It has recently been suggested that her characterization may owe
something to a contemporary Yorkshirewoman whom Emily Brontë
lived very near in 1838–39, the mannish landowner Anne Lister, whose
diaries—not decoded and published till 1988—chart her affairs with a
variety of more ladylike partners.)

When Shirley goes for a walk with Caroline's beloved cousin
Robert, Caroline (clearly well versed in English fiction) leaps to the
conclusion that she will have to sacrifice Robert to her infinitely superior friend, then flee. But Shirley rejects that hackneyed storyline. Not
that she denies that things have been changed by Robert's arrival: she

describes her bond with Caroline as a shining thing like the sun or moon, "but that six feet of puppyhood makes a perpetually recurring eclipse of our friendship. Again and again he crosses and obscures the disk I want always to see clear." Shirley's candor about what she calls "the black eclipse" shocks the reserved Caroline into making her own declaration of

> affection that no passion can ultimately outrival, with which even love itself cannot do more than compete in force and truth. Love hurts us so, Shirley: it is so tormenting, so racking, and it burns away our strength with its flame; in affection is no pain and no fire, only sustenance and balm. I am supported and soothed when you—that is, *you only*—are near, Shirley.

In this interesting passage, Caroline begins by identifying "affection" for a woman and "love" for a man as two different, equal forces that "compete" with each other. But in her next sentence she backs off, trying to recast them as complementary—love burning, affection pouring on the balm. (The vocabulary is highly traditional: in Sir John Suckling's *Brennoralt* [1646] we heard women's love for each other described as "less scortching" than men's.) This ambiguity is fundamental to Brontë's novel: will their friendship "soothe" and "support" Caroline and Shirley as they struggle toward marriage, or will the love of men "outrival" the friendship in the end? For all the originality of the "black eclipse" scene, Brontë ends up resorting to the substitute brother trick, as in *As You Like It;* a brother of Robert's turns up for Shirley to marry, so Caroline can have Robert, the two women can set up a school, and they can all live happily ever after together. The eleventh-hour appearance of a brother—so handy, as we saw, for winding up female bridegroom stories—is just as convenient for bringing two inseparables together again, either by marrying one to the other's brother, or both to a pair of brothers.

Sometimes the narrative sequence is reversed: rather than beloved friends becoming rivals, rivals are transmuted into beloved friends. Here the man begins as a wedge between them, but becomes more like a bridge. The earliest example may be Marie de France's *lai Eliduc* (written sometime before 1189), in which Guildeluec, gazing at her husband's mistress, who is in a coma, is so ravished by her beauty that she heals her with a magic flower, then volunteers to become a nun to allow the other two to marry.

From the seventeenth century to the nineteenth, then, there are few plots in English literature more popular than that of female friendship under fire. Generally women fight to preserve their bond at all costs. That bond may be pre-, post-, or extramarital, or neatly interlocked with marriage in the form of a three- or four-person family.

Only occasionally do writers drop hints that, as Brontë's Caroline says (before correcting herself), the bond may "compete" directly with women's love for men. A buried resentment often comes closest to the surface at the point where one woman tells her friend she is getting married. In *Hedged In,* a novel of 1870 by American spiritualist/feminist activist Elizabeth Stuart Phelps, the mutually devoted factory girls Christina (another of those Christlike names) and Eunice finally manage to form a female household with Christina's mother and Eunice's long-lost child—but then Christina gets engaged. Once over the shock, Eunice praises the bridegroom, and makes the bridal clothes.

> It was noticed, through the day, that Eunice was somewhat more than commonly pale, and that, though she was busy, in and out, here and there, up and down, smiling much, that it was she who tied the flowers, who trimmed the rooms, who dressed and veiled and gloved and kissed Christina, and stopped her (so Christina says) on her way down stairs, to lead her into the gray room, and close the door, and fold her into her arms, and move her lips a little as if she would have spoken; yet, speaking not a word, unwound her arms, unlatched the door, and led her, by the hand all the way, down stairs,—that through all the day she was very silent.

In this long, restless sentence, Phelps allows Eunice's silence to speak with eloquent if frustrated desire. Eunice is found dead of heart failure later that day, as if seeing Christina depart has literally broken her heart.

An 1899 story by Mary E. Wilkins (later Freeman), "The Tree of Knowledge," has an odder premise but a similar resolution. In a hole in a tree, young Annie keeps finding letters from her secret admirer—but it turns out they have been written by Cornelia, her devoted elder sister. Cornelia claims that she went to these bizarre lengths in order to give her little sister an idealized standard of manhood, and prevent her from falling prey to some lowly suitor—but to a modern eye, it seems obvious that Cornelia has adopted a male persona to express the kind of passion for Annie that goes beyond what even inseparable sisterhood would allow. What Cornelia hid in the biblical "tree of knowledge," once revealed, will expel her from the paradise of sisterly love. By the time Annie does marry her admirer, however, Cornelia has wrestled herself into submission, and earned a role (if a humble one) in her sister's life again. In a moving image that alludes to the gospel parable of the bridesmaids, Wilkins tells us that Cornelia "had thrust herself and her own needs and sorrows so far behind her trimmed and burning lamp of love that she had become, as it were, a wedding-guest of all life." Such painful denials and hints of a secret wish to compete with the male suitor are far from uncommon in the fiction of female inseparability.

CHAPTER THREE

Rivals

THREE IS A CROWD, and often an uncomfortable one. We have
looked at the fraught triangle of two women friends and one
man, but it is when the neat distinction between opposite-sex "love"
and same-sex "friendship" starts to break down that the triangle really
teeters. What happens when the tension between a man and a woman
who adore the same woman reveals itself as rivalry, a duel for her heart?
If two is company, three can be war.

Let us begin with a poem of Sappho's variously known as "Fragment
31," "Peer of the Gods," or "To the Beloved," in which a speaker watches
in agitation as a male rival talks to a beloved woman. In the Greek, the
speaker reveals herself as female only in the fourteenth of the seventeen
lines. Here is an English version of 1711.

Blest as th'immortal Gods is he,
The Youth who fondly sits by thee,
And hears and sees thee all the while,
Softly speak, and sweetly smile.

'Twas this deprived my Soul of Rest,
And rais'd such Tumults in my Breast;
For while I gaz'd, in Transport tost,
My Breath was gone, my Voice was lost:

My Bosom glow'd; the subtle Flame
Ran quick thro' all my vital Frame;
O'er my dim Eyes a Darkness hung;
My Ears with hollow Murmurs rung.

In dewy Damps my Limbs were chill'd,
My Blood with gentle Horrors thrill'd;
My feeble Pulse forgot to play;
I fainted, sunk, and dy'd away.

This lyric is one of the few surviving out of what is thought to have been an oeuvre of about twelve thousand lines by Sappho (born 612 B.C.E. on Lesbos; it was because of this famous Lesbian that the Greek word for her people came to be used of women-loving women as early as the tenth century C.E.). Fragment 31 happened to be saved for posterity because Longinus quoted it entire in his treatise *On the Sublime,* so it had more influence on literary history than anything else she wrote. But for all its popularity, the triangle of erotic rivalry in Sappho's poem has made many of its translators and editors deeply uncomfortable. Anne Le Fèvre Dacier, for instance, titled her toned-down 1681 version "A son amie" to present its subject as mere female friendship. Taking a different tack, Joseph Addison added a note to Ambrose Phillips's frank translation (1711, quoted above) to soothe his audience: "Whatever might have been the Occasion of this Ode, the *English* Reader will enter into the Beauties of it, if he supposes it to have been written in the Person of a *Lover* sitting by his *Mistress*." (Addison is both hinting that the poem is about desire between women, and advising readers to banish this idea from their minds.) François Gacon in 1712 heterosexualized the poem itself, rewriting it—to make it "natural," he explained in a footnote—as a woman's jealous denunciation of the woman who sits beside the man they both love, and in 1768, E. B. Greene did the same thing in his English translation. In 1795, Abbé Jean-Marie Coupé offered a different but equally bold rewrite, converting it into a poem of worship of the goddess Aphrodite. And in 1855, in what Joan DeJean calls "the nadir of Sappho's repression in France," Paul-Pierre Rable despaired of this knotty problem and simply cut the poem off after the fifth line.

But over the period in which these scholars struggled to disguise Fragment 31's scenario, a surprising number of playwrights and novelists were taking the risk of laying bare the same triangle. In a competition between a male and a female character for the same woman, the issue is not who gets to sleep with her—as the women in these premodern texts are generally not sleeping with their male suitors anyway—but who gets her primary attention, who wins her heart. Which means that, long before there was widespread familiarity with the concept of a same-sex preference, it was possible to write stories in which male and female rivals duke it out on the battlefield of love.

Obviously this motif is a variation on the ancient plot of two men competing for a woman—but it works rather differently. The two roads are not evenly matched, nor do they wield the same weapons. The woman in the middle stands at a crossroads, and in a sense it is not just an individual, but a whole sex, that will win her.

RAKES VS. LADIES

The eighteenth century was boom time for the novel, and this new genre offered ample room for psychological analysis of complicated situations such as rivalry between a woman and a man for the love of a woman. I want to look at four contrasting works of fiction in which ladies must choose between charismatic but unscrupulous rakes and passionate female friends.

Printer-turned-novelist Samuel Richardson's masterpiece *Clarissa* (1747–48) follows, over eight compelling volumes, a rake's plot to seduce a virtuous beauty. Lovelace (a pun on *loveless*) aims to strip Clarissa of all her armor: her home, her family, her self-respect, and, not least, her Anna. (Jean-Jacques Rousseau, who thought *Clarissa* the most extraordinary novel ever written, borrowed its structure of a correspondence between the angelic heroine and her tougher, proto-feminist adorer for his *La Nouvelle Héloïse* [1761].) When Lovelace steals some of the letters the two women constantly exchange, he is disconcerted to encounter "so fervent a friendship." It is most fervent on the side of Anna, who boasts of loving Clarissa "as never woman loved another," and refers mockingly to male suitors: "How charmingly might you and I live together and despite them all!" But Lovelace clings to the traditional belief that love between young women is only a brief flame, not a "steady fire"; a feeble alliance between the weak, "One reed to support another!" He derides it as a childhood game,

> a cork-bottomed shuttlecock, which they are fond of striking to and fro, to make one another glow in the frosty weather of a single state; but which, when a *man* comes in between the pretended *inseparables,* is given up like their music and other maidenly amusements.

Although he would never admit to taking Anna seriously as a rival, Lovelace treats her like one. Having tricked Clarissa into running away with him, he keeps the two women apart and at times even manages to disrupt their correspondence and make them misunderstand and suspect each other.

Their friendship survives all these obstacles—but the problem is that it is of absolutely no practical use in saving Clarissa from her fate. Like Shakespeare's Celia, Anna at several points shows a wistful awareness that her friend, far from returning this passionate love, is made uneasy by it. Anna wants to take bold action along the lines of *As You Like It,* telling Clarissa, "If you allow of it, I protest I will go off privately with you, and we will live and die together." But the problem with her gallant offer of "knight-errantry"—only one of many she makes in the novel—is the qualifying phrase "if you allow of it," because Clarissa never will. Echoing the book of Ruth, Anna insists she would "accompany you as your shadow whithersoever you go," but Clarissa returns Anna's gifts of money, will not run away with her in case it damages her friend's reputation, and—finally drugged and raped by a desperate Lovelace—refuses to let Anna tell the authorities. She effectively starves and wills herself to death (a ladylike, sinless form of suicide), and will not even allow Anna to visit her on her deathbed. The way Clarissa sees it, the noblest act of friendship she can perform is to keep Anna at a safe distance from all these shameful horrors—and keep up the pressure until Anna reluctantly agrees to marry the suitor who has been waiting faithfully for her. "Love me still, however. But let it be with a weaning love," Clarissa advises. "I am not what I was when we were *inseparable* lovers." Lovelace has failed to tear the friends apart, but he has subtly alienated them, with the result that Anna only gets to embrace her beloved when she finds her laid out dead in her father's house. It is only in this scene that Anna's desire can safely declare itself as both possessive and physical (though in a chaster, more English way than we saw in *La Nouvelle Héloïse*):

> Why [...] was she sent *hither*? Why not to *me*?—She has no Father, no Mother, no Relations, no, not one!—They had all renounced her. I was her sympathizing friend—And had not I the best right to my dear creature's remains—And must Names, without Nature, be preferred to such a Love as mine?
>
> Again she kissed her lips, each cheek, her forehead;—and sighed as if her heart would break.

Despite being the longest novel in English, Richardson's *Clarissa* was a huge success, and had a strong influence on British and other European literatures until well into the nineteenth century. So who wins this, the original duel between rakish rapist and devoted friend? Nobody, really. By the end of the novel, one of the male characters comments that Clarissa and Anna have thoroughly proved "the force of *female friendship*," but it is only a spiritual victory. The irony is that Anna could have saved Clarissa by ignoring her friend's reservations, overruling her, turning up with a carriage and dragging her away—in fact, by acting rather like Lovelace. The exquisite goodness of the women's friendship—its egalitarian, sensitive, honorable quality—wins it a place in heaven (where Clarissa fondly expects to be reunited with Anna), but in this world, it achieves very little.

One of the first stories in which a man openly acknowledges that he has a female rival is found in a very different kind of eighteeth-century text, Anthony Hamilton's *Mémoires de la Vie du Comte de Grammont* (1713; in English, *Memoirs of the Life of Count de Grammont*). This rambling, fictionalized biography by the count's brother-in-law includes a cruelly satirical tale of competition between the sexes in the erotically experimental Restoration court.

Lord Rochester (a rake notorious, incidentally, for his poems about sex with boys as well as women) goes head-to-head with a senior maid of honor, Mistress Hobart. Ugly, and so obviously drawn to women that the ignorant spread rumors that she must be a hermaphrodite, Mistress Hobart has "a *tender Heart,* whose *Sensibility,* some pretended, was in Favour of the *Fair Sex.*" (Hamilton's phrase "some pretended" is a classic example of an author hedging his bets by presenting lesbianism coyly as an unproved hypothesis.) She wins the affection of young Miss Sarah—but quickly loses the girl to the seductive Lord Rochester. In the next round, Mistress Hobart is prepared to play dirty. Charged by her duchess employer with protecting the silly young maid of honor Mistress Temple from Rochester, she sets about it with zeal, offering the girl sweetmeats and flattery, and inviting her to retire with her to the privacy of "the bathing closet." (Terry Castle points out that sweets have been a staple of lesbian seduction in literature ever since the sev-

H. Gray, "Miss Temple Rejecting Miss Hobart's Caresses," in Anthony Hamilton, Memoirs of the Count de Grammont *[1713] (1889).*
    This is one of a series of etchings added to the eighteenth-century satire in a limited edition for the delectation of late-Victorian readers.

enteenth century, to be joined by nude bathing in the early eighteenth.)
She also tries to poison the girl against the whole male sex, and turns
Rochester's reputation as a pornographer against him, convincing Mistress Temple that one of his poems was written to expose the girl's physical flaws; this has the incidental benefit of prompting the girl to strip
naked to prove to her friend that the rake lied. But Rochester sends his
former conquest Miss Sarah to spy on the two women, and then coun-
terattacks by using the old rumor of hermaphroditism to scare Mistress
Temple into the belief that Mistress Hobart has impregnated her own
maid! Finally he ensures that the girl overhears an explicit denunciation of Mistress Hobart:

> Your *Passion* and *fond Desire* for Mrs. *T——e* are known by every
> Body but herself [. . .] 'Tis a scandalous thing that all the Maids
> of Honour should pass through your hands, before they know
> where-abouts they are.

It is more than a little ironic that Mistress Hobart is being denounced
as a lesbian rake here, when in fact she has had no luck getting any
woman into her bed. Anthony Hamilton's tale reaches its ludicrous climax when Hobart, bewildered by Temple's flight, slips into her chambers to embrace the girl while she is changing her clothes. Temple
screams for help, Hobart is suspected of attempted rape—and only the
intervention of the duchess saves her from being exiled from court. We
are left to assume that, having ousted the lecherous chaperone,
Rochester will have his way with the girl.

Perhaps the most interesting thing about this story in *Memoirs of the
Life of Count Grammont* is how similarly Hamilton presents the two
rivals, rake and lady: lusty, unscrupulous liars, for whom court gossip is
a double-edged sword that they grasp even when it cuts them. Of
course, Rochester is a powerful male courtier whereas Mistress Hobart
is a butt of mockery and no match for him—but she does get to take
advantage of the female privileges of private access to, and influence
over, girls.

Pierre Choderlos de Laclos offers a much more suave take on the
rivalry motif in his famous novel *Les Liaisons dangereuses* (1782; in English, *Dangerous Liaisons*). In an intriguing anecdote, Valmont admiringly

recounts one of the triumphs of his fellow rake, Prévan, who "separated 'the inseparables.'" In this case it is not two but three beautiful, talented women whose devoted intimacy arouses general hostility. Some accuse the ladies of sharing their male lovers, but others claim that

> while the three gallants need fear no male rivals they had female rivals to contend with, and even went so far as to say that, having been accepted only for the sake of appearances, they had acquired a title without a function.

It is typical of Laclos's light touch here that he goes no further than citing gossip about the possibility of "female rivals"; sex between women is invoked only indirectly, as the possible reality behind the "appearances," the invisible love, of which the redundant "gallants" only wear the "title." This mysterious bond between the three ladies offends the all-conquering Prévan—not because of its perversity, we gather (since rakes are not prudish), but because it excludes men, or worse, sets them up as merely puppet rulers. He decides to give these inseparable women a double punishment, by splitting them up and destroying their reputations. On the principle of divide and rule, he seduces each woman in turn, then tells the "gallants" and persuades them to abandon their lady friends and broadcast the story. The women are exiled from Parisian society; one retreats to a convent, the other two to their own estates. This nasty little story suggests not just that female "inseparability" could look like sex to sophisticated observers, but that some men were starting to resent it: Prévan's triumph is not just personal but patriarchal.

One remarkable American novel that takes its lead from Richardson's heartfelt *Clarissa*, rather than from Hamilton's and Laclos's cynical anecdotes, is Charles Brockden Brown's *Ormond; or, The Secret Witness* (1799). But Brockden Brown—a Gothic novelist of Quaker background and distinctly feminist views—goes well beyond Richardson in spelling out what is at stake in a duel between obsessed rake and devoted lady. The narrator, Sophia, and her childhood companion Constantia have been out of touch for more than three years, when, despite being newly married to Courtland, Sophia leaves him in England and comes back to America on a quest to find her friend. She hopes to persuade Constantia to return with her, but if not, it is Sophia's "inflexible purpose to live and to die with her" in America, and Courtland will just have to "wait patiently" till he finds out in which country this three-way marriage will take place. As Sophia sums up this heroic narrative of female friendship, "We imagined ourselves severed from each other by death or by impassable seas; but, at the moment when our hopes had sunk to the lowest ebb, a mysterious destiny conducted our footsteps to the same spot." After an ecstatic reunion, the women spend three days

> in a state of dizziness and intoxication. The ordinary functions of nature were disturbed. The appetite for sleep and for food were confounded and lost amidst the impetuosities of a master-passion. To look and to talk to each other afforded enchanting occupation for every moment. I would not part from her side, but eat and slept, walked and mused and read, with my arm locked in hers, and with her breath fanning my cheek . . . O precious inebriation of the heart! O pre-eminent love!

But the inseparables are unaware that their drunk-on-love conversations and embraces are being spied on by the "secret witness" of the novel's subtitle, Constantia's rakish suitor Ormond. Sophia does not like the sound of this mercenary soldier, a "competitor in her [Constantia's] affections." She moves quickly to secure Constantia's promise to settle in England with her and her meek husband. Eavesdropping on this betrayal, Ormond is filled with rage. He confronts Constantia, ranting about having spied on the women's "rapturous effusions" and "romantic passion"; he is well aware "that thy affections and person were due to another." "Person" here means "body"; he is hinting that she has committed herself physically as well as emotionally. In this strange scene, the rake sounds like nothing so much as a cuckolded husband. It is as if the oddity of such an embodied passion between women has canceled out, in his mind, the irregularity of his claim to Constantia's fidelity. Appalled to hear of this accusation, Sophia examines her conscience: "On reviewing what had passed between Constantia and me, I recollected nothing incompatible with purity and rectitude." But the technical chastity of such a bond is no comfort to Ormond, or defense against his outrage; like Brockden Brown's modern readers, the rake glimpses the sexual in what is not strictly sex. (As early as 1949, Harry R. Warfel was complaining of Constantia that

Suffrage Parade, New York City, May 4, 1912.
    This anonymous press photo of one of a number of mass rallies demanding the vote for women (finally won in 1920) emphasizes the suffragists as mothers and captures a moment of intense eye contact.

"emotions of normal love are alien to her nature, and there seems to be a homosexual tendency in her conduct.") In the novel's gripping climax, Ormond corners Constantia in a locked room. Here the plot contrasts with that of *Clarissa* so clearly that Brockden Brown almost seems to be rebuking Richardson for letting his heroine get raped: rather than surrender, Constantia stabs Ormond to death with a penknife. Sophia turns up to shepherd her through a quick trial that finds her innocent of murder, then nurses her through the consequent breakdown before carrying her off to England. Interestingly, in the bellicose triangle of Sophia, Constantia, and Ormond, Sophia has to "win" Constantia away from her "competitor," whereas in the more harmonious triangle of Constantia, Sophia, and Courtland—in which the husband accepts a secondary place—it need never come to blows.

FEMINISTS VS. HUSBANDS

But husbands are not always so meekly compliant, nor are the friends always willing to share space with a marriage. Although most novels, throughout the nineteenth century and into the twentieth, would continue to present marriage as completely compatible with female friendship, sometimes we can hear the rumblings of women's discontent with such an arrangment.

Perhaps the earliest example is Sarah Scott's *A Description of Millenium Hall* (1762), not so much a utopia as a novel about the formation of a small utopian community by various escapees from orthodox womanhood. One of them is Miss Melvyn: forced to marry the horrible, aged Mr. Morgan, she knows that marriage will somewhat constrain her inseparable bond with her childhood friend Miss Mancel, but she has no idea that her husband is harboring a strange jealousy. (I say strange because apart from nasty-minded rakes, men in eighteenth-century fiction tend to view love between women with approval, or, at worst, indifference.) The day after the wedding Mr. Morgan refuses to let Miss Mancel visit, telling his wife, "Madam, my wife must have no other companion or friend but her husband; I shall never be averse to your seeing company, but intimates I forbid." Mrs. Morgan is as "stunned" by this as if hit by lightning, and bursts into tears.

> "I did not want this proof," resumed Mr Morgan, "that I have but a small share of your affections; and were I inclined to grant your request, you could not have found a better means of preventing it; for I will have no person in my house more beloved than myself. When you have no other friend," added he with a malicious smile, "I may hope for the honour of that title."

He is a villain, but almost a tragic one: his resentful logic may make more sense to modern readers than to those of the 1760s, since he has seen what we see, that the friend is indeed "more beloved," leaving him only a "small share" in his wife's affections. He does not phrase it in terms of a same-sex preference—he shows no signs of caring what it means about his wife that her beloved is a woman—but he knows there is a battle going on. The irony is that by fighting so dirty, by keeping his miserable wife away from her friend for years and years, Mr. Morgan is never going to win, since love—unlike marriage—cannot be compelled. Sarah Scott finally punishes him with a mysterious paralysis; speechless, he must submit to being nursed to death by his saintly rival, Miss Mancel, who has returned to claim her beloved.

It is by his hostility to women's intimacy—so peculiar for a husband of his time—that Mr. Morgan proves himself to be as much a tyrant as any wife beater. (It is hard to avoid reading this storyline as autobiographical, although Sarah Scott did not meekly wait for a merciful Providence to release her from her own awful marriage: she walked out after just a few months and spent the rest of her life with a woman.) But it is also political: *Millenium Hall* is a sort of manifesto of the "bluestocking circle"—bookish women, of proto-feminist tendencies.

The women's community in *Millenium Hall* is only founded after the Morgan marriage is over, but in nineteenth-century novels, feminism—the Cause, as those first-wave British activists of the 1850s often called it—sometimes takes hold of the heroine before she gets safely hitched. The best example is *The Rebel of the Family* (1880) by Eliza Lynn Linton, a journalist and novelist (and, again, separated wife) notorious for her attack on the "New Woman" of the day. The young post office worker Perdita, struggling to break free of the expected feminine role, has a name that suggests she is in danger of being "lost." She meets Bell Blount, a garishly dressed separated wife and feminist, whose name suggests her handsomeness and her blunt manners. Bell tells Perdita seductively, "I can give you all you want—work, love, freedom and an object. I want nothing in return but your love and that you will let me guide you." Perdita's mother tries to make her give up this unsuitable friend, but the girl resists, as enthralled as someone "about to be admitted into a secret sect" and "initiated into those hidden mysteries." (This is Linton's nod toward the more lurid French tradition of writing about lesbian monstrosity that I will explore in chapter 4.) Bell claims the girl, with a pseudomotherly "kiss of adoption," as "one of us!—the friend of woman and the enemy of man."

Bell may hate men but the joke is that she models herself on them too, in both blunt manners and lifestyle. What complicates her overtures to Perdita nicely is that she has done this before: she left her own husband and children for a woman called Connie. Far from representing a radical alternative to the stifling codes of marriage, she calls Connie "my little wife" and expects her to act as (as the narrator puts it nastily) "lady's maid, milliner, housekeeper, amanuensis, panegyrist in public, flatterer and slave in private." And like many a Victorian husband, Bell has a roving eye: she invites Perdita to "come and chum with us" as a housemate, masking her sexual intentions by presenting herself and Connie as mentors:

> "And if you want love," said Bell, putting her arm tenderly round Connie Tracy; "You have it here—the best and truest that the world can give—the love between women without the degrading and disturbing influence of men."
> "Yes, I know," said Perdita, a little blankly.

The women's home is bare and messy, bottles of beer and cigarettes everywhere. Despite Perdita's "fascination" with Bell, we are told that the older woman's physical overtures "chilled and repelled" her from the start, because Bell is "one of those sphinxes which are beast and human in one." (As for Connie, she suffers tortures of jealousy. Linton points out snidely that she is as subservient as a man's wife but as insecure as his mistress, since she is bound to "her woman-'husband' " with no legal security.)

Once a male rival presents himself—a gentle pharmacist with the oddly sapphic name of Leslie—it is obvious which way Perdita will go. The crisis of *The Rebel of the Family* comes when Bell tries to force Perdita to join her on the platform at a suffrage meeting, and Leslie turns up in time to dissuade her. But Bell does not give up without a fight. Connie, walking in on Bell and Perdita in an embrace sometime later, takes delight in dropping the bombshell about the male suitor: "She will never be one of us." The outraged Bell punishes her fallen idol by telling Perdita's mother about Leslie, unsuitable husband material because he happens (like Mr. Rochester in Charlotte Brontë's *Jane Eyre*) to have a mad wife in the attic. But hundreds of pages later he is finally freed, by widowhood, to marry Perdita and save her from the feminists. Compared with the creepy, oppressive simulacrum that is marriage between women, ordinary marriage is offered as a safer bet.

Biographers have pointed out the difficulty in classifying such writers as Eliza Lynn Linton as antifeminist, because although they attacked "the Cause," they seemed to endorse female independence in both private and public life. *The Rebel of the Family* is a crude but intriguing commentary on the condition of women and the changing image of their pair-bonds. The novel is marked by an ambivalence not only about feminism but about desire between women: patently hostile to Bell and all she so "bluntly" promotes, it still offers her as a memorable, oddly seductive figure. Interestingly, although Bell is not described as being like a man in features or clothes, her manner is the epitome of what we would now call butch. "The masculine lady who inveigles Perdita into her friendship, is a character too odious, and the scenes in which she appears too repulsive, even for comment," shuddered the *Academy*, but the *Saturday Review* decided Bell was worth commenting on:

> [Linton's] portrait of Mrs Blount, or Bell Blount, as she preferred to be called, is as forcible as it is unsparing. In executing it with complete fidelity, the author has once or twice had to deal with somewhat risky matters, and has dealt with them with marked skill. The scenes in which Bell Blount figures cannot possibly be pleasant, in the sense in which a pretty landscape is pleasant, and some of their features are markedly unpleasing; but Mrs Linton knows where to insist and where to touch lightly, and the whole result is what no doubt she aimed at—to exhibit in a strong light some of the absurdities, and worse than absurdities, connected with a movement which she seems to dislike. The character is, as we have said, drawn with considerable strength, and in many of its touches there is a strong, if grim, sense of humour.

I have quoted this review at such length because its language exhibits a strange overspill of masculinity from Bell to her author: it is Eliza Lynn Linton's writing that is described as "forcible," "unsparing," tackling "risky matters" with "marked skill" and "considerable strength" like some death-defying adventurer. She even "knows where to insist and where to touch lightly," which makes her sound like some bodice-ripping Lothario. The reviewer may find Bell's scenes "unpleasing," but he seems fascinated both by her and by her equally masterful creator. It is hardly surprising that he focuses on this issue, because Linton's characterization of a butch (though not cross-dressing) lesbian was almost unprecedented.

One of Linton's correspondents, on and off for a decade, was the novelist Henry James, an American who spent most of his life in his adopted country, England. Published six years after *The Rebel of the Family*, his novel *The Bostonians* (1886) has a very similar structure—a girl must decide between a feminist activist and a male suitor—and ends with an almost identical showdown over a speaking engagement. But in

James's arrangement, the feminist is much more appealing than Bell Blount and has no other "little wife" to hand, so the stakes are much higher. James conceived of the novel on a visit to his family in Boston in 1883, and later explained his untypical choice of such an overtly political topic:

> I wished to write a very American tale, a tale very characteristic of our social conditions, and I asked myself what was the most salient and peculiar point in our social life. The answer was: the situation of women, the decline of the sentiment of sex, the agitation on their behalf.

He insists that this is not a narrow or minor story, then, but one that says a lot about men, women, America, and the times. Badly reviewed on first publication, *The Bostonians*—with its perceptive characterization, intense drama, and wry narrative style—is now recognized as a masterpiece.

The rich, nervous spinster Olive Chancellor (her name probably echoing Olivia from *Twelfth Night*) and her poor southern lawyer cousin Basil Ransom are both young and single-minded in their pursuit of the innocent and even younger Verena Tarrant, an inspirational speaker from a vulgar family. They each use the weapons of their own sex. The night they both meet Verena, for instance, it is Olive, as a lady with a home and an established name in Boston, who can seize the initiative and befriend her; Basil, the male stranger in town, is kept at bay by protocol. Over the weeks that follow, Olive courts Verena rather frantically, because of "her sense that she found here what she had been looking for so long—a friend of her own sex with whom she might have a union of soul." She is aware that her passion is not yet reciprocated and offers to wait—but a page later she is suggesting that Verena should move in so her "protectress" can shape the girl's talent for oratory. "Olive had taken her up, in the literal sense of the phrase, like a bird of the air, had spread an extraordinary pair of wings, and carried her through the dizzying void of space." The image suggests an eagle stealing a lamb.

For his part, Basil is a misogynist with a chip on his shoulder who seizes every opportunity to undermine Olive. But love between women has a peculiar status in the world of *The Bostonians*. The pairing of educated, New England female couples in what was commonly known as "Boston marriage," and the jealous wish to hold on to one's "friend" for life—this is taken for granted (and not called unhealthy or perverse) by most of the characters. (What James does not mention when describing his choice of theme for *The Bostonians* is that his invalid sister Alice had recently settled into a partnership with a beloved woman, Katherine Loring. It is far from clear whether Alice, as the brilliant hysteric, or Loring—the possessive intruder, as several of the Jameses saw her—is the main model for Olive Chancellor.) By offering the rivals a fairly level playing field, James never makes it clear who will win, which gives the suspense another turn of the screw. He also balances his sympathies cleverly, switching point of view between the two and satirizing everyone.

After Verena moves in with Olive, the two study, go to concerts, and occasionally embrace or kiss, and Olive keeps Verena secluded even from their colleagues. (In one of her seedier moments, she secretly pays the girl's crass parents to stay away.) Verena is more and more enthralled:

> The fine web of authority, of dependence, that her strenuous companion had woven about her, was now as dense as a suit of golden mail . . . Her share in the union of the two young women was no longer passive, purely appreciative; it was passionate, too.

However, Olive keeps looking over her shoulder for potential dangers, longing to "extract some definite pledge" that "would bind them together for life." Her feminist scruples prevent her from letting Verena promise not to marry any man. Instead of admitting that she wants to possess Verena for herself, Olive puts the onus on the girl to work her way through "a certain phase" (meaning interest in men) before choosing a life of dedication and "sacrifice" to the cause, a sort of "priesthood."

Just as with Richardson's Anna, this high-mindedness is Olive's weakness. It becomes clear that "Boston marriage" between women, for all its respectability, is not seen by most people as any bar to the "real" marriage that awaits a charming girl. "Don't attempt the impossible,"

Mrs. Burrage advises Olive, trying to bribe her into persuading Verena to marry Mrs. Burrage's rich, pleasant son; this harks back to the Renaissance notion of love between women as an exquisite *amor impossibilis*. The real threat, however, is from Basil, who takes up his interest in Verena again partly out of animosity toward his cousin Olive. He sees Verena heading toward "ruin" (a highly sexual word) as she trains to be a feminist orator, and he toys with the idea of "rescue": "She was meant for something divinely different—for privacy, for him, for love." In Basil's slow and covert courtship of Verena, he is more strategic than the other suitors, and cleverer than Olive; more playful, less direct. He pumps the women's friends for information about Verena and her whereabouts; he pretends to fully respect both their "tremendous partnership" and Verena's speaking talents, while privately determining that "if he should become her husband he should know a way to strike her dumb."

Verena is no pushover: she is impatient with Basil, and keeps insisting to Olive that she is "more wedded to all our old dreams than ever." But her use of the word *wedded* may remind the reader that female union is no legal marriage. Basil charms her into a secret correspondence, casting "a spell upon her," much as Olive did first; James shows the two cousins as oddly similar in their wooing. As the plot moves toward a showdown, Verena panics, embraces Olive, and cries, "Take me away, take me away!" But Olive lacks Basil's masculine confidence; although she does bring Verena to a rural retreat—a houseful of women on Cape Cod—she does not lock the door the way a husband would. When Basil comes "to take possession," the "double flame" that was Verena's love for Olive and her commitment to feminism is snuffed out into "colourless dust" by his "magical" power. As he sees it, the women's friendship is only a "flimsy" pretext for Verena to refuse him; "he wanted to know since when it was more becoming to take up with a morbid old maid than with an honourable young man." Without ever naming Verena's relationship with Olive as sexual, he portrays it as profoundly unimportant, and "morbid"—which is one of those words (like *sentimental, intense, languid,* and *dangerous*) often used as code for *lesbian* in the late nineteenth century.

By obliging her heart to wear the mask of nobility, by forcing love to go by the name of sisterhood, Olive has found herself unable to hold on tight to Verena:

Olive put forward no claim of her own, breathed, at first at least, not a word of remonstrance in the name of her personal loss, of their blighted union; she only dwelt upon the unspeakable tragedy of a defection from their standard.

From this false position, all she can do is try to hide Verena away from Basil, and when he tracks them down, before a public lecture, he leads Verena away in tears (leaving Olive, a brave martyr, to force herself to give the speech in Verena's place). In case any readers might see this as a fairy-tale ending, a triumph of the prince over the witch who has been holding Rapunzel captive, Henry James ends the book with a famously dry sentence about those tears: "It is to be feared that with the union, so far from brilliant, into which she was about to enter, these were not the last she was destined to shed." *The Bostonians,* then, is a darkly realistic story of the battle between two flawed, uneven kinds of "union."

I have given a play-by-play analysis of Olive Chancellor's game because she is the archetypal lesbian loser. Her gloomy shadow falls not only on later characters whose debt to her is obvious—such as the stylishly mannish feminist Kate Chancellor in Sherwood Anderson's *Poor White* (1920)—but on every woman who gives up her beloved to a man rather than fighting no-holds-barred.

But patriarchal fiat was not the only way the duel could end. One interesting example of a woman quietly triumphing over her male rival is a novel by Florence Converse. (One of Converse's professors at Wellesley College in 1887 was Vida Scudder; more than thirty years later the friends set up home together—along with their two mothers—and the partnership lasted until Scudder's death in 1954.) Converse's *Diana Victrix* (1897) is an unusual "New Woman" novel in which women's love does not have to surrender nobly to the claims of legal marriage. Enid and Sylvia, a lecturer and a novelist, are New England feminists who have lived together for twelve years.

We are a partnership, Sylvia and I. I am the man about town, the planner, the promulgator. Sylvia sits in the counting-room and cashes the checks, and she is to keep the record of events, and lay the affairs of the firm before the public in good literary form.

But behind the flippancy there is tenderness: Enid is described as putting "her arms around [Sylvia], and . . . saying a great many things very softly in the dark." When a man called Jacques proposes to Enid, she turns him down:

> "I share with her thoughts that I have no wish to share with you. I give to her a love surpassing any affection I could teach myself to have for you. She comes first. She is my friend as you can never be, and I could not marry you unless you were a nearer friend than she. You would have to come first. And you could not, for she is first."
>
> "And this is all that separates us," said Jacques, in a tone of entire amazement. "Only a woman?"

Enid spells it out as clearly as she can: "I have chosen my life and I love it."

She is not crass enough to boast to Sylvia of having made this great decision for her sake. Sylvia, rather less committed, starts to fall in love with a man called Jocelyn. Interestingly, it is Jacques who enlightens his rival, more than a year later, warning Sylvia in biblical cadences:

> Do you also be loyal! For I say that the time is not far off—look in her eyes and see!—when she shall need, not you, not you, the woman friend alone, but husband and little children. See that you be all these to her then! If you can!

Despite his scornful tone, despite the way the invoking of "little children" throws more weight on the marriage side of the scales, the effect on Sylvia is to make her fully realize, at last, "how dearly I do love her"—so she turns down Jocelyn. At the end of *Diana Victrix*, as the title makes clear, the goddess of virginity, Diana, has won. And there is an interesting moment of authorial self-consciousness: after all Enid's patient encouragement, Sylvia manages to publish a novel, and plans a second one which features a heroine based on Enid but whom Sylvia will marry off because "the public are more used to it." Enid quips: "But sometimes, Sylvia, I don't marry, even in novels."

THE BEAUTIFUL HOUSE

One reason the female couple in *The Bostonians* seems so insecure is that they are constantly traveling, like criminals on the run; despite

Frank Walter Taylor, " 'You're an unutterably philistine person,' said Sylvia," in Catherine Wells, "The Beautiful House," in Harper's Monthly Magazine *(March 1912).*
Taylor was a major American illustrator during the first two decades of the twentieth century, based in Philadelphia. Note the way the introduction of Sylvia's cousin/ suitor literally pushes Mary into the background, where her hat makes her almost faceless.

owning her own house, Olive keeps decamping in order to yank Verena out of Basil's reach. Although Enid and Sylvia in *Diana Victrix* have achieved a bare-bones domesticity in rented lodgings, in other rivalry stories the impermanent nature of the female couple's housing signals to the reader that the bond is all too breakable. It is a laundry business in a rented basement that a man successfully invades to break up two women in Pauline E. Hopkins's *Contending Forces* (1900), a boardinghouse in J. D. Beresford's *House-Mates* (1917), a women's residential club in Naomi Royde-Smith's *The Tortoise-Shell Cat* (1925), an institution for troubled youth in Klaus Mann's 1925 play, *Ania and Esther,* and a houseboat on the Thames in Mary Renault's *The Friendly Young Ladies* (1944; U.S. title *The Middle Mist*).

The irony is that in many novels and plays, the female couple is fervently domestic: they may not possess a home, but they long for one. In Catherine Wells's extremely sympathetic story from *Harper's Monthly Magazine,* "The Beautiful House" (1912), Mary, an artist of thirty-five, "in a manner fell in love" with a younger student, Sylvia. They find the country house of their dreams, which just so happens to be named "Love o' Women." Listen to the palpable excitement in this passage about real estate:

> Mary looked at her, aflush with sudden daring. "Shall we take it, then?" She tried to throw a note of facetiousness into her voice.
>
> "We could, you know," said Sylvia. Her voice dropped. "Our hearts have taken it," she said. "We could come here together," she went on. "Just whenever we wanted to. Just you and I. Mary beloved," she almost whispered, "wouldn't you like it?"
>
> Her slender hands lay out along the table, palms turned up. Mary gathered them in her own hands and kissed them. "I should—like it!" she said, whimsically insistent on the moderate word.

Here the house is not only a refuge but a metaphor for the urgent feelings the women try to hide behind "moderate words." But they never get to actually move in, because Sylvia casually transfers her affections to a young cousin and announces she will marry him. Mary capitulates at once: "Something far stronger than she had claimed her beloved for its own." (Not "someone" and "he," we notice, but "something" and "it": the primal, sacred force of a man's desire for a woman.) At which point the house called "Love o' Women" fortuitously burns to the ground.

Catherine Wells, incidentally, was H. G. Wells's student and second wife (full name Amy Catherine Robbins Wells, nicknamed Jane); their thirty-three-year bohemian marriage included not only many house moves but his affairs with (and fathering of two children by) other women. Which suggests that perhaps "The Beautiful House" is not a simple fable of the triumph of heterosexuality, but a meditation on the instability of any shared domestic life, and the pain of having to make do with whatever is left of one's beloved after other people's "claims."

When a female couple does find a home, destruction is rarely far behind: it is as if the hubris of claiming a permanent site for love brings on nemesis. This setting-up-house-together plot, though it shows up from the late nineteenth century, becomes more common after World War One decimated the male population, when there was widespread concern about how "surplus" women might live without husbands. Because of the newly widespread awareness of lesbianism as a lifestyle, the emphasis in these stories is not just on the individual man's victory but on the reassertion of heterosexuality itself. (Not that this conversion narrative is entirely new; after all, pornography from the late eighteenth to the twentieth centuries had endlessly replayed the scenario of the unsatisfying sex scene between two women interrupted—and brought to a glorious finish—by a man.)

In *The Rainbow* (1915), D. H. Lawrence wrote about a brief girl-teacher affair in a chapter heavily titled "Shame"; to avoid having the book formally banned for what the crown prosecutor called "immoral representations of sexuality," his publisher (Methuen) had to apologize and surrender all remaining copies. Undaunted, Lawrence returned to this dangerous subject in *The Fox*, a short story drafted in 1918 and published in a truncated form in 1920 before he expanded it to a "novelette" three times its original length, which came out in 1922.

Perhaps because women's relationships had become more culturally visible even in the few years since *The Rainbow*, Lawrence did not need to describe in explicit terms the bond between two women who run a farm together. The rather exploitative teacher-pupil relationship of *The Rainbow* (similar to the pederastic model of man-boy seduction) has been replaced in *The Fox* with what a few decades later would be called a butch-femme pairing. March is the androgynous "man about the place," and the wealthier Banford, "a creature of odd whims and unsatisfied tendencies," is described as the frail and feminine one. (As Terry Castle points out, "odd" has been a code word for desire between women since at least the end of the seventeenth century.) But the difference between the women's personal styles should not obscure their basic similarity as two spinsters in their late twenties, rebelling against the expectation that they will sit around waiting for husbands: in setting up their farm, they are staking out their territory both literally and culturally. Soon, however, the project becomes arduous. They start feeling "tired of one another," and Lawrence drops heavy hints about what they need: March is shown "carrying the eggs on her breast as if they were some heavy child." Their hens stop laying, and a masterful fox keeps carrying them off; this is the whole story of *The Fox* in miniature.

"Don't talk to me about Nature," says Banford disgustedly of the hens, but Lawrence constantly invokes the seemingly irresistible laws of the animal kingdom.

Since it is 1918, the surviving men start coming home, and Henry, grandson of the farm's last owner, turns up and promptly woos March in order to get the property back. If it seems surprising at first that he should choose the androgynous one, this makes more sense if we consider that to Lawrence, March represents not just a woman to win, but a gender problem to be solved. When she announces that she is engaged to Henry, "Banford looked at her like a bird that has been shot; a poor, little sick bird." This glide from injury to illness manages to make it seem as if it is no one's fault that the bird got shot; her weakness was internal. As for March, at first she thrives on being the object of a duel: "She seemed to sit between the two antagonists with a little wicked smile on her face." But as Banford descends into misery, March dithers: "She wanted the boy to save her," yet when he is away for a few days she writes to break it off yet again: "When I think of Jill [Banford], she is ten times more real to me. I know her and I'm awfully fond of her, and I hate myself for a beast if I ever hurt her little finger. We have a life together."

This appeal to the rational is in vain; March may hate herself "for a beast," but that is what she is, what everyone is in Lawrence's world. Henry is described as a maddened animal who must get "the thorn of Banford" out of his foot; here Lawrence presents aggression as self-defense. Finally, in a particularly crude bit of phallic symbolism, Henry manages to crush Banford under a huge falling tree. But this ending is no less ambivalent than that of *The Bostonians;* Lawrence undercuts heterosexuality even as it appears to triumph. "He had won her. And he knew it and was glad," he tells us, echoing the rhythms of the book of Genesis—but Henry is soon feeling tormented by March's inability to relax into passive feminine acquiescence. As a last resort, he takes his wife off to settle in Canada, in the faint hope of restoring her to her natural role of Eve to his Adam.

A comparison between the two versions of *The Fox* is highly revealing. In the short story in *Hutchinson's Story Magazine* in November 1920, Lawrence winds up the conflict with a rapid proposal and marriage; March is left dreamily happy, Banford angry but alive. Paradoxically, the magazine's caption justified the publication by emphasizing both the up-to-date realism of this triangle, and its timelessness as a narrative pattern: "a fine story of a post-war partnership between two modern young women—and the intervention of the inevitable man." But in Lawrence's rewrite, the engagement is longer and more complex—with March struggling to break it off, and hold on to her relationship with Banford—and Henry not only has to kill his rival before the wedding can take place, but finds himself struggling to really possess his melancholy, rebellious wife afterward. All these changes have the effect of making readers take the women's love more seriously, and lifting *The Fox* from a conventional man-wins-woman-from-woman story into an almost allegorical duel between different forms of sexuality.

The Fox had an enormous influence. In Thomas Dickinson's play *Winter Bound* (1929), Tony the mannish lady sculptor glumly donates the farmhouse to the happy couple, and exits wailing that she is "a hundred years ahead of my time." By contrast, in Geoffrey Moss's *That Other Love* (1930), the woman who gets married decides to leave the Normandy cottage as a booby prize for her cast-off beloved. The *New York Times* complained:

> Nothing in Phillida's history accounts for the fact that she loves women more than men; and her subsequent decision to forsake Vera and marry in order to have children is also poorly motivated. Granted that in life people drift in and out of such relationships with little apparent reason, it is the duty of an author to create reasons for everything.

The reviewer's irritation is revealing; it suggests that by 1930 the rivals storyline was so well established that readers had a right to expect it to be strongly characterized, dramatically played out, and illustrative of a clear divide between two sexual preferences. (Interestingly, elsewhere in this review seems to be the first time the *New York Times* ever offered *homosexual* and *heterosexual* as a pair of opposite terms.)

Housing is the territory on which the whole battle is played out in Dorothy Dodds Baker's fascinating melodrama *Trio* (1943)—decried by critics, but winner of the Commonwealth Club of California medal for literature. Janet is a PhD student recovering from a nervous breakdown in the glossy penthouse of her professor and lover of three years, Pauline—the plagiarist author of a brilliant book on the decadent movement. By constrast, Ray, a part-time theater student, lives in a shabby but honest apartment. For three months Janet sneaks out at night to slum it with her boyfriend, until Pauline stalks in to sneer at this "below-stairs liaison" and "take her home where she belongs." Janet finds the courage to stay—but the complication is that when she finally spells out to the obtuse Ray that she has been a prisoner in the "Alcatraz" of lesbianism, he throws her out. She can only think to flee to the neutral third zone of her parents' house. Pauline makes a desperate suggestion that she and Janet should swap their life of luxurious domesticity for one of exotic travel: the tropics or the frozen north. But our hero Ray turns up at the eleventh hour to denounce lesbianism, whatever its setting, as "no place to go . . . a dead-end and a blind alley and a bottleneck of a way of life." (Not the *vagina dentata*, then, but the hermetically sealed womb.)

The motif of the man breaking up the beautiful/hideous "home" of love between women clearly owes a debt to Ovid's *Metamorphoses*, in which Jove penetrates the enclosed female world of Diana's woods to seduce the nymph Callisto. In Ovid's version, it is the nymph who pays for her divided loyalties: pregnant, banished by Diana, Callisto is ultimately turned into a bear. Whereas in these twentieth-century stories, it is the Diana figure who is left bereft, punished for trying to possess a girl, while the Callisto figure goes off with her godlike lover to discover the joys of normality. This is a great example of how plot motifs repeat over thousands of years, even though the ideological message attached to them may have completely changed.

"Go on, then," the man tells his girlfriend sourly in Ernest Hemingway's 1933 story "The Sea Change," releasing her to try a lesbian affair. But this acquiescence is most untypical of fictions and plays in which a man and a woman compete for a woman's heart. Very often somebody has to die. Pauline in Baker's *Trio* shoots herself in the head; the spurned man drowns himself in Guy de Maupassant's satirical story "La Femme de Paul" (1881; in English, "Paul's Mistress"). In *The Dark Island* (1934), Vita Sackville-West winds up her tormented triangle *Hamlet*-style by having the husband drown the woman who loves his wife, whereupon his wife kisses him in order to pass on her diphtheria so they will both die of it. Whether in sparkling social comedy or bloody tragedy, the stakes are high, the weapons are various, and the archetypal forces of masculinity and femininity are unleashed.

Marjorie Garber argues persuasively that in narratives such as *The Fox* the triangle is not an interruption of an erotic relationship but the source of that eroticism. Jealousy generates desire, and therefore plot; it takes a static situation and turns up the heat.

The triangle gets a further layer of tension when family members compete sexually for a woman: father against daughter, mother against son, brother against sister. Sometimes the narrative is heated even more by having all three sides of the triangle involve desire as well as competition: the man and the woman both want and compete with each other. For instance, in a remarkable story published in 1876, Constance Fenimore Woolson's "Felipa," an eleven-year-old cross-dressing Minorcan girl forms a passionate attachment to a couple, and ultimately stabs the man. The narrator insists, "She loved them both alike. It is nothing; she does not know," but the girl's grandfather corrects her: "It was two loves, and the stronger thrust the knife."

The erotic energies of a triangle can switch direction suddenly and unnervingly. The earliest example I know of the man managing to seduce his female rival is Colette's *Claudine en ménage* (1902; in English, *Claudine Married*), in which Claudine's husband, Renauld, indulgently rents her and Rézi a love nest, seeing lesbian sex as "a restful diversion" for women, and then secretly beds Rézi himself—which shocks Claudine right back into the bonds of monogamy. But equally, two women competing over a man can suspend their hostilities and fall in love, in fictions as different as Sylvia Townsend Warner's *Summer Will Show* (1936) and Kingsley Amis's *The Green Man* (1969).

The rivalry motif is still thriving today, and it is still not simply a private duel, but a clash of worlds. Because in Western culture passion between women is always a big deal, whether presented as glorious or shameful, angelic or monstrous.

CHAPTER FOUR

Monsters

Excess, infraction, deviance. From the very beginnings of literature, women who desire other women tend to rampage across the boundaries of the acceptable.

Such characters, in classical, medieval, and Renaissance texts, often lament what has happened to them. Fiordispina in Ariosto's *Orlando Furioso* (1516–32) complains to Cupid, "I sole am found in earth, aire, sea, or fire / In whom so strange a wonder thou hast donne." Notice that it is Cupid she blames, not herself. These characters see their desire—"so strange a wonder"—as the work of fate or the gods, and themselves as random victims. What is new, in the majority of fictions from the eighteenth century on, is the implication that a woman who wants women is inherently strange: a monster who has made the bed of vice in which she wallows.

Why the eighteenth century? Well, the plays and romances produced before that era tend to celebrate the fanciful, the whimsical, the eccentric, which can leave room for quirks of desire. But from the mid-1700s on, and above all in the new popular form of the novel, we find an emphasis on realist narrative, and an endorsement of the moral and the normal. Same-sex desire becomes the scapegoat term: no longer a whimsical anecdote, but a cautionary tale. If love between women cannot be shown to be utterly saintly, it drops into the realm of carnal vice, and is known as (among other terms) *tribadism*—literally, genital-genital rubbing, but more generally referring to the phenomenon of sexual relationships between women. Paradoxically, it is the very fervor of same-sex love for which such heroines as Rousseau's Julie are praised (as we saw in chapter 2) that can cause it to tip over, in the very next text, into evil. And although that evil could be conceived of in various ways—in the Christian terms of sin, for instance, or the medical/psychological discourse of madness—perhaps the most common vocabulary was that of monstrosity.

The lesbian monster's most important source is Sappho: not her writings, but her image. This may sound odd, since the seventh-century-B.C.E. poet was and is such a revered cultural icon, but the idea of the woman who desires women as a perverse, angst-ridden figure clearly originates in a long Latin poem Ovid wrote about Sappho six centuries after her birth, called "Sappho to Phaon" (Epistle 15 of his *Heroides*, 5 B.C.E.). Ovid revved up the drama by showing the poet—a rival to men for the love of girls—as going through a change of life, a late conversion to the love of men. Drawing on references by earlier Greek dramatists, which in turn may be based on a myth about the goddess Aphrodite's passion for the ferryman Phaon, Ovid portrays an ugly, middle-aged Sappho turning away from her female lovers when she falls for the handsome young Phaon—who beds her and dumps her. Here is the crucial verse from Alexander Pope's 1707 translation:

No more the Lesbian dames my passion move,
Once the dear objects of my guilty love:
All other loves are lost in only thine,
Ah, youth ungrateful to a flame like mine!

Ovid's poem ends with Sappho going to throw herself into the sea from the Rock of Leucas, which is said to have the power to cure the leaper of love. She hopes to be healed—but it is always assumed (and first spelled out by Addison in 1711) that her leap killed her, so it is recast as a suicide. It could be claimed that Sappho actually died of heterosexuality, then. However, the most lingering elements of her myth are her angst about her "guilty love" for girls, the sense that it is her whole sexual history for which she is being punished, and the leap from the cliff.

So although Ovid's Sappho is a tragic heroine rather than a repulsive monster, perhaps the clearest mark of his poem on Western (but particularly French) literature is the seemingly endless line of texts in which lesbians rant, rave, and end up dead by means of illness, accident, murder, or suicide. Jennifer Waelti-Walters, in her study *Damned Women: Lesbians in French Novels* (2000), puts it bluntly: "From 1796 to 1929 the male-created lesbian was depicted unrelentingly and almost without exception as a monster with no hope of redemption."

Of course, to call these characters lesbians does not fully account for them; the queer and the monstrous are overlapping, rather than identical, cultural shadows. The bogey in these texts is not simply desire between women but every fault that could plausibly be associated with it (immaturity, deception, abuse of institutional or aristocratic power), every fashionable vice (sadism, pedophilia, drug abuse), every social change (women's leadership, racial integration). And authors clearly enjoyed creating these memorable villainesses to intrigue and appall their readers. The monster tale is one of the most interesting branches of the literature of desire between women—marked by sympathy as well as indignation, glamour as much as horror.

Sex Fiends

In the late eighteenth century, two French authors simultaneously invented the lesbian fiend: the woman whose lust for her own sex is so all-consuming that it leads to destruction. Their two prototypes, the defiant fiend and the guilt-wracked, both hit print in the post-Revolutionary 1790s.

A woman dressed as a man goes up to a beggar in an alley:

> "Frig me," I ordered, conveying her hand to my cunt, "I am a woman, but one who stiffens for her own sex. Put your fingers in there and rub."
>
> "Oh, Lord! Leave me be, leave me be, I shudder at all these horrors. Though poor, I am honest; don't humiliate me, for pity's sake!"

Achille Devéria [attributed], in Alfred de Musset, Gamiani *(1833).*
   One of a series of twelve colored lithographs, more ebullient in mood than the death-driven pornographic novella they accompany. Unsigned, they are generally attributed to Devéria, the son of a student of Girodet-Trioson's (see page 5) and a noted watercolor painter, lithographer, and erotic illustrator.

> She endeavours to break away from me, I seize her by the hair, raise a pistol to her temple: "Be off, buggeress," I say, "off to hell with you, and tell them there that Juliette sent you."
>   And she fell, blood gushing from her head.

The speaker is the fearless, endlessly orgasmic heroine of the Marquis de Sade's *Juliette,* which appeared in ten volumes between 1797 and 1801, and prompted Napoleon to incarcerate the author for the last thirteen years of Sade's life. A Revolutionary aristocrat, this paradoxical author was both utterly modern and writing in the old libertine tradition.

   The libertine authors of the seventeenth century, James Grantham Turner argues, often focused, in a way that is as philosophical as it is bawdy, on the erotic education of a girl: the unflowering of mind and body. It is generally a woman who takes the girl's education in hand; Turner shows how erotica by authors such as Nicolas Chorier celebrates desire between females as "an aestheticized, voluntary, Epicurean sexuality, an *amour philosophe* removed as far as possible from mammalian 'necessity.' " Yes, these seventeenth-century texts present sex between women as a rehearsal for the real thing, but also revere it as a form of physical and mental arousal which can never be quite sated, so never ends; they veer between what Turner names the "phallocentric" and "philosapphic" modes.

But if in its phallocentric mode libertine literature can trivialize lesbian sex as pointless "foolery from woman to woman" (in the words of the immortal Fanny Hill), the Marquis de Sade broke with that tradition violently. Same-sex acts (between men as between women) are exalted, in Sade's works, alongside other illicit, nonprocreative forms of sex: whatever turns the social order upside down. For the same reason, he celebrates the liberation of women from their traditionally passive role.

The heroines of *Juliette* are entirely free of the shame that dogs so much of the literature of desire between women. "You simply have no idea, my dear one, to what point I am contemptuously indifferent to whatever may be said about me," Madame Delbène (the abbess of the convent) tells Juliette (the thirteen-year-old pupil she is seducing). And it has clearly never occurred to them that there is anything *impossibilis* about *amor* between women; their orgasms are like fireworks displays. *Juliette* is more an education than a novel: our heroine simply soaks up the lectures (hedonism, atheism, nihilism) and practical demonstrations (scatology, child abuse, torture, cannibalism, mass murder) offered by a series of male and female mentors. The libertine women vary in their tastes—Delbène prefers sodomy with women, Clairwil is a man-hater who gets her real thrills from killing young males, Juliette is equally attracted to both sexes—but these do not amount to sexual identities; these women are all tribades, but in the broadest sense.

The Sadeian tribade is a woman who seeks out pleasure in all its forms—clitoral, oral, vaginal, anal, but especially the suffering and (much more so) inflicting of pain. She is a beautiful, aristocratic, intellectual serial killer. She is also unnervingly protean: she plays any role she chooses. After all, in the marquis's equal-opportunity, nightmarish universe, all a woman has to do is pick up a few tools and she can rape and slaughter men, women, children, and animals as easily as a man can. All roles are swappable: "We girded on dildoes," says Juliette of herself and Honorine on their second date, "and fell to dallying now as lover and mistress, now as master and mate, now in the style of bardash and tribade, we coupled in every imaginable manner." The result is that one character blurs into the next in this endless, exhausting novel: "My libertinage is an epidemic," Delbène tells Juliette, "whosoever is in my vicinity is bound to be infected by it."

In the relationships between women Sade shows us, lust produces enthusiasm, sometimes even romantic attachment, but these feelings soon give way to boredom, revulsion, and a craving to kill. Juliette does develop long-term, devoted bonds with two older women, Clairwil and Durand, but when Durand—a sorceress with a giant clitoris—tricks her into killing Clairwil, Juliette bears no grudge:

> Mistresses of all a universe we shall be; through our alliance I feel we shall become the superiors of Nature herself. Oh, dear Durand, the crimes we are going to commit! The infamies we are going to achieve!

Perhaps the most revolutionary aspect of *Juliette* is its happy ending: the circle of surviving libertines, male and female, are left rich and richly satisfied. But although Juliette and Durand have pledged to live in a sort of sexually open partnership, one gets the impression that our heroine would hear of the older woman's agonizing death—as she did Clairwil's—with indifference bordering on amusement. The paradox is that, despite the rich bonds between sex fiends, ultimately each stalks alone.

Precisely because Sade was so extreme—so deeply shocking, even today—his narrative pattern represented rather a dead end for the literature of desire between women. We can see his influence in elements of what was published after him—the grandiose cult of vice, or sex culminating in murder—but later fictions did not so much follow on from *Juliette* as retreat from it. In particular, his notion that a woman is just as able as a man to seduce, molest, have orgasms with, or torture women proved too radical for later authors, who when depicting desire between women preferred to fall back on the older notions of confusion and *amor impossibilis*.

If Sade's *Juliette* epitomizes the fiend at her most exuberant, Denis Diderot took the opposite tack in *La Religieuse* (in English, *The Nun*) by showing her as broken on the wheel of her own desires. As much erotic thriller as anticlerical exposé, this novel was begun in 1760 but only published posthumously in 1796, when the Revolutionary climate encouraged exposure of all the abuses of the ancien régime.

The most protracted of our heroine Suzanne's string of sufferings at the hands of the Church is her relationship with the superior of her third convent—the novel's only unnamed character, designated in the original as "Mme ***." Diderot creates an atmosphere of claustrophobic humidity, as for instance when Sister Thérèse, the superior's discarded favorite, is reduced to begging her in coded terms for "a moment of consolation before Vespers." Suzanne fails to understand what kind of story she is in, even on the first night, when the superior undresses and fondles her. What tempts Suzanne into compliance is the idea of using her powers for good: she buys forgiveness for the other nuns by granting the superior "innocent" favors, such as kisses. Despite her confessor's warnings, and despite the fact that Suzanne has accused other nuns of "suspicious intimacy" before and been accused of the same thing herself, she remains obtuse—even when the superior presses against her and gives every sign of being on the brink of orgasm. Suzanne will not let herself think of these convulsions as anything but—that omnipresent metaphor in the literature of desire between women—illness: "It was probably an affliction to which she [the superior] was subject, then another thought came, that perhaps the malady was catching, and that Sainte-Thérèse had caught it and I should too."

Unlike Sade's Juliette (unshockable at thirteen), Suzanne is an innocent narrator of a kind often used in eighteenth-century social critique, such as Voltaire's *Candide* (1759), but she reminds us more specifically of the heroine of, say, Honoré D'Urfé's *L'Astrée* (1607–27), who refuses to see any evil in her romantic friendship with a woman. Suzanne fits even better into the libertine tradition of the ingénue who claims to have no idea what another woman's caresses may mean or where they are likely to lead; in literature, this pattern prevailed right through to the end of the nineteenth century, and has lingered in pornography to this day. (And like their heroines, the narrators in fiction and other prose genres can display the same faux naïveté, pretending not to understand what could be suspicious about a scene of eroticism between women: David Robinson calls this the convention of "mock-unknowing, a tongue-in-cheek ignorance.")

Christopher Rivers, in a brilliant essay on *La Religieuse* and *Made-*

moiselle de Maupin, probes this more deeply. He points out that such male-authored novels focus on epistemological questions for good reason:

> "We" as men, the author seems to say, with a wink, know more about what goes on between women than they do; male dominance is asserted then, not only in the sexual realm, but more importantly in the realm of knowledge from which it is inseparable.

Like Gautier in *Mademoiselle de Maupin,* Diderot tries to pull off the trick of keeping homosexuality unspeakable while nonetheless speaking of it: not only do they constantly present lesbianism as inexplicable, but each keeps his heroine faux-innocent till an implausibly late point. The moment the heroine loses her innocence, the joke is over: it is significant that shortly after this point, in both these novels, the narrative breaks off.

But though he may share this rhetorical strategy with Gautier, Diderot has a sternly moral agenda of his own. The superior is good-looking, intellectual, charismatic, and erotically involved with several of her nuns, just like Madame Delbène in *Juliette*—but she proves to be unlike her Sadeian equivalent in that behind her apparent confidence lies a profound unease. At the moment she is first introduced in the book, she is described in terms of asymmetry (the size of her eyes, the position of her head, the fit of her clothes) and twitchiness:

> She wriggles on her chair as though something were bothering her, forgetting all sense of decorum she lifts her wimple so as to scratch, crosses her legs, asks you questions but does not listen when you answer . . . she is in turn compassionate and hard, her ever-changing expression indicates the disconnectedness of her mind and all the instability of her character.

Consumed by manic emotions that go as fast as they come, the superior is a walking bag of nerves. At first her infatuation with young Suzanne lifts her spirits; according to the other nuns, she "seemed to have lost her moody character and they said I had steadied her." But she does not just want to feel young Suzanne up; she wants to seduce her into knowledge, into a fully conscious affair. So when Suzanne's innocence proves impermeable, the superior shows signs of being on the verge of a breakdown, "lamenting" and "sighing" in the corridors at night like a ghost.

Suzanne is so passive that it takes the interference of a man—her confessor Father Lemoine—to bring this plot to a crisis: it is on his orders that she starts to avoid the superior. At first the superior fights back eloquently, sneering at the priest for his paranoid inventions.

> I only have to get attached to somebody in an affectionate friend-
> ship for him to make a point of driving her out of her mind . . . I
> cannot see how this Father Lemoine of yours can see my damna-
> tion all signed and sealed in such a natural preference.

The preference she means is her liking for one nun above all the others, but she may be hinting at lesbianism as her "natural preference" too. It is an interesting moment: we half expect the superior to launch into a Sadeian dissection of the arbitrariness of moral codes. But a few days later, unable to persuade Suzanne to accept her obsessive and self-abasing love, she starts going into a decline, passing "from melancholy to piety and from piety to frenzy."

One suspects that the superior behaves erratically because Diderot's sympathies are erratic: he is not sure what to make of, or do with, his own monstrous creation. Her guilt is oddly unconvincing, because belated; we know that she never used to mention her "natural preference" in confession because she did not consider it a sin, but now she fasts, scourges and mortifies herself, begging Suzanne to "trample me underfoot." The new confessor, Dom Morel, is acute enough to see through all this psychic smoke and mirrors to the impossible task of repression: he predicts that the superior will either "soon go back to her first inclinations or go out of her mind." Though he blames the unnatural nature of monastic life for having turned her into a "maniac" with "monstrous affections," he offers gender segregation as a contributing factor, not an excuse. During months of delirious fever the superior is terrorized by visions of devils coming to get her, and yet longs for it all to be over: "If only I could lose my memory! . . . If I could go back into the void, or be born again!" Her death is soon followed by that of poor Sister Thérèse. Even the technically innocent Suzanne cannot escape;

after running away from the convent she ends up a miserable laundress. As in the book of Genesis, forbidden knowledge leads to exile; all who have as much as tasted the lesbian fruit must be punished.

The pattern Diderot established, of the evil lesbian who lures a younger woman into a relationship which can only end in disaster or death (perhaps with a deathbed repentance), was to be lastingly popular in fiction and drama. Unlike Sade's *Juliette,* it offered the best of both worlds—titillation, plus a morally satisfactory ending.

We find Diderot's grim plot even in pornography, which might be expected to operate outside the parameters of respectability. The perfect example is *Gamiani* (1833), a slim fiction attributed to Alfred de Musset, published with frank illustrations and reprinted forty times by 1928. It was said to have been the result of Musset's accepting a bet that he could not write an erotic novel without obscene words; it took him just three days, so the story goes, and he based the character of his Countess Gamiani on his lover George Sand. But it seems more likely that he really borrowed her from Sade, since this aristocratic "wild beast" has a repertoire that includes nuns, monks, whips, dogs, and dildos that ejaculate hot milk (a popular eighteenth-century notion, though unfortunately no examples survive in museums). But what is new is Musset's emphasis on the inherently terrible nature of lesbian sex. Before Sade, it is generally a tantalizing, unfinished business; in Sade, it is one act among many; in *Gamiani* it becomes a dark and almost supernatural force. If Musset's tribade antiheroine is an "unconquerable harpie" (a vengeful monster from classical myth, half bird, half woman), she is also prey: "a female Prometheus, having her heart torn out by a hundred vultures at once." Having no religious context, she cannot proclaim herself (like Diderot's antiheroine) to be damned, but she expresses the secular equivalent: she feels "divorced from nature," and this brings her not Sadeian triumph but psychological torment.

> Nothing that is not extravagant, unnatural, can appeal to me now; I am ever seeking the unattainable. Oh, I assure you it is dreadful to feel as I do! To spoil one's inmost feelings, to be consumed with a desire that is not to be appeased.

Musset describes her as "half-satisfied" and therefore "always tormented." But interestingly, Gamiani turns this technical problem into an asset, boasting that her girlfriend Fanny will keep returning to her because, unlike a man who comes and then collapses, a tribade is always hard, always ready to give more pleasure. This is reminiscent of what James Grantham Turner identifies in libertine literature of the seventeenth century as the "philosapphic" mode, in which lesbian sex is celebrated for the fact that it never quite ends. But what is new, in *Gamiani,* is the existential fury associated with it. Peter Cryle calls this the moment when the Lesbos theme and the Messalina theme (female insatiability) overlap for the first time, and he shows how the notion of fearsome lesbian hyperstamina emerges from the older, more wistful notion of *amor impossibilis:* "The (supposed) inability of women to achieve climax and denouement without male help is thus bound up with their (supposed) capacity to maintain endless desire in exclusively female company." Gamiani's superpower is also her damnation; as in the poems of Baudelaire, the tribade's punishment is a temporal one, a narrative loop in which she is trapped without hope of reaching a dénouement.

But Gamiani does finally bring her story to a resounding climax, by dosing herself and Fanny with a poisonous aphrodisiac so they can die together in the act. Musset probably killed off his monster to make the story more acceptable to his readers, but the effect is oddly glorifying. Unlike Sade's steely Juliette, who slaughters and moves on, Gamiani is a Byronic hero who stakes her life on the meaning of this perverse "martyrdom." "Don't you understand. I only wanted to know, if I could not do more in the rage of agony!" Rather ludicrously—but thrillingly—the lesbian has here become a symbol of the defiance of nature that the decadent movement would champion half a century later.

Gamiani was a best seller in France. But Musset's peers in the British Isles had a problem: their readers would never stand for this kind of explicitness, particularly about goings-on between women. When Maria Edgeworth wrote about a lesbian fiend in 1801, for instance, she did so in a subplot to a courtship novel (*Belinda*), and left the sex out: all that remains are scattered, indirect hints about the unsubtly named Mrs. Harriot Freke, a brash, crass feminist and occasional cross-dresser, who flirts with every girl in sight and persuades one to run away with her.

Charles Dickens used the same strategies in *Little Dorrit* (1857), but he approached his lesbian seriously rather than satirically, and the result is a fascinating portrait of a woman intelligent enough to analyze her own unhappiness and cruelty: a sort of homoerotic Frankenstein's monster. (This sober novel, judged to be Dickens's worst by many nineteenth-century critics, found its first real champion in George Bernard Shaw, and is now considered a masterpiece for its critique of corrupt institutions, prison being only one among them.) Miss Wade is a minor character in *Little Dorrit,* appearing in only eight of the novel's seventy chapters, but disproportionally memorable. Her story is told nonchronologically, in jigsaw pieces that only fit together late in the book. No doubt Dickens used this structure to increase suspense around the mysterious Miss Wade, but it also had the convenient effect of avoiding setting off early warning bells about this erotically perverse character.

Introduced as a handsome, fierce young loner, Miss Wade does not speak for herself until the fifty-seventh chapter (book 2, chapter 21)—a memoir she writes on the pretext of justifying herself to the novel's disapproving hero, Arthur Clennam—entitled "History of a Self-Tormentor," a curiously memorable coinage which is probably meant to hint at "self-abuse." Raised on sufferance by an adoptive grandmother, Miss Wade is furiously possessive from the time of her very first crush on a schoolmate:

> She would cry and cry and say I was cruel, and then I would hold her in my arms till morning: loving her as much as ever, and often feeling as if, rather than suffer so, I could so hold her in my arms and plunge to the bottom of a river—where I would still hold her after we were both dead.

Jealousy here segues into murderous death wish; Miss Wade's passion sounds impossible to satisfy, intrinsically morbid.

In the sentence quoted above, "hold" is repeated three times, but Miss Wade never manages to hold on to her love objects (male or female) for long, because her real sexual preference is for emotional abuse. As soon as she gets to know a young maid, Harriet (fondly nicknamed Tattycoram by her employers, the Meagles), the two are drawn together by a sense of "a singular likeness." Tattycoram is more than ready to hear Miss Wade's trenchant analysis of Tattycoram's humiliating position as a rescued foundling, expected to be perpetually grateful to the Meagles—an analysis which readers will find convincing even if they sense the older woman's hidden agenda. But Tattycoram fears her new friend's sympathy is bad for her: "You seem to come like my own anger, my own malice, my own—whatever it is." Miss Wade here sounds like the return of the repressed: unfeminine feelings made flesh. She watches the girl "as one afflicted with a diseased part might curiously watch the dissection and exposition of an analogous case." This is a variation on the idea of desire between women as disease: Miss Wade plays the helpless patient and the cerebral medical student at the same time.

There are many references to the women looking at each other intensely, but few to them touching; if Dickens means to imply a sexual relationship, he chooses to preserve the decencies. But there is an interesting scene, after Tattycoram runs away with Miss Wade, when Clennam and Meagle track down the couple in a stuffy little London flat. Miss Wade's "composure" suggests to the visitors "(as a veil will suggest the form it covers), the unquenchable passion of her own nature." The image of the veil implies that the calm outside of the relationship—domestic companions in an equal, feminist, and mutually beneficial arrangement—hides a much murkier dynamic. Meagle warns his prodigal maid:

> That lady's influence over you—astonishing to us, and I should hardly go too far in saying terrible to us to see—is founded in passion fiercer than yours, and temper more violent than yours. What can you two be together? What can come of it?

He asks Miss Wade whether she is "a woman, who, from whatever cause, has a perverted delight in making a sister-woman as wretched as she is (I am old enough to have heard of such)." While the first half of the sentence could be interpreted to refer to pimping, his claim to be "old enough to have heard of such" hints at a more rare and murky way of being "perverted." Answering this euphemistic charge with a gesture rather than words, Miss Wade "put her arm about her [Tattycoram's] waist as if she took possession of her for evermore. And there was a visible triumph in her face when she turned to dismiss the visitors."

So what can these two be together? Only unhappy, Dickens seems to say. Though Miss Wade's memoir insists on the language of romantic friendship—"fidelity," "common cause," "confidence"—the relationship is fundamentally unequal, because Tattycoram is financially dependent and comes to realize that she has swapped the confinement of service for a new jail. Ironically, the only form of rebellion she can imagine is to renounce the relationship as "madness" and run back to her old employers. Unlike Diderot, however, Dickens feels no need to show the rejected lesbian beating her breast or falling into delirium: Miss Wade simply disappears from the novel, presumably in search of another love object to torment.

Thomas Hardy in *Desperate Remedies* (1871) allowed himself a little more leeway in describing the behavior of Miss Aldclyffe, a handsome, friendless, eccentric spinster of forty-six, who hires the inexperienced Cytherea as a lady's maid (her seventh that year) on the basis of the girl's beauty. Her interest in Cytherea is shown from the start to be inextricably bound up with the dominance and submission of service, and the physical intimacies it involves: "She murmured to herself, 'It is almost worth while to be bored with instructing her in order to have a creature who could glide round my luxurious indolent body in that manner, and look at me in that way—I warrant how light her fingers are upon one's head and neck . . .' "

There are several heavily erotic scenes of Cytherea dressing and undressing Miss Aldclyffe that describe the girl looking at and touching her mistress; the desiring gaze goes both ways. She is uncomfortable with her role in this household, however, and resents "her dependence on the whims of a strange woman." But when the two discover that Cytherea is the daughter of the man Miss Aldclyffe loved and lost, they become obsessed with each other, feeling that their histories are even more "romantically intertwined." Miss Aldclyffe's passion is described sometimes like a mother's, sometimes like a male lover's. She climbs into Cytherea's bed, asking, "Why can't you kiss me as I can kiss you?" When Cytherea admits that there is a man she loves, Miss Aldclyffe loses her temper:

I—an old fool—have been sipping at your mouth as if it were honey, because I fancied no wasting lover knew the spot. But a minute ago, and you seemed to me like a fresh spring meadow—now you seem a dusty highway.

Nonetheless, the older woman hopes to reclaim Cytherea: "Try to love me more than you love him—do. I love you more sincerely than any man can." She begs the girl to stay, not as a maid but as a companion. "Now will you promise to live with me always, and always be taken care of, and never deserted?" But the day after this long, frank scene, Miss Aldclyffe apologizes for her "absurd feeling" of possessiveness. Her behavior changes so abruptly, in fact, that one senses Hardy is backing off from the topic, at a high cost to consistency of characterization. For the rest of the novel, Miss Aldclyffe is more an interfering employer than a lover; she promotes Cytherea's marriage with first one and then another man, before begging the girl's forgiveness on her deathbed.

Some of the awkwardness of *Desperate Remedies* can be explained by the fact that it was Hardy's first novel and very much an experiment, written to cash in on the popular successes of sensation novelists such as Wilkie Collins, and perhaps the French school of lesbian fiend fiction. The first publisher he sent it to (Macmillan) rejected it as too highly charged; Tinsley Brothers agreed to publish it only if Hardy contributed to the printing costs. When the *Spectator* damned the novel for sensationalism, Hardy wished that he were dead, and for the rest of his life he would make attempts to evade this charge. In a new edition of 1896, for instance, he toned down the description of Miss Aldclyffe's affection from "too rank, sensuous and capricious" to "too rank and capricious." In 1912, he made more substantial alterations to the bedroom scene which provide a fascinating insight into the mechanics of bowdlerization. First he softened some wording: "love and be loved by" became "care for and be cared for by." He also added explanations which are not entirely convincing: to Miss Aldclyffe's demand "Now kiss me," he added, "You seem as if you were my own, own child," and to justify the line "I can't help loving you" he preceded it with "I am a lonely woman, and I want the sympathy of a pure girl like you."

The French influence is even more obvious in *A Sunless Heart* (1894), a fascinatingly hybrid work published anonymously by Scottish author Edith Johnstone. This "New Woman" novel is set at a girls' college where Mona, an eighteen-year-old student, is in love with her lecturer, Miss Lotus Grace. Significantly, Mona is a Creole, technically white but ethnically exotic: "a creature of flame and water, genius and strung nerves; a mad, lovable thing; a West Indian heiress, who owned a pitch lake in Trinidad." Lotus responds impatiently to Mona's declarations that "we shall always be together—in life and death"; she assures the girl that "in a few years you will find man is the right and legal object of these hysterics." Interestingly, this does not stop her from kissing Mona and spending the summer traveling with her. Mona is characterized rather unevenly as having both a "tender heart" full of "noble, idealizing love" for Lotus, *and* a sinister possessiveness. She warns off a rival (another lecturer, called Gasparine) in no uncertain terms: "She is all I have—all I want. If you go between her and me . . . do you hear? She is mine. She was always mine in the College. A girl tried to take her from me once. *That girl's gone.*" Mona's erotic greed contrasts and competes with Gasparine's radiant affection: they come across as characters from two different books, representatives of two different traditions, the (mostly French) lesbian fiend tale and the (mostly English) inseparables story. But Lotus can return neither form of love fully because she is damaged goods, her heart rendered permanently "sunless" by sexual abuse in her teens.

After a year abroad, Mona marches back in and invites her beloved to travel around the world with her. But a man has come between them—a middle-aged professor with whom Lotus has fallen in love and whom Mona has already turned down. Urging Mona to marry him and *"be as others are,"* the grief-stricken Lotus shares a bed with her one last time, then leaves, to return to Gasparine and live a chastened, quiet life. But fate intervenes; her train crashes into Mona's, and the girl, in a particularly creepy moment, tracks her down: "In the darkness, she felt a mouth touch hers, and two wet hands groped over her body." Horribly injured, they cling together in the wreckage, Mona in ecstasies that her fantasy of simultaneous death is coming true. During the long night of agony Lotus's chilly heart finally melts and she tells Mona, "Because you did not leave me, now I have faith in love!" This is an oddly romantic climax to a bloody scene.

"But why, it may be asked, does the writer deprive us of two interesting personages by such a thing as death in a collision on the railway," complained the reviewer for the *Scotsman*. Clearly Edith Johnstone had difficulty imagining any other solution to this "interesting" couple's stormy relationship: instead of marrying off either of them to the blundering professor, she preserves their fervid romance by letting them die together, which may be a cliché but in this case does suit the material. *A Sunless Heart* was widely reviewed, and we can deduce that the lesbian theme was what the *Academy* promised would "inspire exceptional interest" in the reading public, and what the *Athenaeum* found "nauseating when not ridiculous." The *Glasgow Herald* was unusual in spelling it out in excited tones: "Few writers seem to know so thoroughly what one woman may be to another, or to have explained it so completely."

Similarly, a boarding school for girls is the setting for the unequivocally hostile *Regiment of Women* (1917), the best-selling first novel by "Clemence Dane" (Winifred Ashton) that established the stereotype of the predatory lesbian teacher. The coldly glamorous Clare Hartill has a surname that suggests the sickness of her heart, and her preference for candles over electricity gives her more than a touch of the vampire. Taking up a new colleague (the boisterous eighteen-year-old Alwynne Durand), Clare draws her into a close partnership. Her secret agenda is not sex—Clare never goes beyond a rare, rough kiss on the lips—but domination. Becoming "a very real tyrant," she binds Alwynne "ever more closely to her," planning to "master" and break this sunny spirit: as Dane puts it sardonically, "She had acquired a lover with a sense of humour and she felt that she had her hands full. Her imperious will would, in time, she knew, eliminate either the lover or the humour." First Clare tackles the maiden aunt Elsbeth, whom Alwynne lives with; she takes her on over such tiny but significant points as where the girl will spend Christmas Day. "Alwynne, by fair means or foul, should be detached . . . should become Clare's property . . . should be given up to no living woman or man."

The tension of this tightening bond, and worry over the suicide of Clare's thirteen-year-old pet, Louise, sends the young teacher into a decline: "The changing Alwynne, whitened, quieted, submissive, the sparkle gone from her eyes and the snap from her tongue." Aunt Elsbeth steps in to rescue her niece, sending her to convalesce with relations, where she will meet a nice gardener called Roger. Here Clemence Dane piles on the agricultural—in fact, borderline eugenicist—metaphors. Roger makes Alwynne realize that her school is "a rabbit warren" and "a tray of unthinned seedlings." He persuades her without much difficulty that "she must show him all the weeds that were choking her before he could set about uprooting them and planting good seed."

As is traditional in the rivalry plots discussed in chapter 3, Roger is comically obtuse about the "sorcery" by which the older teacher holds

Alwynne in thrall. He is shaken when Alwynne turns down his proposal in faltering, borrowed phrases.

> You see, she [Clare] thinks—we both think, that if you've got a—
> a really real woman friend, it's just as good as falling in love and
> getting married and all that—and far less commonplace. Besides
> the trouble—smoking, you know—and children.

(This is the only example I have found of men's tobacco habits being a reason to prefer women!) Alwynne immediately undermines this rather faltering coming-out speech of hers when she admits to hankering for children, but she continues to insist that she is committed: "There can never be anyone but Clare . . . I've let her be sure she can have me always." (Privately, Clare is prepared for the day Alwynne gets broody: "A brat to play with? Let her adopt one, and I'll house it. I'll give her anything she wants.") However, one last bit of nastiness from Clare—a curt refusal of a nightgown that Alwynne has painstakingly handsewn—shakes the scales from the girl's eyes and frees her to run off to Roger. It is Aunt Elsbeth, the knowing observer, who denounces Clare for her "vampirism": "Who will your next victim be? . . . What will you do when your glamour's gone? I tell you, Clare Hartill, you'll die of hunger in the end."

But Clemence Dane's take on her villainess is rather subtler than this. Clare ends the novel sitting at her desk all night during a storm, looking at Alwynne's telegram telling her she is going to marry Roger. She cries briefly, she writes to the headmistress accepting a partnership in the school, and she resigns herself to a future of "loneliness and work" . . . perhaps enlivened by "other fish in the sea," including "that child in the Fourth." This is no lurid death, but a credible plan for survival.

Even if some of the English fiends manage to cheat death, they are—like their French sisters—a frail breed. By the late nineteenth century, sex between women was generally assumed to produce a fraying of the nerves (due to all that unsatisfied arousal) and exhaustion. Cora Linn Daniels's *Sardia: A Story of Love* (1891), Naomi Royde-Smith's *The Island* (1929), and Helen Anderson's *Pity for Women* (1937) end with sudden mental breakdowns. Madness often proves fatal, as in Diderot's *La Religieuse* (1796), though the mechanism is obscure. Many characters show awareness of the conventions of their story: "Ah!" sighs Hélène in Adrienne Saint-Agen's *L'Affolante illusion* (1906; in English, *The Terrifying Illusion*), "I am only too sure of the denouement of my utopian passion: a madhouse or the . . . grave!" Having watched her lover expire in delirium brought on by sexual exhaustion, Aline in Charles Montfort's *Le Journal d'une Saphiste* (1902) draws the obvious moral:

> I have seen to her last resting place the dear victim of my sapphic love and now I shall not rest until I find in solitude or in death the supreme expiation for this tragedy. My last plea will be: Women seek only the Unique and Powerful Love that sways all mankind: the Wholesome and Honest Love, Comforting and Sublime because it is Procreative, that of Man.

That last sentence shows curious capitalization; it is as if Montfort (or his translator) is trying to give his conclusion the weight of some ancient scripture.

If desire between women has difficulty directly killing its victims, it pulls off the trick with the help of prostitution, in, for instance, Emile Zola's scandalously successful *Nana* (1880), which includes the first dyke bar scene in literature. Drugs help too: opium and eau de cologne in Algernon Swinburne's unsubtly titled *Lesbia Brandon* (written 1864–67); aphrodisiacs in Jean-Louis Dubut de Laforest's 1884 novella, *Mademoiselle de Tantale;* some poison which brings ecstatic oblivion in Adrienne Saint-Agen's *Amants féminins* (1902; in English, *Women Lovers*).

Destruction must come down one way or another: it is as if desire between women is a land mine, harming innocent and guilty alike. For instance, when the husband of the bisexually promiscuous heroine of Ernest Feydeau's *La Comtesse de Chalis* (1868) commits her to a sanatorium, it is not she but he and their two children who promptly drop dead. In an Italian novel, Enrico Butti's *L'automa* (1882; in English, *The Robot*), an androgynous aristocrat drives her husband to suicide by taking a variety of lovers, including an even more mannish female singer. Another story of marital breakdown, August Strindberg's *Le Plaidoyer d'un fou* (1895; in English, *A Madman's Manifesto*), is an extended suicide note by a frail writer who only gradually realizes that his cross-dressing suffragist actress wife is cheating on him with every woman in sight. (Despite these last examples, the lesbian fiend is only rarely described as cross-dressing; in the benign tradition of the female bridegroom, a woman in breeches may be comical, romantic, or tragic, but she is almost never evil.)

By the beginning of the twentieth century, violent death is even more popular than a slow decline. Fiends can commit or incite suicide, or wind up a relationship of mutual misery with a murder-suicide (as in *Gamiani*), for instance by gas oven in the backstory to Jean-Paul Sartre's *No Exit* (1945). My own favorite scene of fusion in death is the climax of Jane de la Vaudère's *Les Demi-sexes* (1897), when Madame Saurel turns up in Camille's drawing room to try to force her to leave her beloved husband, and Camille embraces her, pulling them both into the fire: afterward, "their bodies were so strangely shrunken and twisted that it was impossible to distinguish one from the other." This is desire between women as the melting of identity boundaries, the ultimate narcissism.

SECRET ENEMIES

So the lesbian monster can be placed in various narrative frames: the pornographic novel, the school story, the anticlerical exposé, the tragic bildungsroman. But the most popular is a variant on the rivals plot, in which a male point-of-view character has a secret competitor who turns out to be not a man but . . . a lesbian. This storyline offers mystery, narrative suspense, titillation, and moralism all wrapped up in one appealing package.

We have seen writers such as Isaac de Benserade, Honoré D'Urfé, and Denis Diderot struggle to preserve a narrator's innocence even as she is being drawn into an affair with another woman. Honoré de Balzac's clever innovation in *La Fille aux yeux d'or* (1835, one of his History of the Thirteen trilogy; in English, *The Girl with Golden Eyes*) was to keep up the tension without sacrificing as much plausibility, by telling the story from the point of view of a figure who still shows up in lesbian-themed literature and films today: the oblivious boyfriend. (Roger in *Regiment of Women* at least grasps that Clare is a bad influence on

"Your strength will wear out against my will and you will exhaust yourself in useless struggles," in Adolphe Belot, Mademoiselle Giraud, My Wife *(1891).*

This image from Belot's adultery story with a twist is by the illustrator and groundbreaking photojournalist Ernest Clair-Guyot; it first appeared in a French edition of 1889 and was included in the Chicago translation of 1891.

his beloved, even if he is foggy on the specifics, but the man in secret-enemy storylines does not even realize that his unknown rival is a woman.) Balzac's narrator Henri is the opposite of innocent—a decadent Parisian rake, in fact—but it does not occur to him that the one who has preceded him in the affections of the golden-eyed (Spanish and African-American) Paquita could be other than male. He knows the girl is guarded by the large staff of a mansion belonging to the absent Marquis de San-Réal, so he decides—with a certain logic—that the aged marquis must be his rival, and that they are enacting "that eternally old but ever new comedy featuring the stock characters of an old man, a young girl, and a lover."

To give her credit, his beloved Paquita does offer many heavy hints that her captivity is psychological as well as literal: "Listen, I'm chained like a poor animal to its post; I'm amazed I've been able to throw a bridge across the abyss that divides us. Make me drunk, then kill me." She is careful to use gender-neutral terms for the person who has kept her as a sex slave since the age of twelve, "the monster who will devour me," the one who sends Paquita mysterious letters written (as a concession to the girl's illiteracy) in hieroglyphs. Henri is hilariously slow to put the pieces together, even when, having deflowered his beloved, he deduces that she was technically a virgin but "certainly not innocent." As if trying to tell him her secret, she dresses him up in a red velvet frock, and later tells him, "You're forgetting the power of the feminine." But this oblivious boyfriend remains so until, in the throes of sex, Paquita screams out the nickname not of the marquis but of his beautiful young wife. Mortified by his sudden realization, Henri makes a bathetic attempt to strangle Paquita with his cravat.

The marquise returns later that night, like some female Bluebeard with a nose for betrayal, and she avenges the infidelity as Henri failed to do, by stabbing her captive over and over. Though we never see the two women having sex, blood acts as its sign; by the time Henri bursts in, the room is covered in red prints, and the half-naked, magnificent marquise is marked by the girl's bites: "She was too intoxicated by warm blood, too stimulated by the struggle, in too great a state of exaltation to have noticed had all Paris formed a circle around her." The fact that this is the marquise's way of outdoing Henri at defloration is suggested by her send-off to Paquita: "For the blood you've given him, you owe me all of yours!" In a final twist, Paquita's "execution" allows the rivals to reconcile. Almost comically, the Sadeian bloodbath is turned into a sentimental recognition scene as the two alter egos, seeing their features reflected in each other, discover that they have the same father. (So was it her female lover's face in her male lover that Paquita chose? Although at the level of plot this story opposes man to woman and heterosexuality to homosexuality, in the details Balzac clearly relishes blurring such lines.) In a rather unconvincing nod to Diderot, the marquise announces that for love of God she will retire to a Spanish convent. Where, presumably, she will seduce young nuns and go insane? One bizarre indication of the popularity of Balzac's nasty, clever novella is that his description of the boudoir was reprinted in a women's magazine article on decorating tips.

Thirty-five years later, serialized in *Le Figaro, Mademoiselle Giraud, ma femme* (1870; in English, *Mademoiselle Giraud, My Wife*) was a huge success for Adolphe Belot, a divorced lawyer from Guadeloupe whose potboilers financed his travels and his gambling; the novel was reprinted thirty times in the following decade. Belot's title hints at the paradox of Adrien Giraud's wife, Paule, being still a "mademoiselle," fundamentally unmarriageable, still unwon.

The novel's real innovation is in the characterization of the secret enemy. The stylish, witty young Countess de Blangy—a separated wife who jokes about being "allergic to all men"—exhibits none of the lurid traits or twitching neuroses of a lesbian monster. All she does is continue, under cover of friendship, her school-days affair with Paule. It is

Adrien's profound obtuseness—even when the two inseparables come out flushed from long conversations in locked bedrooms—that makes him so easy to cuckold. Unknowingly, he confides in his rival, repeatedly asking her for help with the marriage he has not yet managed to persuade his wife to consummate. Even when he finally forbids Paule to see the countess, it is only an attempt to provoke his serene, enigmatic wife. The punch line of the joke comes when Adrien tracks Paule to a secret apartment—draped decadently with black satin, bookshelves crammed with such sapphic classics as *La Religieuse, La Fille aux yeux d'or*, and *Mademoiselle Maupin*—and though he finds the countess there, the penny still fails to drop. Throughout this novel, the countess's brilliant technique is to tell the literal truth, but flippantly, letting Adrien continue to believe women's friendship harmless:

> If you forgive us for loving each other since our days in the convent and for not being able to live apart from each other, drop that forbidding expression that reminds me of Bluebeard, and take this cigarette.

Only a chance meeting on his travels with the worldly and melancholy Count de Blangy enlightens Adrien about their wives' long-term affair. Unable to use the legal system—because to raise lesbian possibilities in court would bring them nothing but ridicule—the husbands drag their wives apart by force. At this point *Mademoiselle Giraud, ma femme* goes through one of those lurching changes of gear common in lesbian-themed literature: Belot halts his saucy comedy of adultery and tacks on a stern ending. Paule, laid low by a brain disease caused by sexual exhaustion, repents in the arms of her husband (who has still not managed to consummate the marriage), before choking to death on a piece of food: this makes literal her morbid appetites. The Countess de Blangy, as the active seductress, gets a more deliberate dispatch: Adrien, fortuitously happening across her in difficulties out swimming with her new girlfriend, drowns her under cover of lending aid. Her husband writes to thank him for ridding the world of this "reptile." The novel, narrated by Adrien to a male friend, restores the bond of men against the unnerving trickery of women.

The sapphic fictions of Balzac, Gautier, Zola, and Belot all began appearing in widely available U.S. translations in the 1890s. It was on a

Memphis street in 1892 that the notion of the lesbian monster moved into the spotlight of popular culture, when Alice Mitchell took a razor to the throat of Freda Ward, the girlfriend who had backed out on a promise to elope with her. (Ward died on the spot; Mitchell was presumed to be insane and sent to an asylum, where she died, probably by her own hand.) Mitchell was not the first woman to kill a girlfriend rather than lose her; the fact that her case became an international phenomenon suggests that—prompted by the medical interest in homosexuality as either an innate or an acquired perversion—the time was right for stories of evil lesbian killers. Interestingly, it was to *Mademoiselle Giraud, ma femme* that most commentators turned (even though, in Belot's novel, the lesbian is in fact the murder victim, not the killer). As the *New York World* marveled:

> In the Criminal Court of Memphis, Shelby County, Adolphe Belot's *Mlle. Giraud Ma Femme* will be the only textbook at hand. Judge DuBose, of Tennessee, will have cited to him, as bearing on the case of an American girl, the creations of French writers whom he and all his associates have looked upon as perverted creatures, dealing with matters outside of real life, or at least outside of American life.

Here genre and nationality are conflated; real life moves uncannily close to fiction, and American women's sexuality is revealed as horribly similar to the foreign kind.

In *Mademoiselle Giraud,* the rival is seen but not recognized; in *La Fille aux yeux d'or,* she is unseen until the last moment. In his 1925 play *La Prisonnière* (in English, *The Captive*), Edouard Bourdet went one better and kept his predator offstage throughout: Madame d'Aiguines— the older married woman holding Irene in her thrall—is represented only by the bunches of violets she sends her. (Sales of the flower in both France and America were said to have plummeted as a result of this play.) This invisibility of the fiend was clearly the secret of the play's success with audiences; one reviewer, Pierre Brisson, chose not to name its "bold and strangely embarrassing subject," since "by spelling it out one is likely to give it that brutal appearance that M. Bourdet has managed to avoid with such fine skill."

But unlike many other devices for evading censorship, the unseen quality of Madame d'Aiguines makes her all the more fascinating and the play more profound in its effects: she is a bogey, a blank screen on which we project all our fantasies and fears. Though *La Prisonnière* is clearly indebted to *Mademoiselle Giraud*, it comes to a very different conclusion. The invalid, world-weary Monsieur d'Aiguines warns Irene's naïve suitor Jacques to give up and leave these lesbians "to dwell among themselves in the kingdom of shadows":

> It's mysterious, terrible! Under cover of friendship a woman can enter any household, whenever and however she pleases—at any hour of the day—she can poison and pillage everything before a man whose home she destroys is even aware what's happening to him . . . A secret alliance of two beings who understand one another because they're alike, because they're of the same sex, because they're of a different planet than he, the stranger, the enemy!

This is the lesbian monster as an alien, wielding unlimited Terminator-style powers that appear to include invisibility—but also, curiously, the lesbian as any woman, Everywoman. Jacques himself uses an interesting image when finally conceding the battle after a year of marriage to the emotionally numb Irene:

> You're breathless—your eyes are dazed—your hands are trembling—because you've seen her again, that's why! For a year I've been living with a statue, and that woman had only to reappear for the statue to come to life.

Here the monster is elevated to a deity: Aphrodite, who turned the statue Galatea into a real woman. Popular opinion credits the sculptor Pygmalion with this miracle, but he only shaped the statue and prayed to the goddess: in the myth, the power to give life is female. Here, hostility toward the monstrous lesbian tips over the edge into a kind of rapturous fascination.

Bourdet claimed he had been inspired by a comrade of his in World War One, a soldier who wanted to die rather than return to his sham marriage. But Paris gossip said *La Prisonnière* was really about war hero Denys Trefusis, who married Violet Keppel in peacetime in 1919 and endured her affairs with both Vita Sackville-West and the Princesse

Edmond de Polignac before his death ten years later. *La Prisonnière,* despite simultaneous hit productions in half a dozen European cities, was banned in Britain. The 1926 Broadway production of *The Captive* attracted enormous crowds, and a firestorm of publicity. American reviewers, whether they approved of the play or not, followed Bourdet in their avoidance of such unambiguous words as *lesbian* or *homosexual:* instead they offered sterner terms (*sex perversion, abnormality, aberration, psychopathic relationships, warped infatuation*) or euphemisms (*adult subjects, advanced subjects, an indecent theme, a revolting theme*). Many of them suggested, with more than a hint of self-congratulation, that the "man in the street" would be unlikely to understand what the play was about even after sitting through it. Perhaps what was shocking, finally, was the ending: Irene bangs the door behind her as she runs off to join her lover, in an obvious echo of Ibsen's *A Doll's House* (1879). A New York State Supreme Court justice pronounced against the play, but with audible regret:

> Justice Mahoney gave the opinion that the drama had excellent literary quality and that it might not harm a mature and intelligent audience. On the other hand, he held that it might have dangerous effects on some persons in an indiscriminate, cosmopolitan audience.

Meaning that the "mature and intelligent" would deduce the true horror that awaited Irene, but the young and the uncultured might be misled into cheering her on? In the end, the production—along with Mae West's show *Sex*—provoked a law that would ban "sex perversion" on the New York stage from 1927 to 1967.

Bourdet borrowed more than his title from Marcel Proust's posthumous novel of 1923, *La Prisonnière.* In that and other volumes of his *In Search of Lost Time,* Proust broods over the perverse position of the man who suspects, denies, but finally cannot help knowing that his beloved's most erotic feelings are reserved for other women. His narrator, Marcel, makes mistakes that remind us of his oblivious predecessors in Balzac and Belot: at one point, for instance, he denies Albertine access to all her female friends *except* Andrée—who turns out to be her lover. Proust's women, for all their prettiness and playfulness, are straight out of the French tradition of lesbian decadence. After Albertine's death, Andrée speculates to Marcel that Albertine had vainly hoped Marcel would guess that she needed Marcel to save her by marrying her:

> She felt in her heart that her obsession was a kind of criminal lunacy, and I have often wondered whether it wasn't after an incident of that sort, having caused a suicide in a family, that she had committed suicide herself.

Similarly, in a story called "Before Dark" published much earlier, in 1896, Proust squeezes dark comedy from the obtuseness of a man (unfortunately called Leslie) whose beloved Françoise, dying from a gunshot wound, is trying to make him face the fact that she is a lesbian. (The surprise ending is that it turns out to be she who fired the gun.) One of the ironies is that she was encouraged, in her first stirrings of curiosity, by Leslie's own tolerant statements on lesbianism, such as "We cannot say that because most people see things we call red as red that those who see them as violet are mistaken." Might this line have suggested the bunches of violets that stand in for the woman lover in Bourdet's play? Violet, lavender, and purple—as in the title of Alice Walker's 1982 novel, *The Color Purple*—are traditionally associated with desire between women.

Not Quite Human

The woman who desires women is not just metaphorically monstrous; there is a long tradition of characterizing her as nonhuman.

Sometimes she is subhuman, for instance in H. Rider Haggard's *Allan's Wife* (1889)—one of his fifty-eight adventure novels, and so eagerly awaited by fans that two pirated editions appeared before publication. Hendrika is a black ape-woman, but endowed with more dignity than such a crass premise would suggest. Raised by baboons in South Africa, then rescued by a white family, Hendrika has ended up as evolution's missing link, a "devil-woman" in the eyes of the natives. "Mistress" or "Star" is how she addresses her beautiful white foster sister Stella, with a worship which manages to be abased and domineering at the same time, and she is determined to thwart Stella's marriage to

Allan Quatermain, the small, wiry, and unattractive adventurer nicknamed "Macumazahn" (Watcher-by-Night). Our revolted hero claims that Hendrika speaks in "grunts" and "clicks," but on the page she comes across like a Shakespearean tragic hero.

> She drew herself up till her teeth gleamed in the moonlight. "Have I not watched her these many years, Macumazahn? Shall I cease to watch because a wandering white man comes to steal her? Why were you kissing her in the garden, Macumazahn? How dare you kiss her who is a star? . . . They say in the Kraals that men love women better than women love women. But it is a lie, though this is true—that if a woman loves a man she forgets all other love."

This rivals story signals its ending: Hendrika must lose. If Hendrika owes much to Othello, Stella is a Desdemona figure, for instance when she pleads for Hendrika's life after the ape-woman's knife attack on Allan: "I have been very fond of her, and bad as she is, she has loved me. Do not have her killed on my marriage day." Once banished to the jungle, and denied Stella's civilizing influence, Hendrika goes wild and goes mad. (As usual, the lesbian's doom is overdetermined.) Rounding up a huge troop of her baboon relatives, she returns to kidnap the newlywed, pregnant Stella, and holds her captive in a highly womblike cave. Readers hoping for at least a hint of a lesbian ape rape scene must have been disappointed; all the gallant Hendrika does is cook Stella tasty meals. Even after her husband has rescued her, Stella dies in childbirth, as if unable to bear the internal conflict of her two loves. Restored to sanity and the correct use of English, Hendrika stabs herself on Stella's grave. The magnanimous victor, Allan, plans to give her a Christian burial, but the natives throw her body to the vultures instead.

Of course, *Allan's Wife* is a racist, homophobic parable. It is never quite clear whether Hendrika's unnatural desire drags her down to the bestial level, or is the consequence of her bestial upbringing, but either way the connection is clear: as Allan observes thoughtfully, "the lower one gets in the scale of humanity the more readily this passion thrives." However, Hendrika is by far the strongest character, and every statement about her savagery is contradicted by a demonstration of her nobility— which suggests that Haggard could not quite make up his mind whether he was writing about a disgusting passion or a glorious one.

It was more usual for writers to write about lesbians as nonhuman in the sense of the supernatural: an eerie turning away from nature's law. The link goes back at least as far as Samuel Coleridge's *Christabel* (started in 1798, published in 1816), in which a beautiful stranger, Geraldine, tricks her way into Christabel's bed and works some appalling spell on her. The poem gains its power partly from the fact that—left unfinished—it never clarifies what is going on or whether Christabel escapes.

Later writers preferred to spell it out. Ghosts, for instance, are handy devices, because they can be wistful or stern, comforting or horrifying, or an unnerving mixture of them all. The specter keeps an author's options open, since she can be read (by those who believe in that sort of thing) as a real spirit, and (by those who do not) as a personification of the longing, sorrow, desire, or guilt of the one being haunted. Ghost stories can put the culturally semi-visible—desire between women, for instance—briefly in the spotlight.

Victorian ghost stories sometimes stage a weird, passionate encounter between a living woman and her dead friend: examples include Ada Trevanion's "A Ghost Story" (1858), Rose Terry's "My Visitation" (1858), Elizabeth Stuart Phelps's "Since I Died" (1873), and Alice Brown's "There and Here" (1897). Often what makes the ghost walk is unfinished business to do with a close friendship.

In a notable twentieth-century example, Elizabeth Bowen's 1934 story "The Apple Tree," Mrs. Myra Wing's newly wedded life is rendered intolerable by the nightly apparition of an apple tree which paralyzes her and terrifies anyone who comes near it. The tree is eventually revealed as standing for the intense bond she had at school with a "queer-looking" spectacled girl called Doria. Both she and twelve-year-old Myra were unpopular and they formed a pact, becoming "quite proud of ourselves, of being different." They used to hide high up in the branches of an old apple tree where no one could find them, and tell stories. But as soon as Myra managed to make other friends, she dropped Doria and betrayed her by joining in the others' mockery. One night she followed Doria out to the gardens and found her hanging from the apple tree. In the aftermath, Myra got brain fever and almost died. The young bride now explains her "haunted" state to the kindly, older Mrs. Bettersley; every now and then, she confesses, she dreams that she wakes up in the dormitory and sees Doria tying the cord around her waist and going out. "I have to go after her; there is always the apple tree. Its roots are in me. It takes all my strength." The way a relationship from school days has become a permanently blighting force on the heroine's adult life and marriage suggests that same-sex attachment, once planted in a girl's character, cannot be easily uprooted. Interestingly, the cure turns out to be a mysterious interaction between women; Mrs. Bettersley (whose name suggests that she will make Myra better) says, rather mysteriously and romantically, "come away with me." After some weeks she brings Myra back to her husband, cured, but "by what arts" we do not learn. The Wings live happily ever after in "sublime nonentity," as Bowen puts it drily; being haunted may be a ghastly business, but it is more exciting than happily married life.

Betrayal between women is the backstory to Shirley Jackson's *The Haunting of Hill House* (1959), considered by many the best ghost story of the twentieth century. The house's spinster mistress, we learn, "took a girl from the village to live with her, as a kind of companion," but died neglected while the girl was dallying in the garden with a man. Inheriting the house brought the girl no happiness because of accusations that she had tricked her doting benefactor, so she killed herself. Hill House is already throbbing with lesbian unhappiness, then, by the time an investigator brings along a group of psychic sensitives. It is no surprise that the ensuing psychodrama focuses on the turbulent relationship of two of the sensitives, timid Eleanor and cocky Theo (Theodora). Theo has arrived fresh from a row with the "flatmate" who ripped up "the volume of Alfred de Musset" Theo gave her for her birthday—no doubt a wink-wink reference to the murderous tribade in Musset's *Gamiani* (1833). One of the book's scariest moments comes when Eleanor and Theo are gripping each other's hands in the dark, listening to ghosts babble outside the door—but when the lights come back on, Eleanor realizes she is alone. "Good God—whose hand was I holding?" Desire and revulsion, the live and the dead, touch here to produce a delicious shudder; what if the true monster is not outside but right beside you, pretending to be your friend?

The ghost is not the only uncanny figure used to suggest the invisibility of women's romantic relationships. In an oddly domestic fantasy novel from 1927, Edith Olivier's *The Love Child*, Agatha is lonely enough, at thirty-two, to summon back her sole childhood friend—an imaginary one, aged eleven, called Clarissa. (The name echoes not only Richardson's novel of 1748–49, but the heroine of Virginia Woolf's *Mrs. Dalloway* [1925], preoccupied with the memory of kissing her best friend.) Defying the convention that girlish things must be put away as a woman matures into heterosexuality, Agatha plunges into a playful but secret relationship with her "love child." This novel is often read as a parable of mother-child relationships, but Olivier describes the bond in terms more romantic than maternal: "It was as if a shaft of light had shot into a darkened room." It is at night that Agatha is free to focus on Clarissa, and this makes it sound even more like a sexual affair: "She found herself looking forward to bedtime as if something wonderful was going to happen, something which she did not even try to define to herself."

The problem arises when others gradually start noticing Clarissa. Their love, now visible, needs a cover story—so Agatha calls herself the girl's mother by adoption. Increasingly obsessed, she cannot take her eyes off Clarissa for a second; she thinks of them as planets bound by cosmic "attraction," or as "musician" and "instrument." In a nice twist, the girl starts growing up—and the plot morphs into a rivals story in which Agatha has to fight a male suitor for the unaware Clarissa. Young David's ranting betrays his half-formed knowledge of the nature of the women's bond: "Clarissa spends half her life shut up in a dark room, mopping that old maniac's head with a wet rag. It isn't safe. It isn't decent. It isn't healthy." Ironically, he sees Agatha, not Clarissa, as the supernatural being: a "vampire," a witch of "uncanny power" who has put a "spell" on his beloved.

In a conventional novel of 1927 David would probably win Clarissa, but in this peculiar fantasy she tells him, "I belong to Agatha," and she means it literally: the moment he presses a kiss on her, she disappears back into nothingness, as if he has cut the psychic umbilical cord between her and her mother/lover. David, clearly well-read in the literature of the lesbian monster, keeps accusing Agatha of having murdered the girl. But once David has gone away, Clarissa appears to come back into Agatha's life: we are told from a maid's point of view that Agatha seems to be playing happily with someone invisible in the garden. With this ambiguous ending, Edith Olivier may be asking whether love between women is a mere game of let's pretend, or more real than obtuse observers think.

David Henry Friston, in J. Sheridan LeFanu, Carmilla, *in* The Dark Blue *(March 1872).*
LeFanu's vampire tale first appeared in installments in this short-lived journal with an
impressive roster of contributors. This illustration focuses on the moment when Carmilla
looms in a predatory way over a sleeping figure—not our innocent heroine, Laura,
interestingly, but a minor character named Bertha, who could be shown bare-breasted without
shocking readers as much. An English figure painter, Friston went on to be the very first
illustrator of the Sherlock Holmes stories.

The vampire, too, has often been used as an allegory for the Other, especially a member of a distrusted, invisible minority such as Jews. Queers fit the vampire profile even better: a hidden identity revealed only by subtle signs, a nocturnal subculture of predators looking for naïve victims to recruit into their lifestyle. And it is hardly a stretch to draw an analogy between same-sex desire and the vampire's thirst for blood: a secret craving for the exchange of fluids by mouth, a nonreproductive melding of bodies, associated with disease, sterility, and death.

The lesbian vampire first appears in Joseph Sheridan Le Fanu's *Carmilla* (1872), but Le Fanu was probably influenced by Coleridge's *Christabel* (the mysterious frail beauty begging the young heroine to give her refuge) and Diderot's *La Religieuse* (the heroine who maintains her innocence through a series of increasingly steamy encounters). In turn, his novella was an important source for Bram Stoker's *Dracula*

(1897), a quarter of a century later. Laura, Le Fanu's narrator, finds her new friend Carmilla's passion for her "unintelligible":

> It was like the ardour of a lover; it embarrassed me; it was hateful and yet overpowering; and with gloating eyes she drew me to her, and her hot lips travelled along my cheek in kisses; and she would whisper, almost in sobs, "You are mine, you *shall* be mine, and you and I are one for ever." Then she has thrown herself back in her chair, with her small hands over her eyes, leaving me trembling.
>
> "Are we related," I used to ask; "what can you mean by all this?"

But even if Laura's mind stays closed, in the traditionally ever-innocent way, her body is awakening; in her dreams she experiences orgasmic sensations which we guess mean that Carmilla is sucking her blood. This is a lushly romantic novel in which, even after Carmilla has finally been laid to rest with a stake in her heart, Laura is haunted by memories of her seductive friend. Filmed half a dozen times since 1932, *Carmilla* launched the subgenre of the lesbian vampire movie.

In the 1970s, many lesbian critics lamented the lack of "positive images" of love between women. In a provocative essay, novelist Bertha Harris turned that on its head: complaining about the insipidity of much of the literature, she argued that the lesbian should represent "the Female enraged," and posited that the lesbian equivalent of the literary hero is, in fact, the monster. The last twenty years of the twentieth century saw a wholesale rethinking of lesbian monstrosity along those lines.

In particular, the supernatural lesbian moved to center stage, as heroine and narrator. In her fascinating study *Lesbian Gothic* (1999), Paulina Palmer analyzes how writers since the 1970s have reworked the conventions of the Gothic (including vampires, witches, ghosts, and other spectral visitors), using them not to hide or denigrate eroticism between women but to celebrate its transgressive physicality.

It is the lesbian vampire, already popularized in cinema, who has appealed to the widest range of writers in the past few decades. She is at the center of such contrasting texts as Whitley Strieber's *The Hunger* (1981), Jody Scott's *I, Vampire* (1984), Anna Livia's *Minimax* (1991), and Charles Busch's *Vampire Lesbians of Sodom* (1985)—the five-year run of which made it the longest off-Broadway production ever. Katherine V.

Forrest's novella *O Captain, My Captain* (1987) is a particularly clever genre-blender: a lesbian romance between the naïve lieutenant of a spaceship and the reclusive, androgynous Captain Drake, who turns out to be a vampire with a craving for . . . vaginal juices. "Your body is not my food," she reassures the lieutenant charmingly. "Your pleasure is."

But the most thorough and original reworking of the motif is Jewelle Gomez's *The Gilda Stories* (1991), which takes on race and sexuality by way of history and fantasy. Its picaresque heroine "the Girl" journeys from 1850s slavery into twenty-first-century environmental wars as one of a multiracial, underground "family" of male and female vampires. Not lonely killers but scrupulous, politicized telepaths, they give ideas, dreams, and healing in exchange for blood. When Gilda first invites the Girl to join them, her stern speech makes the lesbian/vampire analogy clear: "There are only inadequate words to speak for who we are. The language is crude, the history is false. You must look to me and know who I am and if the life I offer is the life you choose."

It is Gomez's emphasis on ethics, on the tough, moment-by-moment choices entailed by all relationships, that makes *The Gilda Stories* really stand out from its literary tradition. Because from the start, solipsism has been the lesbian monster's hallmark. The monster's attraction to her own sex is presented as a dreadful narcissism; love of the similar is read as love of the self. In Dickens's *Little Dorrit*, for instance, Tattycoram describes her beloved as a warped reflection: "I have had Miss Wade before me all this time, as if it was my own self grown ripe—turning everything the wrong way, and twisting all good into evil." Narcissus starves to death gazing at his own reflection, and similarly the lesbian monster is the instrument of her own punishment, most literally in the case of that popular ending, suicide. Miss Wade "writhes under her life," and titles her memoir "History of a Self-Tormentor." Similarly, in Diderot's *La Religieuse,* the superior is described as "fighting a losing battle against herself," and the heroine of Musset's *Gamiani* claims that "my diseased imagination is slowly killing me." These ringing phrases are probably meant to prevent the reader from wondering whether it might not be other people who in fact are punishing, tormenting, and killing the lesbian, because they cannot see her as anything but a monster.

CHAPTER FIVE

Detection

IT'S A CRIME—OR IS IT?

Although lesbian sex has rarely been criminalized in law, it has often been presented as at least borderline: vaguely, murkily criminal. And in literature it is often associated with murder. Lesbians kill their male rivals, their own husbands or suitors, even their own mothers. Often they murder their women lovers. And they can be victims just as easily: done to death by their male rivals, their own husbands, brothers, or simply male strangers. Not to mention the various frauds, kidnaps, rapes, druggings, impersonations, thefts, and blackmailings in which they get involved.

But what I want to explore in this chapter is not lesbian crime so much as lesbian detection: narratives shaped by the double helix of homoeroticism and the discovery of a crime. Desire, like crime, lurks beneath a respectable surface, and only a knowing eye can spot its clues, break its codes. How suitable, then, that detective fiction in English, from the genre's beginnings in the mid–nineteenth century— whether in the most sedate mystery or the most adrenaline-fueled thriller—has so often relied on plots about attraction between women.

Irving Politzer, jacket of Gladys Mitchell, Speedy Death *[1929] (1932).*
For the New York (Mason Publishing Co.) edition of Speedy Death, *the popular illustrator Politzer produced a stylized image of the victim in "his" bath that managed to hint at sexual ambiguity without giving away the plot. Gladys Mitchell used bathtubs for murder in several of her novels, and on one occasion even made do with a small hand basin.*

Now You See It . . .

Some crime stories are puzzles about the protagonist's gender, riddles that readers—along with the other characters and especially detectives—must shed their own blinkers in order to solve. Perhaps the earliest is *Speedy Death* (1929), the first novel by schoolmistress Gladys Mitchell, featuring her witty psychoanalyst sleuth Mrs. Adela Lestrange Bradley. It begins with the drowning in his bath of the famous explorer Sir Everard Mountjoy (his surname implying the "joy" he takes in "mounting" to unknown places, and his first name possibly suggesting that he is "ever hard"). It is a ridiculous end for such a brave traveler— especially when the naked body is discovered to be female. Now, most of the other characters consider that the real crime was Sir Everard's, against his fiancée, Eleanor; how could this cross-dressing freak have taken such advantage of an innocent girl? But in a witty undermining of the conventions of the female bridegroom story, the unshockable

Mrs. Bradley discovers that in fact it was Eleanor who forced the engagement, and Eleanor—appalled to discover her nervous husband-to-be was female—who committed the murder. Having unmasked the ladylike victim as a villain, the decisive Mrs. Bradley dispatches her by poison, and is acquitted, to go on to star in sixty-five other mysteries.

Similarly, in later titles such as John Evans's *Halo in Brass* (1950) and Pamela Frankau's *Colonel Blessington* (1968), it is not until the detective solves the puzzle of the cross-dressed woman's secret identity—developing considerable sympathy for her along the way—that he can figure out who killed whom, and why. Marjorie Garber has shown that cross-dressing in detective fiction often concerns itself with language, using a word or phrase (whether spoken or written) as "a hieroglyph of transvestic impersonation." She offers a fascinating example from Ruth Rendell's *A Sleeping Life* (1978): while investigating the death of a woman who will turn out to have had a part-time, hidden "sleeping life" as a man, Inspector Wexford mishears the word *eonism* (cross-dressing, from the eighteenth-century Chevalier D'Eon) as *aeonism,* which he thinks must have something to do with transcending time; as Garber points out, the "telltale diphthong" *ae* here becomes "the ortho-graphic mark of cross-dressing: two-in-one, two-as-one, inaudible as difference—passing."

Inspector Wexford should have consulted his files, because he made the same mistake back in Rendell's first novel, *From Doon with Death* (1964). This plot is not about sartorial cross-dressing but a textual equivalent. "Doon" is the prime suspect, the name on a series of frus-trated letters sent to a woman called Margaret who has ended up dead. There are no male pronouns in the letters—but the police still believe Doon to be a man because these are love letters; it is not the writer of the letters (a woman called Fabia) who disguises her sex, then, but the readers who misread it. This false assumption makes the police miss comically obvious clues, such as the fact that Doon's gifts to Margaret included luxuriously bound classics of same-sex love such as Oscar Wilde's *Picture of Dorian Gray,* Walt Whitman's *Leaves of Grass,* and the *Poems* of Christina Rossetti. Here the police are the forensic equivalent of the obtuse husband in "secret enemy" stories such as Belot's *Made-moiselle Giraud, ma femme* (1870). *From Doon with Death,* for which Ren-dell was paid only seventy-five dollars, was considered thrillingly modern in its theme, and won her international critical attention.

In gender puzzles, everything can be a trick; even the crime may not have really happened. In *To Love and Be Wise* (1950), a mystery about the disappearance and possible murder of a witty, attractive young man called Leslie Searle, "Josephine Tey" (Scottish schoolteacher Elizabeth MacKintosh) drops many hints that Searle is not what he seems; she calls him a demon, a fallen angel, "the creature," and his name is both androgynous and a pun on *lesbian*. Interestingly, unlike the cross-dressing women in *Speedy Death* and *A Sleeping Life*, Leslie does not have to die to be understood. The detective Alan Grant acts as a sort of therapist, discovering not only that "Leslie" is the part-time male persona of a woman photographer called Lee, but that Lee staged the disappearance as an attempt to frame Walter, a male rival, for the murder of the fictional "Leslie." Walter's crime was to take up and then abandon Lee's beloved cousin Marguerite, a glamorous actress who then committed suicide: it is significant that the only actual death in this psychologically probing novel is self-inflicted. Lee presents her passion for Marguerite as having been fervently sisterly, but Alan Grant sees past that to its queerness: "You were so devoted that you couldn't think quite straight about her." However, no one in *To Love and Be Wise* condemns or sneers at Lee's cross-dressing or her feelings for Marguerite, and the detective is not interested in arresting her, only in helping her find self-knowledge and get "cured" of being "green." He brings Lee to the point of realizing that the cousin she idealized was actually a selfish heartbreaker. She concludes ruefully, "It is very growing-up to find that someone you loved all your life never existed at all." In this extremely unusual crime novel without a crime in it, Josephine Tey casts both the lover and the beloved as figmentary: erotic performances rather than solid selves. And she suggests that if, as the proverb of the title puts it, it is impossible "to love and be wise," then on the other side of love a certain wisdom, and a maturity that comes of blending one's masculine and feminine qualities, may be possible.

Cynthia Asquith, in a remarkable short fiction from 1947, "The Lovely Voice," plays the opposite trick on her readers: an apparently same-sex story masks one that is about desire between the sexes. The narrator remembers being a thirteen-year-old girl at a French country hotel and forming an overwhelming crush on a sweet-voiced, black-haired fellow guest—the more beautiful of a pair of ladies visiting from Paris. Hearing them exchange such endearments as *"chérie"* and *"ange,"* the girl cannot work out what the bond can be that keeps such two contrasting characters traveling together, and decides that family is the only plausible connection: "They must be related."

Readers by now will be congratulating themselves on having solved the simple puzzle, detected the lesbian relationship that the obsessed child does not understand even when, eavesdropping on the couple at night, she hears them exchange "repeated kisses." But wait. The girl also hears that her beloved recently dyed her red-gold hair black in preparation for going to a costume ball as Medea—an extreme measure, one might think, but the lovely woman insists that wigs never look fully natural. The girl is thrilled by this secret information, this foretaste of her beloved's authentic self: "I longed to see her as nature had designed her." She gets her wish the next day in a way that disconcerts her: when the beautiful lady holds her hand walking through the forest, and a tree branch knocks her hat sideways, her black hair moves too, revealing red underneath: the black was a wig after all. But later, when the beautiful woman leaves the hotel in a carriage, kissing her hand to the girl, "my damped devotion flared up. Let her wear as many wigs as she chose and make any sort of fool of her dull friend, what cared I?" Several days later, when the body of the "dull friend" is finally discovered in the forest—murdered with a hat pin—the girl says nothing, out of a mixture of terror and guilt. Adoring the killer, she feels complicit—but she also identifies with the dead woman, because the beautiful redhead had treated them both with the same casual flirtatiousness, and abandoned them both.

Only gradually does the narrator piece together the whole story, from gossip and newspapers. What she discovers is that the dead woman was the wife of a famous, handsome young poet. At fifteen, the girl is strolling through another forest, this time in Paris, when she sees the red-haired beauty lying beside the poet, reading to him in blissful intimacy: she is his new wife. The narrator finally figures out the full plot: in league with the poet, his red-haired mistress sought out, befriended, lived in some unspecified intimacy with, and then killed his wife. So all along there has been a perverse heterosexual story hiding inside the lesbian one, like the red hair inside the black wig. The girl makes no attempt to bring her beloved to justice: it is enough to have seen her truly with "her own wonderful colouring," to have finally figured out this bewitching Medea who can play any sexual role she likes.

CRIMES OF PASSION

I would like to nominate, as the most glamorous lesbian killer in literature, the heroine of an undeservedly forgotten novel-in-stories, *The Sorceress of the Strand* (1903). The inexhaustible "L. T. Meade" (Elizabeth Thomasina Meade Smith), an Irish author of more than three hundred popular novels, co-wrote it with Robert Eustace and published its six distinct episodes in the *Strand* magazine; she was probably inspired by Madame Rachel, a notorious con artist of the 1860s and '70s. This

Gordon Frederick Browne, " 'The great Madame Sara is dead,' she said," in L. T. Meade, The Sorceress of the Strand *(1903).*

The son of Dickens's illustrator "Phiz," Browne was a popular illustrator of children's books in the late nineteenth and early twentieth centuries. Here he presents with the utmost glamour both Meade's beautician antiheroine and the animal tamer who finally brings her down.

Edwardian *Nip/Tuck* features a beautician and cosmetic surgeon (and, it is darkly hinted, abortionist), Madame Sara, who—a touch of the vampire, here—though past fifty, looks radiantly twenty-five, "a young, fresh and natural girl." To make matters worse, she is obscurely foreign (an Italian-Indian mix), and has many loyal Brazilian and Arab male assistants. Unlike the typical villain of turn-of-the-century detective fiction, who is the detective's suave alter ego, Madame Sara is an unknown quantity. She repeatedly foils the private eye and his doctor friend; they soon realize what an evil thief, blackmailer, and killer she is, but they cannot prove anything. Nor can they break her hold on the ladies of London, who remain fanatically devoted to her and refuse to credit any evidence of her crimes; women's intimacy gives Madame Sara access to social circles that the men hunting her lack. She is a "magician" who has "cast a spell" over girls. In this outstanding potboiler, femininity, and all its dark arts of beautification, is a mask for desire between women.

Madame Sara's crimes are highly original. Agnes Dallas, a spinster of twenty-nine who feels a fearful "idolatry" for her, dies of poison that Madame has inserted in Agnes's tooth during a dentistry session. "I love her very much," insists another girl, Antonia, in the next story, giving the beautician "the fascinated look of a bird when a snake attracts it," but Madame repays her in a fiendish act of blackmail, during an operation to remove a mole, by writing the awful truth of Antonia's parentage in silver nitrate on the girl's neck, so it will show up under the bright lights of a party. Here women's bodies betray them, literally spelling out their shameful secrets. On the one occasion when the intended victim of Madame Sara's complex plots is a man, she still works by means of her hold over girls: she has the lovely young Donna Marta literally "mesmerized," put in a trance, as a lure to tempt Professor Piozzi into marriage, so that Madame Sara can steal his scientific formulas and then murder him by means of a fake potted plant that puffs carbon monoxide during his lecture.

"Hunting her as a recreation is as good as hunting a man-eating tiger," the detective and the doctor agree ruefully toward the end of the book; unable to bring the invincible Madame Sara to justice, they seem doomed to do nothing but bear witness to her triumphs and watch her disappear at the end of each of the first five episodes. But if she is a wild beast, she makes a fatal mistake when she allies with a woman who is a match for her: the six-foot, mannish, widowed animal tamer Mrs. Bensasen, who wears a fearsome set of false teeth and keeps her own daughter tied up in a cellar. In a bloody climax that outdoes Balzac's *La Fille aux yeux d'or,* the sleuths turn up to find that Mrs. Bensasen's pet wolf has ripped Madame Sara's throat out, and the dying beautician has shot Mrs. Bensasen through the heart. As Jennifer A. Halloran points out in one of the only articles about *The Sorceress of the Strand,* Meade breaks with crime-fiction convention by having the detectives completely fail to bring this uniquely slippery villainess to justice, and the bloody dénouement is none of their doing.

Lesbian killers are not rare in crime fiction, but interestingly, they are almost never presented as simply evil by nature. The causality of lesbian murder is usually a matter of narrative rather than characterisation: the crime is prompted by the peculiar, strained circumstances of a closeted relationship. For instance, in Ruth Rendell's *From Doon with Death* (1964, discussed above), by the time we learn that Fabia (aka Doon) strangled her beloved Margaret for refusing to consummate their passion after Margaret strung her along through long years of secret, fervid correspondence . . . we are rather inclined to forgive her. In such stories, the detective, working backward from an apparently motiveless crime, has to "solve" the mystery of the women's relationship.

Sometimes, like a clue hiding in plain sight, the sexual passion is masked by a highly respectable friendship or domestic arrangement. This is the case in what seems to be the earliest detective story to hinge on a lesbian relationship, "The Long Arm" (1895), which won Mary E. Wilkins (later Freeman) a prize of two thousand dollars from a newspaper syndicate.

Sarah Fairbanks, a spinster of twenty-nine, is the fascinating narrator/suspect/investigator of this murder story. Her father has been shot dead, probably—according to a professional detective who offers her his help—by someone with an arm abnormally long enough to open the door from the outside. Her neighbors are two elderly unmarried dressmakers who have lived together since girlhood, Phoebe dominating the timid Maria. It is they who point the finger of suspicion at Sarah herself, suggesting that she killed her father because he was standing in the way of her marriage. Sarah does not return the favor by accusing Phoebe, not even when she discovers that her father recently got Maria to change her mind (after rejecting him forty years ago) and agree to marry him. She cannot believe Phoebe is the killer, even when she notices the woman's arm is "seven inches longer" than Sarah's own. (This suggests that Phoebe has a hint of the ape about her, and the "seven inches" is strikingly phallic too.) "There is no motive," Sarah continues to insist; as a spinster whose whole community has turned against her, she may identify too strongly with Phoebe and Maria to let herself see through the façade of their Boston marriage. Like many fictions of desire between women, "The Long Arm" is an epistemological puzzle: the knowledge of lesbianism is constantly evaded and postponed, until Phoebe—seizing the power of narration from Sarah in a two-page confession—chooses to explain her motive herself.

> I stopped it [the marriage] once before. This time I knew I couldn't unless I killed him. She's lived with me in that house for over forty years. There are other ties as strong as the marriage one, that are just as sacred. What right had he to take her away from me and break up my home?

Still in some denial, Sarah turns not to sexological science but to the older discourse of religion to make sense of these "other ties": she blames Phoebe's jealousy on "demoniacal possession." But actually Phoebe sounds remarkably self-possessed: it is as if she is relieved to declare herself as the killer, in what we could also call a coming-out speech. Hauled off to prison, however, she pines away and dies in a month, leaving Maria—as if being punished for her dithering—bereft of either kind of marriage, the official or the unofficial kind.

"The Long Arm" is often contrasted with a piece Mary Wilkins published eight years earlier, "Two Friends" (1887). In this benign domestic comedy, as in the murder story, a devoted partnership between two middle-aged spinsters is overshadowed by an old secret. Thirty years ago, Sarah was at the deathbed of Abby's mother, and heard her give permission for her daughter to marry John Marshall. The crime Sarah confesses now, in the face of Abby's own serious illness, is that she was too greedily possessive of her beloved to pass the message on: "I couldn't have her likin' anybody else, an' gittin' married." The joke of the story—the happy ending, despite Abby's aproaching death—is that the threat was an illusion, and so the crime was no crime:

The poor sick woman laughed out, with a charming, gleeful ring.

A look of joyful wonder flashed over Sarah's despairing face. She stood staring.

"Sarah," said Abby, "I wouldn't have had John Marshall if he'd come on his knees after me all the way from Mexico!"

Wilkins was writing from personal experience, having lived with her childhood friend Mary Wales (and Wales's family) for four years already when she wrote "Two Friends." But for three years she had known a businessman called Charles Freeman, and in 1889 she would agree to their engagement; they finally married (with Mary Wales as witness) in 1902. The marriage was overshadowed by his alcoholism, and ended after a few years when she had him committed to an asylum. When she wrote "The Long Arm" in 1895, reusing the name of the possessive partner (Sarah) for the narrator this time, she was reworking a rivals plotline in a new, darker light. But as Lillian Faderman points out, the abyss that separates "Two Friends" from "The Long Arm" may be attributed not only to the changes in Freeman's life, but to the seismic shift in interpretations of love between women around the Alice Mitchell murder trial of 1892 (discussed in chapter 4), which was a clear influence on the story of "The Long Arm."

A very similar plot shapes the last Miss Marple mystery Agatha Christie wrote, *Nemesis* (1971, first serialized in *Woman's Realm*). A young man called Michael has already served ten years for the brutal murder of his girlfriend Verity. The investigation brings the elderly sleuth to a sinister house of three sisters—one widow, two spinsters— and it turns out that one of them, the handsome and learned Clotilde, took the orphaned Verity in, at eighteen, as a beloved protégée. Miss Marple, discovering that Verity and Michael had been on the point of getting married, manages to look past the cliché of the brutish man who kills the woman he desires—to the possessive woman who kills the girl she is about to lose to a man, and frames him for it. "You loved Verity too much," Miss Marple tells Clotilde bluntly. She sees it as inevitable that the girl should have tried "to escape from the burden of the bondage of love she was living in with you," as she explains with uncharacteristically awkward grammar. Maurice Richardson, writing in *The Observer* on October 31, 1971, particularly relished this scene in which the aged sleuth, "alone in bed, quite defenceless with not even a knitting-needle . . . is confronted by a brawny great fiend of a butch." But Christie has a subtler take on Clotilde than her reviewer; ultimately Miss Marple judges Clotilde not as a monster (the way the police do), but—even before her suicide with drugged milk—as a "poor, lost soul," haunted for ten years by the beautiful girl buried in her garden. The crime is shown as springing not from malice but from the unbearable pressure of an ill-defined, only semirequited love between two women of different generations. Across eight decades, what links the killers of "The Long Arm" and *Nemesis* is that neither has a socially legitimate language in which to insist *Don't marry him, stay with me.* Their jealousy, partially gagged, finds expression in murder.

Interestingly, it is not always the domineering member of the couple who does the killing; sometimes the meeker woman is the one who lashes out. *Death of a Doll* (1948)—the best of the four novels that "Hilda Lawrence" (Hildegarde Kronmiller) published in her fifties, before lapsing into silence again—is a subtle and atmospheric thriller set in a hostel for New York workingwomen. The sweet-natured Miss Angeline Small (her names suggesting virtue and timidity) has a passionate relationship with the older, richer manager, Miss Monica Brady, which has promoted her from a boarder almost to the status of a partner in the boardinghouse. "Angel" and "Monny" exchange loving notes during the day, meet for cocoa every night, and are planning to resign their exhausting jobs and go off to live in Europe together as soon as Monny's inheritance comes in. "Does anybody in the world have one half as much fun as we do?" cries Angel. Hilda Lawrence misleads readers about this relationship by presenting Monny as the dominant giver of orders and of treats, Angel as the childlike, lower-class one who takes the marshmallow out of her cocoa when Monny expresses disapproval. However, she does drop hints that point the other way: "Everybody thinks you're the strong one," Angel tells Monny, "but I am." The detective who comes to investigate the death of a girl called Ruth is bewildered by this strange environment; in one nightmarish party scene, the girls all dress up as identical masked dolls, like interchangable ghosts who haunt the corridors. And he misunderstands the bond between the manager and her partner, because he assumes that it is Monny's money Angel is after. It is only when he learns to take their passion seriously that he can figure out killer and

motive: the saccharine Angel murdered Ruth to avoid being exposed
to Monny as a shoplifter with a prison record, because she feared losing Monny's love.

In P. D. James's claustrophobic mystery *Shroud for a Nightingale*
(1971), Detective Adam Dalgliesh invades the closed world of a nurses'
residence to solve a series of murders, much more confident than his
opposite number in *Death of a Doll* of his ability to interpret the emotional terrain. Ironically, it is his modern awareness of what can go on
between women that knocks him off course; titillated, he pays most
attention to the overtly sexual involvement between the man-hating
Sister Rolfe and the promiscuous bisexual Julia Pardoe. But it is a red
herring; he should really be looking at the much quieter, pseudomarital bond between the boring Sister Brumfett and the beautiful
Matron. Brumfett's knowledge of Matron's Nazi past has the effect of a
loaded gun, winning her a cozy intimacy with her beloved: as Dalgliesh
comments wryly when he finally figures it out, "A more orthodox
blackmailer, merely demanding a regular tax-free income, would have
been infinitely preferable to Brumfett's intolerable devotion." This
unholy yoking drives both women to murder—Brumfett to kill various
people, in a deranged attempt to protect her beloved from exposure,
and Matron to finally throw off Brumfett's suffocating embrace by
killing her and making it look like suicide. Love not only involves
blackmail, in *Shroud for a Nightingale;* it is blackmail.

It Takes One to Know One

Interestingly, Dalgliesh figures out the complex affiliations in the closed
world of *Shroud for a Nighingale* only with the help of his informants
and friends, the birdlike Miss Beale and the sturdy Miss Burrows, who
have spent their adult lives in mutual devotion, each convinced that
her partner is an exceptional nurse: "The happiest marriages," P. D.
James jokes urbanely, "are sustained by such comforting illusions." In
the same way, the male detective in *Death of a Doll* is aided by two amateur sleuths: an eccentric, squabbling pair of women in their sixties.
Hilda Lawrence seems to be including a benign image of lesbianism to
set in the scales against the sinister twosome at the heart of her story.
But by making their male detectives rely on the insights of female cou-

ples, both authors may also be implying that love between women is a knot that only knowledgeable insiders can untangle.

This pattern is particularly striking in Dorothy L. Sayers's *Unnatural Death* (1927). Both Agatha Dawson and the grandniece, Mary Whittaker, who murders her live in rural female couples, but of different generations and kinds: Agatha in a fifty-year Victorian idyll as "*domestic partner*" (i.e., housewife) to a mannish horsebreeder, Mary in a stormy relationship with an infatuated girl called Vera. To probe these subtleties, the sleuth Lord Peter Wimsey has to call on the experience of his female assistant, Miss Climpson. But the subject is a fraught one for her; she describes herself defensively as "a spinster made and not born—a perfectly womanly woman." After some preliminary investigation she derides Vera's feelings for Mary as a " 'pash' (as we used to call it at school)" and pronounces their plan to set up a chicken farm together (shades of Lawrence's *The Fox*, published just five years earlier) as "unhealthy" on the basis of having "seen so much of that kind of thing in my rather WOMAN-RIDDEN existence!" Tactfully, Miss Climpson makes absolutely sure Lord Peter—and of course the readers—know she is talking about lesbianism by mentioning Clemence Dane's "*very clever book* on the subject," i.e., *Regiment of Women* (1917). Overinvested in this particular case, Miss Climpson soon goes beyond her sleuthing duties and starts trying to save young Vera. Here Sayers's persistent interest in the subject of relationships between women causes her to go off on a tangent and give us six whole pages of a conversation in which the girl boasts that she is "*absolutely* happy together" with her beloved Mary, and Miss Climpson counters that it would be "more natural— more proper, in a sense" to feel this for a man. It is significant that the normally cogent Miss Climpson is almost stuttering at this point, and finds it impossible to spell out exactly what she means or ask Vera directly whether she and Mary have become lovers.

Later, when she just so happens to come across some words Vera has scribbled down in preparation for the Roman Catholic sacrament of confession, Miss Climpson extrapolates from them an elaborate proof that Mary has seduced and then dumped her girlfriend.

Humiliating, degrading, exhausting, beastly scenes. Girls' school, boarding-house, Bloomsbury-flat scenes. Damnable selfishness wearing of its victim. Silly *schwärmerei* swamping all decent self-respect. Barren quarrels ending in shame and hatred. "Beastly, blood-sucking woman," said Miss Climpson viciously.

This paragraph is a strange excess, in a book that is otherwise witty and worldly. It is not so much a summary of the relationship as an associative swarm of possibilities: a nightmare world of lesbian abandonment (in both senses). With its alliteration, its piling-up of hackneyed adjectives—"beastly," "blood-sucking," and "barren"—it sounds rather as if it has been badly translated from the Anglo-Saxon. Ultimately, it tells us less about Mary and Vera than about what Miss Climpson herself may have endured in her own "WOMAN-RIDDEN existence."

It is very suggestive that Mary's method of killing her great-aunt turns out to have been the injection of an air bubble into her bloodstream. "There's nothing in that," insists Mary when she is shown the empty syringe. The weapon in this very "unnatural death" is a mere absence, undetectable except to educated eyes—much like lesbianism, you might say. Sayers's original title for *Unnatural Death* was *The Singular Case of the Three Spinsters,* but that was an underestimate: the novel has at least five significant spinsters, who could be categorized along affectional axes (the four woman-loving ones vs. the insistently heterosexual Miss Climpson) or moral ones (the two good Victorians and Miss Climpson vs. the hapless Vera and the wicked Mary). Working as a copywriter during this period, Dorothy Sayers is popularly credited with having invented the catchphrase "It pays to advertise," and certainly the title she finally decided on, *Unnatural Death,* advertises the novel's chief preoccupation. The paperback reprint in the homophobic 1950s bore the more discreet title *The Dawson Pedigree,* which nonetheless does manage to suggest a sort of lesbian line of descent, from Agatha's Boston marriage to Mary's sordid Bloomsbury-flat scenes.

So a male detective is often provided with female assistants who have insight (whether placid or paranoid) into relationships between women. But for the first novel that puts a sapphic sleuth in the lead role, we must go . . . no, not forward, but all the way back to the mid-nineteenth century. To the title that has been called the first thriller, in fact: Wilkie Collins's masterpiece *The Woman in White* (1860). A sensation on first publication—bonnets, cloaks, perfumes, and dances were immediately named after it—the novel has never been out of print. Its

"The strangeness and peril of my situation," in Wilkie Collins, The Woman in White *[1860] (c.1900).*

    This unsigned illustration in the New York edition of Collins's works captures the moment when Marian undertakes surveillance in a rainstorm for the sake of her beloved Laura.

real heroine is not the lovely, sensitive (and often rather feeble) heiress Laura Fairlie, but her half sister Marian Halcombe: yet another woman-loving character whose name derives from the Virgin Mary. Collins, perhaps thinking of his friend George Eliot, took the risk of matching all Marian's traditionally womanly traits (sympathy, tenderness, tact) with manly ones: she is sensible, frank, flippant, energetic, and . . . ugly, with "almost a moustache." She constantly describes herself, or is described by others, as having masculine attributes, from her firm grip to her taste for chess and billiards—but she has none of the crude, blustering mannishness of a character like Bell Blount in *The Rebel of the Family* (1880).

Marian and Laura exchange passionate words and caresses throughout the novel. Marian's love may be technically half sisterly but it is also fiercely romantic: "I won't live without her, and she can't live without me," she declares at the start. Notice that for the frail Laura it is a matter of need—she "can't" live without Marian—whereas for the tireless Marian it is a matter of will, "won't." All Marian can offer men is a comradeship that is entirely lacking in flirtatiousness. But when, out of duty, Laura lets herself be married off to the sinister Sir Percival Glyde, Marian erupts in language that, visceral and political at once, has the ring of 1970s lesbian feminism:

Men! They are the enemies of our innocence and our peace—they drag us away from our parents' love and our sisters' friendship—they take us body and soul to themselves, and fasten our helpless lives to theirs as they chain up a dog to his kennel. And what does the best of them give us in return? Let me go, Laura—I'm mad when I think of it!

Marian sees this marriage as a "death"; what devastates her is the idea that the beloved "will be *his* Laura instead of mine!" She has to break it to the naïve Laura that she will not be coming along on the honeymoon:

I was obliged to tell her that no man tolerates a rival—not even a woman rival—in his wife's affections, when he first marries, whatever he may do afterwards. I was obliged to warn her that my chance of living with her permanently under her own roof, depended entirely on my not arousing Sir Percival's jealousy and distrust by standing between them at the beginning of their marriage, in the position of the chosen depositary of his wife's closest secrets. Drop by drop I poured the profaning bitterness of this world's wisdom into that pure heart and that innocent mind . . . The simple illusions of her girlhood are gone, and my hand has stripped them off. Better mine than his—that is all my consolation—better mine than his.

Here, Laura's discovery that a beloved woman might be seen by a nasty husband as his "rival" is presented as a kind of "stripping" or "profaning"—a deflowering, in other words—and it is Marian who has been "obliged" to do it, tenderly but firmly.

By portraying his heroine as a feminist spinster with manly traits, possessively devoted to a woman, Wilkie Collins must have known that some of his audience, at least, would read her as a woman who desired women. (Though not, presumably, the handful of male readers who sent Collins proposals of marriage to pass on to Marian, who they were convinced was real.) So how did he get away with it—how did he make her so obviously sapphic, and yet so universally popular? It could be argued that he pulled his punches: by making her Laura's half sister, he harnessed the incest taboo to keep the idea of lust between them virtually unthinkable. But as I see it, his real trick was to channel all Marian's passion away from sex and into detection.

She is a sleuth in search of a crime, her unused mental energies so pent up that the moment she hears about the mysterious stranger called the woman in white, she declares, "I am all aflame with curiosity, and I devote my whole energies to the business of discovery from this moment." At first Marian values her rationality above her more feminine traits such as intuition, but as the story goes on she learns to use both sides of herself in her "investigations and discoveries." Having repeatedly failed to "root out" her "prejudice" against Sir Percival, for instance, she gives in to it and starts looking for evidence that he means his wife some harm. Marian's position in his home is so precarious that she cannot play the hero. When he insults her, for instance, she thinks, "If I had been a man, I would have knocked him down," but being a dependent woman, tied to the spot by her devotion to Laura, she is forced into the covert role of an eavesdropping sleuth instead.

Sir Percival goes to the lengths of wrenching Laura's arm, and Marian insists on seeing the bruise, to steel her resolution; she tells Laura in apocalyptic tones, "our endurance must end, and our resistance must begin today." Stripping down to a single petticoat and cloak, Marian crawls along a roof in a rainstorm to listen in on Sir Percival and his co-conspirator Count Fosco, reminding herself that "Laura's honour, Laura's happiness—Laura's life itself—might depend on my quick ears and my faithful memory tonight." From this point in the book, Marian—despite almost dying of fever, as invariably happens to heroines who get caught in the rain—is a full-blown action heroine. Uncovering an elaborate plot of swapped identities and springing her beloved from a madhouse, she works with Laura's devoted suitor, Walter, but always insists on taking "my share in the risk and the danger." And even at her most impoverished and frightened, Marian shows every sign of enjoying her "investigations and discoveries" far more than her old ladylike life.

For a modern equivalent to Marian Halcombe in *The Woman in White,* readers would have to wait for the lesbian detective novel, part of the boom in tough-woman-detective fiction which began in the late 1970s and is flourishing today. If two of the strongest conventions of crime fiction are that the villain is the detective's alter ego, and the femme fatale his object of desire, then lesbian crime fiction can have it all ways: the (female) detective is often linked to the (female) victim and/or criminal and/or prime suspect by longing as well as identification. The detective's sense of her own sexuality can complicate the matter further. Very often she discovers her preference for women at the same time as her powers of detection; it is by digging up a lesbian plot that she unearths her own secret. We see this pattern from the very beginning of the lesbian detective genre. For instance, in Sheila Radley's *The Chief Inspector's Daughter* (1981), Alison figures out that her employer, Jasmine, was killed by a female lover's jealous fiancé—and, retrospectively, that Alison's own feelings for Jasmine went beyond the professional. Similarly, Vicki P. McConnell's sleuth Nyla Wade in *Mrs. Porter's Letter* (1982) discovers that an apparently opposite-sex love affair was really a same-sex one, and in the process decodes her own sexuality.

It is standard protocol for the heroine of a lesbian mystery series— such as the two that really launched the genre in 1984, by Barbara Wilson and Katherine V. Forrest—to fall for a woman in the course of her first investigation. In Forrest's Kate Delafield novels, great tension is wrung from the police detective having to weigh her loyalty to the judicial system against her involvement with an oppressed subculture. Notably, in *Murder at the Nightwood Bar* (1987), Kate has to investigate the murder of a young hooker called Dory outside a dyke bar. Kate's being in the closet makes the whole case fraught to the point of absurdity; as the bar owner points out, "You could get killed tomorrow doing your job. And you tell me you can't go to a Gay Pride parade. Doesn't that strike you as a little weird?" Equally, the community's resentment of the police is a form of prejudice. "Enjoy being one of the boys?" one of them asks Kate. "Kicking your own sisters around?" When thugs invade the bar to drag off one of the women, Kate bashes the face of one of them against a car. Her unprofessional behavior

could potentially wreck the case, but it will prove to be the key to getting the dead woman's friends to open up to her. Ultimately *Murder at
the Nightwood Bar* reverses readers' expectations, revealing the under-
world of the bar as a homey refuge, and exposing the nuclear family as
a site of horror—because it was Dory's own homophobic mother who
battered her to death, to stop her from naming her father as a child
abuser. The book ends with Kate on the sidelines of a Pride march
looking longingly at parents who carry a sign that says, "We Love Our
Gay Daughter."

Kate Delafield is atypical: many lesbian investigators are private
eyes, who occupy an uneasy position on the margins of official investigation. Others are amateur sleuths, completely outside the judicial system. Perhaps the most stylish is Emma Victor, the heroine of Mary
Wings's Chandleresque series, which began in 1986 with the first in a
series of double-entendre titles, *She Came Too Late*. But in any of these
roles, the lesbian makes a suitable investigator, because she may be
socially invisible or stigmatized, with divided loyalties; she sympathizes
with and understands outsiders; she is a subtle reader of behavioral
signs, and above all, she has a nose for secrets and lies. The similarities
between dyke and private dick are amusingly presented in Penny Sumner's *The End of April* (1992):

> If people can't imagine what lesbians actually do, they're even
> worse about the realities of my second profession. They tend to
> suspect that you're going to start unearthing guilty secrets, or
> maybe steaming open their mail. Sometimes, of course, they're
> right.

Lesbian detective fiction is a highly self-conscious genre: just as
lesbians can never take their sexuality as a given (having had to dis-
abuse themselves of the myth of universal heterosexuality to discover
it), so they tend to be critical of the conventions of the heroic, crime-
fighting supersleuth. Self-referential parody is common in such postmodern mysteries as Sarah Schulman's *The Sophie Horowitz Story* (1984),
Barbara Wilson's gender-bending *Gaudi Afternoon* (1990), and Dorothy
Porter's clever verse novel about treacherous poets, *The Monkey's Mask*
(1995).

But in a way, the literary tradition which began with Wilkie

Collins's *The Woman in White* (1860) culminates not with lesbian detective fiction but with the critically acclaimed and best-selling Victorian-era thrillers of Sarah Waters. Her heroines are not sleuths, but they investigate each other. Above all, they are doubles: their identities blur together in a frightening, sexy way that owes much to nineteenth-century popular fiction and Wilkie Collins in particular.

In *Affinity* (1999), for instance, Margaret, a plain, nervous "lady visitor" to Millbank women's jail, becomes obsessed with the beautiful Selina, who is serving time for being a fraudulent medium. Over the course of this ghost story for those who do not believe in ghosts, the differences between these two women fall away. Selina is as much a lady as her visitor, and Margaret (bullied by her paternalistic family ever since her suicide attempt) is both criminal and prisoner. But Waters goes beyond merely merging the two: winning Margaret's love lets Selina suck power from her in a vampire-like way, and ultimately run away with Margaret's whole fortune. With another woman, to add salt to the wound: Margaret's own maid. Margaret only realizes the truth when she looks into the missing servant's trunk and finds

> a mud-brown gown, from Millbank, and a maid's black frock, with its apron of white. They lay tangled together like sleeping lovers; and when I tried to pull the prison dress free, it clung to the dark fabric of the other and would not come.

In its combination of class-consciousness and identity confusion, creepiness, and sensuality, this paragraph is vintage Waters.

For *Fingersmith* (2002)—the only British novel on the Man Booker Prize shortlist that year—Sarah Waters borrows the central motif from *The Woman in White:* a husband conspires to switch his wife's identity with another woman's and incarcerate her in an asylum so he can steal her fortune. But Waters reworks this lurid plot (meaning both a plan for a crime, and the unfolding narrative of a novel) with a postmodern sophistication, without denying her readers any of the genre's old-fashioned thrills. The following passage, for instance, comments on—even as it builds up—narrative suspense.

> I feel the mounting pressure of our plot as I think men must feel the straining of checked machinery, tethered beasts, the gathering

of tropical storms. I wake each day and think: Today I will do it! Today I will draw the bolt and let the engine race, unleash the beast, puncture the lowering clouds!

Fingersmith (thieves' slang for a thief) is a complex machine, perfectly constructed from the interlocking perspectives of a rich girl (Maud) and a poor girl (Sue) who are victims and swindlers, allies and enemies all at the same time. A man (Richard, aka Gentleman), acting as agent for the Machiavellian Mrs. Sucksby, persuades the girls to try to trick each other into a madhouse. Which they do, but not before throwing a wrench in the works by falling in love. What is so fascinating is that this passion is not some unexpected addendum to the crime, but part and parcel of it: by watching each other, by spying and eavesdropping and living cheek by jowl as they plot against each other, Maud and Sue come to want each other. Detection is not just accompanied by desire: it is a form of desire. And the girls' passion is real enough to cut through the layers of pretense and reshape the narrative. Maud wonders if she and Sue can take Richard's plot and "make it ours" or "give it up entirely."

"She has made a fiction of herself," comments one of the asylum doctors of the patient he thinks is claiming to be her own maid. *Fingersmith* is an investigation into the psychology of plotters: the smugness as well as the guilt, the performing and the second-guessing. Like their author, Maud and Sue are hyperconscious at every moment about who possesses what valuable or "counterfeit knowledge." "When did you know?" Sue finally demands of Maud. "When did you know everything, about us, about—Did you know, at the start?"

A question, in my experience, that women who fall in love with women constantly ask each other, and themselves. Which leads us finally to the quest for self-knowledge, the coming-out story.

CHAPTER SIX

Out

T HE TERM "COMING OUT OF THE CLOSET" only seems to
have reached print in 1963. By the 1990s it had been simplified to
"coming out." But the notion of owning up to a persistent desire for
people of the same sex—and of recognizing that as an important fact
about oneself—is centuries older. "I love, and only love, the fairer sex;
my heart revolts from any other love than theirs," Yorkshirewoman
Anne Lister put it, with clarity and finality, in her Regency diary. Not,
of course, that the woman aware of her attraction to women might not
be interested in men too; not that her preference would necessarily be
permanent; not that she would have to see herself as a certain personal-
ity type or a member of a social minority; not that her taste would necessarily be central to her sense of self or shape the rest of life. But this
storyline—the discovery, recognition, and acknowledgment (whether
private or public) of a same-sex preference—has been part of Western
consciousness and Western literature since at least the second half of
the nineteenth century.

The fact that the phrase "coming out" is now used, by analogy, to
refer to owning up to any hidden trait ("coming out as a smoker/

bulimic/Christian," et cetera) suggests how culturally pervasive the idea has become. Freud may have recommended discovering what one has repressed, in the privacy of a psychoanalyst's office, but the current pressure to bare all on television may be considered at least partly a legacy of the twentieth-century lesbian and gay movement. Luckily, the coming-out motif has produced literature that is far subtler than the *Oprah Winfrey Show.*

The discovery of same-sex desires can be presented as an awakening (rude or gentle), a splitting off from ordinary womanhood, a puzzle to solve or a grueling quest, a trial (in the broadest sense of the word), a daring escape, a tragic exile, or a homecoming. There are losses as well as kisses, suicides as well as honeymoons. Although a late branch on the family tree of plots about desire between women, the coming-out story has been the dominant one throughout the twentieth century and still lingers in the twenty-first. It seeds itself within many genres (from the school story to tragedy, the coming-of-age novel to pulp romance) and takes many narrative forms, of which this chapter explores half a dozen of the most popular. Despite what you might expect, when considered in order of publication these texts do not form a simple progress narrative: some of the earliest show heroines attaining a surprising ease with themselves, while some of the most recent are marked with painful confusion.

What has made this storyline fruitful for writers for so long is that the acknowledgment of same-sex desires generally starts a fight: a battle against the forces of convention, religion, or law, or simply a battle within the self. Women in these novels, stories, and plays struggle to understand their desires (not just for other women but for certain clothes, jobs, ways of being in the world); they wrestle to suppress or express them; they struggle to understand what difference these desires make to who they are. They fight for love, and for freedoms social or existential. The fact that the coming-out story is generally a heroic one does not mean it cannot also be ambivalent, humiliating, or downright absurd.

The elements vary: the story does not always begin with falling in love, nor end with sharing the news with family or friends, or even getting the girl. Many of the characters I look at in this chapter could not be said to live in "the closet," nor to step out of it; it is all a lot muddier than that dramatic metaphor would suggest. But what is common to almost all of them is a recognition of same-sex desire, and a movement outward, upward, toward coming to some kind of terms with it.

CASE HISTORIES

The case history is a medical genre: a collection of symptoms in meaningful association and sequence, apparently neutral but always meant to lead to a diagnosis. In the second half of the nineteenth century, doctors began offering case histories of female members of the "third

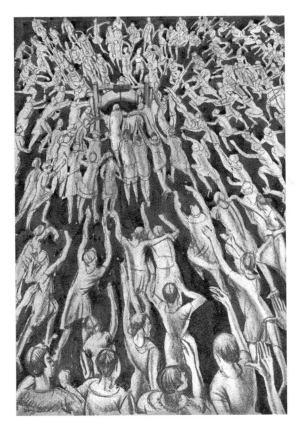

John Cosmo Clark, in a review of Radclyffe Hall, The Well of Loneliness, *in* The American Sketch *(March 1929).*
   Cosmo Clark was a distinguished English artist who spent 1928–29 in New York; at home he designed posters for London Transport and achieved his greatest success with a series of pub paintings during World War II. Here, although he draws these women as rushing in an ungainly and possibly suicidal way toward the "well of loneliness," he wittily suggests that it is in fact a highly social spot.

sex," or "inverts" (women born masculine, highly strung, and attracted
to women). Interestingly, before World War I very few novelists took up
these terms, or presented desire between women as a matter of congenital masculinity. What many of them did borrow was something of the
case history's narrative structure: they started shaping their own treatments of desire between women as probing investigations of troubled
individuals.

One early example is George Moore's *A Drama in Muslin* (1886)—a
satirical Irish novel about the marriage market, which has rarely been
out of print since publication. Writers who want to interest a broad
readership in the grueling process of recognizing one's attraction to
one's own sex typically adopt a softly-softly approach. They begin with
a friendship, eliciting our liking for both parties, and only then comes a
fork in the road, a parting of ways between the one for whom it is really
only friendship . . . and the one for whom it is revealed as something
more. Often, in rivals stories such as Henry James's *The Bostonians*
(1886), it is not a gentle drifting apart but a forcible parting by a man
who comes to separate the innocently homoerotic sheep from the neu-
rotically lesbian goat. This is the case in *A Drama in Muslin:* our heroine Alice's dearest friend is Lady Cecilia, a deeply religious, ascetic
hunchback, filled with panic on leaving the safe haven of school and
nauseous at the very mention of men or marriage. Cecilia feels for Alice
"love that was wild and visionary, and perhaps scarcely sane. And the
intensity of this affection had given rise to conjecturing." Cecilia is as
aware as anyone that something is wrong with her, and the news that
Alice has a male suitor sends her into a hysterical crisis.

Moore is writing in the French tradition of the monstrous lesbian,
but with a new sympathy: he sees Cecilia as a victim of bad influences
(in fact, a confusing plethora of them). The narrator interrupts the
scene here to blame Cecilia's "misshapen body," plus her father's age
and decrepit sperm when he sired her (bad genes), plus her mother's
revulsion against him (fetal conditioning), plus the bitterness of late-
nineteenth-century feminism (social conditioning). Just about the only
explanation he does not offer, interestingly enough, is inversion. He
lays it on thick, assuring the readers that Cecilia has "the eyes of the
deformed, deep, dreamy depths of brown, luminous with a strange
weariness, that we who are normal, straight and strong, can neither feel
nor understand." The prose is purple, but the tone is high-minded: the

author seems to be trying to help "normal, straight" readers "understand" what they can never "feel." Alice, lacking this understanding, rebukes Cecilia for her "absurd" feelings, sending her into depression. But at this point Cecilia does some hard thinking: the trauma of losing Alice brings a compensatory breakthrough in self-knowledge. At their next meeting, she confesses to Alice that "I desired to possess you wholly and entirely." She announces that she plans to suppress her guilty passion by becoming a nun. Moore, well aware of Diderot's *La Religieuse,* may be hinting here that Cecilia might find in convent life not so much sublimation as a discreet outlet for her desires. Cecilia—acknowledging her preference for women, and choosing a life that will not subject her to the horrors of marriage—is a subtly different creature from her literary foresisters, and seems less likely to die frothing at the mouth.

Perhaps the earliest novel to take the discovery of a lesbian identity as its central theme, *Méphistophéla* (1890) by Catulle Mendès, grafts the salaciousness of French sex-fiend literature onto the structure and analysis of a coming-of-age novel. Like George Moore, Mendès offers a bewildering range of origins for his brooding heroine's perversion but does not describe her as an invert. He presents Sophie at some points as genetically warped (descended from a long line of evildoers), at others as simply holding to the truth of her own nature (forced into an engagement to her beloved Emmeline's brother, she fears that marriage will feel like a bird trying to live underwater), at others as a traumatized victim (raped on her wedding night). Fleeing to Emmeline, Sophie stands watching her friend sleep, and suddenly recognizes her feelings as sexual: "The monster which had always been inside her wanted to come out and satisfy itself." The rape has awoken Sophie to the dreadful knowledge of male lust, and—paradoxically—to her own, not unsimilar desire to be her friend's husband/rapist.

That night, Sophie persuades Emmeline to run away with her. But this romantic interlude leads to a frustrating stalemate, as they cannot figure out how to get past arousal to satisfaction. Sophie, very sensibly, does not assume that lesbian sex is an *amor impossibilis* but that she needs some technical advice, being a "stupid creature, incomplete, crippled, loving without knowing how to love, coveting without knowing how to possess," ignorant of "the mysterious rites of the cult in which she was an instinctive oblate." Again, in phrases like this, Mendès hedges his bets: is lesbianism an inborn trait or a subcultural institution—or a bit of both? When Emmeline creeps back to her family, Sophie accepts her destiny and joins the "cult," by finding a network of Parisian lesbians whom she reluctantly recognizes as her sisters.

Her first girlfriend, the lower-class, kindly Magalo, renames her Sophor, as if to mark her new identity. Guessing that Sophor is pregnant as a result of her wedding night, Magalo looks forward to bringing the child up with her; here the novel gestures toward possibilities that would not be fulfilled in fiction until the second half of the twentieth century. But Sophor, already hardened by her experiences, has the child fostered far away. Over the years of promiscuity, quarrels, wealth (she becomes a baroness), social stigma, and a morphine habit, she grows increasingly "sullen in her terrible joys," "ever more proud" of being "detestable." Relishing the paradox of an unwanted craving, a reluctant drive, Mendès claims that his heroine's vice "repels her, even, but she must do it, she submits to it as if to a unbreakable law." Here is the old idea of the lesbian trapped in a vicious circle, as in Musset's *Gamiani* (1833). But as Peter Cryle notes, *Méphistophéla* does something new with it. Sophor has no difficulty in getting or giving sexual satisfaction—and in this she is typical of lesbians in late-nineteenth-century literature—but she does have Gamiani's restless, tortured libido, what Sophor calls "forever unsated desire." So she sets out to seduce every young woman she can, turning lust into, as Cryle puts it, "a whole life's project . . . making the problem of desire into its own (final) solution, producing damnation not as poetic stasis but as a powerful narrative dynamic."

On one level *Méphistophéla* is trashy fiction, the last gasp of the tradition of lesbian monstrosity: Mendès promises readers at the start that Sophie will plunge "straight to her damnation, without pause, like a falling stone." But in fact the journey is more circuitous than that, and his method anticipates twentieth-century narratives of diagnosing lesbianism, mulling it over, gradually dragging it into the light. This is a complex portrait of a woman who lives as a loner within a community of the like-minded, who chooses and acts but thinks of herself as a slave. It is hardly surprising that Mendès finally shuts down on these paradoxes in the way that Diderot made so popular a century before: when Sophor finally tracks down her long-lost daughter, now a teen-

ager, she is so appalled to find herself lusting after the girl that she goes
barking mad.

As if to distinguish themselves sharply from this tradition of lurid
sexuality, many British writers emphasized the idealistic in their
coming-out stories. Sylvia Stevenson's *Surplus* (1924) is a "fork in the
road" story of two friends; its title refers to the population imbalance
after the war killed so many men, and more broadly to unmarried
women as cultural ballast or waste product. At the beginning, Sally
Wraith—an intense, nervous woman in a man's job (taxi driving)—
knows only that she is "not a marrying woman," although sophisticated
readers would have marked the various symptoms of inversion. When
she moves in with Averil, she thinks of the two of them as "partners,"
but Averil calls them "pals" and shrugs off all Sally's romantic or possessive actions as "little eccentricities." Both women are equally slow
to register the profound difference between their perceptions, and between their natures.

All that changes when Sally loses her beloved to a doctor, the
unsubtly surnamed Barry Hope. Dr. Hope casually diagnoses his rival
as "abnormal," one of many cases of what in the fashionable, pseudo-
Freudian terms he describes as repressed sex instinct, "people who
aren't running straight on nature's lines." (In 1920s gay slang, "straight"
was already beginning to mean heterosexual, several decades before
"bent" took on the opposite meaning.) But if the man gets the girl,
Sally gets the key to her own heart. It takes her some time, and a lot of
reading. She has to wade through grim sexological texts, such as "a har-
rowing description of an 'unmated' woman who thought she was perfectly happy with a girlfriend, but later found what she had missed and,
in despair, ended her career in an asylum." However, Sally finally
comes to the conclusion that this is who she is, and it is not her fault. "I
love a woman with all the strength of my heart, and I'm sneered at,
laughed at, condemned to solitude as if I'd committed a crime!" She
concludes, "I may be queer, but I'm not quite mad yet." (Just as
"straight" was coming to signify heterosexual, "queer" was taking on
same-sex overtones by the 1920s.) Here knowledge of homosexuality
reveals itself as a consolation prize. After a last-ditch grasping at normality in which she gets engaged to a nice man, Sally chooses to accept
her destiny: she will break off the wedding, buy into a motor business,
and wait for the right woman to come along. By committing to a tradi-

tionally masculine career, as much as by staying a spinster, she is accepting her tendencies as they are. Where once she felt like a "pariah" and a "pitiable freak," now she counts herself among the company of "dreamers" and "rebels."

Notice that although this is a coming-out story, by any definition, it is a private one. Sylvia Stevenson presents her heroine's sea change as psychologically healthy, but a personal matter; Sally feels no urge to tell anyone, or seek out a community organizing itself for political emancipation. It is not as a lesbian, invert, or Sapphist (just three of the possible labels) that she names herself, but as one of a mixed bag of "dreamers." If she is a "rebel," she is not the banner-waving kind but one who chooses a highly modern lifestyle in discretion and silence. I think Stevenson is not being timid here—as there is nothing euphemistic about the "I love a woman" passage quoted above—but is making a broader point about resistance to cultural norms. And, of course, trying to appeal to all the readers who may in their different ways count themselves as "rebels" or at least "dreamers" too.

On publication in 1924, *Surplus* received reviews that varied according to the critics' attitude to its theme: the small-town *Daily News* in Greensboro, North Carolina, sneered that the author was "mistaken in thinking that the mere characterization of a more or less perverted woman is sufficient content for a good novel," whereas the *New York Evening Post* heralded Stevenson's "skill," "sanity," "insight," and "courage" for tackling an emotion "that, although not common, is doubtless commoner than we believe." *Surplus* struck the *New York Times* as utterly contemporary: "Fifty years ago such a novel . . . would have been impossible, for girls fashioned of such emotional timbre as Sally Wraith simply did not exist." But in the next sentence the reviewer falters, conceding that women may have desired each other before now: "Or if they did exist they never dared to express themselves. It is only in modern times and since Dr. Freud flung the gates open to many a chafing inhibition that the Sally Wraiths began seriously 'expressing' themselves." The point is highly debatable: it could be argued that the newly publicized notion of the lesbian, based on sexology as well as popularizations of Freudian theory, scared as many women away from a same-sex partnership as it attracted. But what is important is that the reviewer offers the coming-out story as not merely modern, but constitutive of modernity.

It is no accident that the fiancé in *Surplus* is a doctor, as he is in H. E. Bates's story "Breeze Anstey" (1937, a less cruel rewrite of Lawrence's *The Fox* from the point of view of the loser) and in Aimee and Philip Stuart's 1937 play, *Love of Women*. The doctor, as guardian of modern knowledge about what is "abnormal" as opposed to "healthy" and "straight," parts the straight woman from her friend, but does his rival a sort of backhanded favor by enlightening her about her sexuality. No longer innocent, cast out of Eden, the lesbian is freed to go off in search of an alternative paradise.

In an Irish novel set in Spain, Kate O'Brien's *Mary Lavelle* (1936), it is—appropriately enough—a priest who plays the doctor's role, forcing the androgynous, "nunnish," and "queer" Agatha to realize that her love for Mary, a younger au pair, is the "very ancient and terrible vice" of lesbianism. Interestingly, after Agatha tells Mary the truth, the two friends experience "a certain relaxation." Mary comes to see Agatha's desire as equivalent to her own passion for a married man: "You take one kind of impossible fancy, I take another," she tells Agatha. By the time Mary is leaving for Ireland, Agatha is confident enough to ask for a photo of her, and refuses to wish herself cured: ruefully, she jokes that she is going to age into "the sort of muttering hag children throw stones at!"

But for most authors, medicine remained the pole around which the coming-out story revolved. Austrian author Aimée Duc's *Sind es Frauen? Roman über das dritte Geschlecht* (1903; in English, *Are These Women? A Novel of the Third Sex*) uses both the sexological model of inversion and the very different insights of feminism to make sense of the careerist, woman-loving lives of some unapologetic "inverted women" who meet as students in Geneva. This novel is a peculiar mix of political debate and lesbian romance, with far more space devoted to the former. The Russian-French protagonist, Minotchka, is an ambitious scholar who has switched to art from medicine because she cannot stand the way most doctors (sexologists aside) maintain a conspiracy of silence about homosexuality. Described as both tomboyish and coquettishly feminine, Minotchka is a passionate cyclist despite her weak left ankle (a hint of hereditary taint?). At one of her parties, Minotchka—despite the fact that she once made a rash and brief marriage herself—reacts badly to news that a fellow third-sexer, Elise, has just got engaged: this "turns everything into a lie and slaps all our faces." Her friend Dr. Tatjana is more blasé about marriages of convenience, arguing that if Elise really loves her fiancé, that proves that "she is a normal being and was mistaken up till then," just as Minotchka and Tatjana were mistaken about being heterosexual. But Minotchka, a feminist who believes all marriage is oppressive, argues that in a patriarchal culture desire is never a matter of unconstrained self-discovery. For her it is "the sacred duty of each one of us who belongs to the third sex to warn our undecided wavering sisters against marriage, those whose conditions we easily recognize with knowing eyes and the feeling of solidarity."

The Countess Marta, an older Polish aristocrat studying music for pleasure, who has followed Minotchka to Geneva for love, seems to be an even more out-and-proud third-sexer. She speaks up in stronger terms about the political obligation to come out.

> We have to try to fight our way into the public, to be acknowledged and not to be ignored! . . . We have to speak up at all times, we have to assert ourselves and we must not let ourselves be intimidated into believing we are sick.

But the punch line is that Marta, too, will turn out to be one of those "undecided wavering sisters." While Marta is away looking after her dying father and then sorting out his estate, Minotchka buries herself in work in traditionally masculine fashion, and despite being aware that Marta's letters are getting rarer and shorter, and that there is a young officer hovering around her, Minotchka makes no effort to fight for her. News of Marta's sudden wedding to the officer sends Minotchka into a nervous breakdown. Marta has married not for love but "for the sake of outward appearances" and companionship with a fellow music lover who knows she is a lesbian, but she comes to the conclusion that even such a marriage is "a fetter, a rape, an outrage." Duc grants her troubled heroines a second chance: when Marta's husband dies after a couple of years, the women meet again coincidentally in a Paris graveyard and Marta begs her beloved's forgiveness. Marta describes them as like a married couple, who "separate for long times out of some terrible error, only to stick together ever closer afterwards." She proposes that they split their time, spending six months a year in each of their home places: "Do you want to set out on this new venture with me, will you trust your life to me?" Minotchka—amusingly, put in the position of the bride in this proposal scene—says yes. By holding firm to her nature, she has won not only the argument but the girl.

Like Aimée Duc, "Christopher St. John" (an Englishwoman, Christabel Marshal) and "Renée Vivien" (Pauline Tarn, another Englishwoman, living in France) linked desire for women to gender nonconformity, but they rejected the language of inversion. Vivien's *Une Femme m'apparut* (1904; in English, *A Woman Appeared to Me*) casts her as the androgyne San Giovanni, poet and prophet, votary of Sappho and "the cause" (feminism); she is presented as brave enough to live the kind of woman-loving life that all women would prefer if only they could resist the pressure to marry. In this very odd, fragmentary work, Vivien anticipates many of the ideas of what would be called lesbian feminism six decades later, but her tone is often Wildean. When a man predicts that San Giovanni will end up with one of the opposite sex, her lover Vally (based on salon hostess Natalie Barney) quips, very deadpan, "That would be a crime against nature, sir. I have too much respect for our friend to believe her capable of an abnormal passion."

Like *Une Femme m'apparut*, Christopher St. John's *Hungerheart: The Story of a Soul* (written from about 1896, while she was working as secretary to Winston Churchill and his mother, and published anonymously in 1915) is a roman à clef and an apologia, if a more cautious, British one. Joanna, aka John, aka John-Baptist, reasons that because she has spurned the "merely female" destiny of marriage and children, and always loved women, she must have the soul of a man. She knows there must be others like her: "Brotherly minds of mine, neglected in the study of womanhood, this was written for you!" But, interestingly, this masculine woman scorns the idea that two women together will play "husband" and "wife," and she also rejects the doctors' focus on lust. John's relationships with a series of contrasting women, whether fiery infatuations or domestic ménages, are above all that. "It was *to love* I yearned more than to *be loved,* and I was entirely free from sexual instincts." But the lack of sex should not be mistaken for a lack of passion; when her companion Sally is tempted by the prospect of marrying a man, John describes it as "a bomb hurtling through the serene air of my paradise, exploding with a noise of devil's laughter, tearing up immemorial trees by the roots, laying waste the greenery of hope and faith—then filth, stench, corruption." Fleeing to Rome, where she converts to Catholicism, John finally directs her feelings into worship of the Virgin Mary and a pure-minded friendship with a nun. Although *Hungerheart* has much in common with the case-history-style fictions we have been looking at, this "story of a soul" insists on being read as a spiritual autobiography.

In Jacques de Lacretelle's fascinating *La Bonifas* (1925; in English, *Marie Bonifas*), Marie's problem has multiple roots. She is a robust, ugly, masculine woman—but she has also been turned off men by her brutish father. While the lesbian's intensity caused only "conjecturing" in *A Drama in Muslin,* these French villagers are knowing enough to assume (incorrectly) that Marie's infatuations are full-blown affairs. People make up satirical doggerel about her, and one man kills her kitten and tries to push Marie into a canal. It is persecution, rather than love, that opens Marie's eyes and moves the plot along. In public she rides astride, smokes, and defies her tormentors, but in private, she is busy poring over medical histories.

> Exaggerating her actions, recalling insignificant details, mere trifles, she discovered deep down in her being all manner of signs which she considered criminal . . . No, no, she denied it no longer, they were right. The whole of her past revealed to her a certain inclination, immanent, an integral part of her very being . . . Bending over the fire as if she could read her destiny in its flames, she admitted to herself that the one ray of romance in her life came from the attractiveness of women.

Marie considers having sex with a woman for the first time, maybe a prostitute: " 'Why should I not?' she repeated. 'Since it is so, since they say it is, since I feel it.' " But (like the heroine of *Hungerheart*) she steps back from temptation. A lonely pariah, she finally wins back the respect of her neighbors in middle age, when she chases off the Germans. (Paradoxically, World War One almost always represents a golden period in lesbian storylines, a moment when unfeminine behavior becomes briefly acceptable.) Lacretelle ends his novel on a wistful note, with Marie weeping during a visit to her old school: there is at least a hint that she may have been foolish to choose dignity over happiness.

But by far the most famous coming-out novel is *The Well of Loneliness,* published in 1928 by Radclyffe Hall (born Marguerite, but she preferred "John"), and banned in Britain and the United States as obscene. Hall drew on her personal experience, but also on other fiction (probably including *Hungerheart,* and possibly *La Bonifas*), as well as the medical literature on homosexuality (primarily inversion, but also prenatal conditioning and family dynamics, including the Oedipal complex). Her protagonist, Stephen, not only discovers what she is in the pages of Krafft-Ebing's *Psychopathia Sexualis,* but is similar in many ways (a writer, well-born, raised more or less as a boy) to "Sandor," the subject of one of Krafft-Ebing's vivid case histories. In fact, the novel is so preoccupied with Stephen's gender troubles—rather than merely desire for women—that it is often read nowadays as a transgender narrative rather than a lesbian one.

Even before she falls madly for a housemaid at the age of seven, Stephen has a nature that everyone but she seems able to diagnose. Her governess, Puddle, held back by "that wilfully selfish tyranny of silence evolved by a crafty old ostrich of a world," longs to tell the child:

> You're neither unnatural, nor abominable, nor mad; you're as much a part of what people call nature as anyone else; only you're unexplained as yet—you've not got your niche in creation. But some day that will come, and meanwhile don't shrink from yourself, but just face yourself calmly and bravely.

There is the book's moral (and political agenda) in a nutshell—but of course Stephen has to figure all this out for herself, by leaving home, becoming a novelist, driving an ambulance in France in World War One, and surviving a series of painful affairs with feminine women. They range from the double-crossing dabbler Angela Crossby to the devoted, underwear-darning Mary Llewellen, whom Stephen—in the novel's sacrificial climax—finally drives into the arms of a man so he can give her children and an ordinary life. Radclyffe Hall was not the first and would not be the last author to purchase the reader's sympathy for her protagonist by means of a noble renunciation. In such novels as Ethel Arnold's *Platonics: A Study* (1894), Gale Wilhelm's *We Too Are Drifting* (1935), Mary Renault's *The Friendly Young Ladies* (1944), and Kate O'Brien's *As Music and Splendour* (1958), the man conquers by default because his female rival is so generous—or, one might say, a sucker.

Many novelists followed Hall in drawing on medical literature for the language—and structure—of their coming-out narratives. The psychological sciences, in particular, could offer novelists a language for the coming-out process. Debby, in *Wasteland* (1946), the first novel of "Jo Sinclair" (Ruth Seid), has an easier time of it than Hall's Stephen, because she is guided by a refreshingly pragmatic psychiatrist. Debby is not so much the novel's protagonist—that role belongs to her brother Jake—as its guiding light. An androgynous writer just like Radclyffe Hall's heroine, but a Jewish American one, she is troubled by the sense that her "difference" (by which she seems to mean her butchness, as much as her intimacy with a Jewish poet called Fran) makes her "isolated, as part of a tiny minority of people who did not dare lift their eyes to the level of the rest of the world. No matter how clean I kept myself. No matter if I loved beautiful music and beautiful words." Despite her psychiatrist's theory that it was her weak father who turned her into a "lesbian," he encourages her to accept herself anyway and "get her hands on what she wants." Debby relaxes into a sense of solidarity not only with fellow same-sexers but with black people and the disabled: "all the odd ones, the queer and different ones." (This sounds a startlingly 1970s note in a 1940s text.) Jake loves his sister, but feels ashamed of her oddity; she sends him to talk to her psychiatrist, who cures him of that, as well as his shame about being a Jew. There is a moving moment when Jake asks to take a photo of Debby; she volunteers to change out of her slacks into a skirt—but no, he prefers to record her "just the way you are." *Wasteland* won the Harper Prize; it was reprinted many times and translated into six languages; readers of all stripes wrote to Jo Sinclair to say how touched they were by Debby. If in *A Drama in Muslin* (1886) George Moore doubted whether "we who are normal, straight and strong" could ever understand a lesbian, a mere sixty years later the world had changed enough that troubled readers all over North America were hoping a lesbian might understand them.

On Trial

"My love for Marie is as natural to me as your love for me is natural to you."

"I know, I know!" said Frank with evident embarrassment, "I meant abnormal, as people generally view such things."

"Yes," said Norma, "it is abnormal in the eyes of the community."

"That was all that I meant," said Frank.

Take a guess at the date of this calm little exchange about the relativism of the "natural" and the "normal": 1960? 1980? Guess again: 1895. The remarkable *Norma Trist; or, Pure Carbon: A Story of the Inversion of the Sexes* is a "dime novel" by John Wesley Carhart, a Texas minister, physician, and inventor of a forerunner of the automobile. Despite the subtitle's mention of the fashionable concept of inversion, Norma is not your tormented, mannish invert at all. In fact, this heiress is an all-rounder whose traditionally masculine strengths (gymnastics, mathematics, carriage driving) are matched with feminine ones (beauty and sensitivity). Elected valedictorian, she gives such a great speech that it wins her immediate job offers in journalism. She is also having a blissful affair with her "inseparable" music tutor, Mrs. LaMoreaux. Carhart describes his heroine's nature as a "beautiful blending of the sensuous—not to say sensual—and the truly, sublimely, religious and poetic." Her preference seems innate (she has desired girls and only girls since the age of twelve), but not inherited (given the lack of anything of the kind in

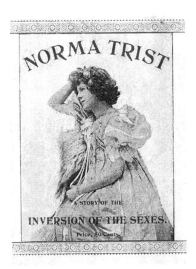

Jacket, John Wesley Carhart, Norma Trist; or, Pure Carbon: A Story of the Inversion of the Sexes *(1895).*
   The anonymous cover art of this novel defies readers' expectations about "inversion" by presenting Norma as an icon of charming femininity. The photograph is said to be of Gertrude Haynes, who set up an all-women theater company in 1905.

her family history), and not marked by either masculinity or neurosis. In one of the very few essays on this little-known novel, Kim Emery argues that although Carhart often echoes the literature of the sexologists, and shares their zeal to shift homosexuality from the moral/legal to the medical arena, he also offers a profound challenge to that discourse. He presents his heroine as so profoundly healthy and successful that, according to the medical literature of the 1890s, "the existence of an individual like Norma Trist was impossible."

Carhart uses familiar elements of the school story, the rivals plot (casting Norma's farmer neighbor, Frank Artman, in the role of oblivious suitor), and the case history (inserting, almost verbatim, excerpts from Krafft-Ebing's case history of "Sandor" in the love letters of Norma's that the school authorities confiscate). He is careful to distinguish between guilt and mere self-consciousness: as Norma puts it, "I feel no condemnation for aught I have done or for aught that I feel. But oh! I dread the criticisms and scoffs of society."

The storyline briefly dips into the French fiend tradition when the faithless Mrs. LaMoreaux gets engaged to a Mexican army officer, and Norma stabs her, but—unlike Alice Mitchell, whose 1892 conviction clearly inspired this novel—not fatally. At this point *Norma Trist* also mixes in the thrills of another genre—the courtroom drama—as Norma's coming out moves from private process to public debate. The first verdict is (like Mitchell's) criminal insanity, but when she is retried, her lawyer argues that her preference for women is merely "psychopathia-sexualis," an "abnormality" (whether congenital or acquired, he says, hedging his bets). The asylum director testifies that Norma is a freak of nature perhaps, but no more culpable than any man who committed the same kind of jealous *crime passionel*. A doctor claims, on the other hand, that she could be cured by hypnosis. Taking the stand, Norma shows guilt only about the stabbing; she speaks with eloquent pride about her relationship with Mrs. LaMoreaux, which she describes as "according to my nature; therefore, God-given and right"—just as worthy as any male-female relationship, "and I may modestly say, as intelligent." In answer to a question about sex, she explains that her "love for and relations with Marie afforded the highest and profoundest satisfaction."

The bewildering discussions in the courtroom lead to a hung jury, and *Norma Trist* has a similarly confused ending. Having spent much of the novel arguing for a sympathetic acceptance of homosexuality, and amassing evidence for its being permanent in the case of his heroine, Carhart suddenly changes tack and resorts to a deus ex machina. As a favor to the devoted Frank, who has bailed her out, Norma allows the hypnotist Dr. Jasper to assess her (he decides that it was all her doting father's fault for educating her like a son), and treat her three times a week, implanting in her the following heavy-handed suggestion: "I abhor the love of my own sex, and shall never again think women handsome. I shall and will become well again, fall in love with Frank Artman, be happy and make him happy." Abracadabra—Norma is *normalized* as fast as any Stepford wife—and she and Frank (like poster children for what a century later would be called the ex-gay movement) have a blissful and fertile marriage. As Kim Emery points out, her married name—Norma Artman—may imply "that all this normalcy is artifice." Carhart may have hoped this eleventh-hour swerve would make his radical story acceptable to the authorities, but in fact it did not prevent his being arrested on obscenity charges.

Although sex between women has very rarely been forbidden by law, courtrooms play an important role in many coming-out stories—but often an offstage one. This might seem like a paradox; perhaps it is that having a protagonist interrogated about her tastes in the dock would read like a debate, whereas showing the complex ripple effects on her whole life of even a threatened exposure on the stand makes for a better narrative.

In Lillian Hellman's critical and commercial hit play *The Children's Hour* (1934)—loosely based, like John Wesley Carhart's novel, on a real case, this time from early-nineteenth-century Edinburgh—two headmistresses fail to convict a pupil's grandmother of libel for destroying their school by spreading a rumor that they are lovers. (In a neat nod to literary tradition, their child accuser has been made aware of such possibilities by Gautier's 1835 novel *Mademoiselle de Maupin*.) But just as the accusation is only whispered, never spoken aloud onstage, the trial is not shown; it is the terrible gap between two acts of the play. When we see the teachers again in the trial's aftermath, living as recluses in the empty school, one of them has gone through an unwilling metamorphosis. Here a play about the evils of gossip suddenly changes course.

MARTHA   I love you that way—maybe the way they said I loved
           you. I don't know. (*Waits, gets no answer, kneels down next
           to Karen.*) Listen to me!

KAREN   What?

MARTHA   *I have loved you the way they said.*

KAREN   You're crazy.

MARTHA   There's always been something wrong. Always—as long
           as I can remember. But I never knew it until all this
           happened.

The *New York Times* reviewer saw this shift as a fundamental flaw in *The Children's Hour,* and advised the producers to bring down the curtain before the confession scene. But I believe this is what keeps the play interesting today: that Hellman takes a tale of persecuted innocence and—by digging more deeply—turns it into a complex parable about scapegoating and identity formation. We can also place *The Children's Hour* in the context of "fork in the road" plots about two friends who both win the audience's sympathy before one of them is gradually revealed—to herself as much as anyone—as a lesbian. Because the fact is, if Martha were a declared lesbian in the first scene, *The Children's Hour* would not have worked the same way on its 1934 audience—in the highly unlikely event that the censors had let the curtain come up in the first place. As it is, she has to bow to tradition and shoot herself— offstage, of course.

Sometimes a relationship between women does not even have to result in a court case; the mere threat of having one's sexuality named in a public forum casts a paralyzing shadow. For instance, in Anna Elisabet Weirauch's groundbreaking, grim trilogy *Der Skorpion* (1919–21; in English, *The Scorpion* and *The Outcast,* and many pulp editions under various titles), young Myra's family tries to break up her affair with the older Olga by a variety of means. The first kind of authority they invoke is medical: they put pressure on Myra to let a sexologist check her for "physical abnormalities," and call in a psychiatrist to convince her that lesbianism leads to death. Once the relationship has been consummated, Olga guesses that their next attack with be legal: "You're going to incriminate me," she tells her lover, who will not come of age for another six months. Sure enough, Myra's family burst into Olga's house, then have her shadowed by a detective and threaten her with jail, until—having heard that Myra has given in and got engaged—she puts a bullet in her head.

But in fiction the main way for a relationship between women to be put on trial is indirectly, through a child-custody battle. The first example is *The Price of Salt* (also known as *Carol*), a classy romance published under the pseudonym of "Claire Morgan" by Patricia Highsmith in 1952. Carol is already separated, living with her small daughter, when she falls in love with a young shop assistant called Therese. This is not her first relationship with a woman, but the first for which she risks rocking the delicate balance of her life. Carol's husband, plotting to gain full custody, sends a private eye to follow the couple on a road trip and record their conversations and lovemaking. Again, the legal battle takes place behind the scenes, and we only catch glimpses of it. Carol writes to Therese to confess that she has surrendered, letting her husband take full custody: "It would be useless to try to face a court with this. I should be ashamed, not for myself oddly enough, but for my own child, to say nothing of not wanting you to have to appear." Notice that she tries to recast her shame about being a lesbian as a form of morality, compunction for her lover and daughter. Although Carol has avoided going into court, her backroom negotiation with the lawyers—hers as well as her husband's, merged in one disapproving, euphemistic brigade—is staged as a nightmarish courtroom scene:

> The question was would I stop seeing you (and others like you, they said!). It was not so clearly put. There were a dozen faces that opened their mouths and spoke like the judges of doomsday— reminding me of my duties, my position, and my future.

By sacrificing her relationship with Therese, she has dearly bought a few weeks' access to her child every year. In her next letter Carol changes tack, arguing that the women's relationship was too new, not yet substantial enough to fight for.

> I say I love you always, the person you are and the person you will become. I would say it in a court if it would mean anything to those people or possibly change anything, because those are not the words I am afraid of.

She is not afraid to say "I love you," that is—but what scares her is the idea of saying it and being misunderstood and crudely labeled as a lesbian by "those people" (the same lawyers, presumably, but gloves off this time). She goes on to tell Therese what it is that she thought she could not express to the lawyers, "the most important point I did not mention and was not thought of by anyone," that some people simply prefer their own sex, just as some prefer "a Beethoven quartet versus the *Mona Lisa.*" The lawyers imply that Carol is heading toward "the depths of human vice and degeneration," but in the calm and privacy of this letter she is able to make a powerful rebuttal:

> It is true, if I were to go on like this and be spied upon, attacked, never possessing one person long enough so that knowledge of a person is a superficial thing—that is degeneration. Or to live against one's grain, that is degeneration by definition.

The letter is eloquent and confused at the same time, unconvincing in its logic but moving nonetheless. In her rhetorical flourishes and her profound unease, Carol is a memorable portrait of a woman uncertain of how to be a lesbian, a mother, and a person of dignity all at the same time.

Although it reads like a final statement, the letter turns out to be the opposite: it records Carol's last attempt to be respectable. When the two women meet again after some time, it emerges that the negotiations finally broke down: faced with elaborate lists of "silly promises" demanded by her husband, the family, and the lawyers, Carol "didn't promise very much" at all in court (which "wasn't a court, you know, just a round-table discussion")—and has been punished by having her access to her daughter reduced to "a couple of afternoons a year." After receiving the letter discussed above, Therese had concluded that "Carol loved her child more than her," and now, she revises that: "Carol loved her more than she loved her child." But the way Highsmith writes this story—despite its famous happy ending—does not support either statement. As if refusing to make a Hollywood movie of this tug-of-love story, she keeps the legal process out of the spotlight and murky in its details (whose lawyers? which promises? in court or out?). Readers are left with a painful, complicated sense of what it means to have one's private sense of self exposed to scrutiny (whether personal and professional, sympathetic or hostile). Carol charts a difficult middle course, ultimately holding neither to girlfriend nor to child but to the truth of her own nature, the salt of it. The "price of salt" to which the novel's title alludes is almost—but not quite—unbearably high.

In Sheila Ortiz Taylor's surreal feminist comedy *Faultline* (1982), Arden is a wonderful mother of six who leaves her husband for his best friend's wife; her husband claims the phrase "lesbian mother" is "oxymoronic" because the two words contradict each other. In works about this apparent contradiction between the 1970s and the 1990s, the custody battle would remain a popular way of making the coming-out story concrete and dramatic, and testing the heroine's strengths and affiliations.

First Love

Ever since Ovid wrote about Diana's band of nymphs in his *Metamorphoses,* writers have been fascinated by the idea of a private world of girls, ruled by one charismatic woman. As Terry Castle has observed, narratives about same-sex desire often start with the "islanding" of women or girls: their physical and social isolation in institutions such as convents, schools, and colleges. School can be a paradise for same-sex love, or a hell, or a memorable combination of the two, as in the founding text of the tradition, Charlotte Brontë's *Jane Eyre* (1847). Against the nightmarish background of Lowood's burned porridge and whistling drafts, young Jane's emotional education takes the form of a dual passion for an older girl (the sternly saintly, dying Helen) and their headmistress (the compassionate Miss Temple). It is here that one of English literature's most famous romantic heroines learns "the love of human beings," as Brontë has Helen put it in a carefully gender-neutral phrase.

In schoolgirl fiction—a popular genre of the late nineteenth and early twentieth centuries, devoured by women as well as girls—the crush (also known as pash, smash, and *Schwarm*) on a teacher or schoolmate is ubiquitous, and often central to the plot. Some critics dismiss the phenomenon by arguing that the girls only choose girls for lack of

Elsie Anna Wood, "To the music of Karen's fiddle, they danced on the turf," in Elsie J. Oxenham, The Abbey Girls Go Back to School *(1922).*
   This bucolic image in the fourth of Oxenham's widely loved Abbey Girls series (1914–59), by a famous English Bible illustrator, captures the context of all-female intimacy from which stories of schoolgirl love arise.

opportunity—which seems like lamenting the fact that Juliet had to make do with Romeo because her social circle was limited to the men of Verona.

These school stories are not about a coming-out process, but when the coming-out story did begin to appear at the end of the nineteenth century, it grafted itself onto some established forms such as the school story, with its atmosphere of emotional intensity and its intricate web of connections among girls and women. Generally the girl who falls in love at school is a blank slate: her lack of emotional history gives her a clean, shining quality, and a lack of self-consciousness (at least at first) about the gender of her beloved. In *Regiment of Women* (1917) by Clemence Dane, discussed in chapter 4—a brilliant thirteen-year-old, Louise, declares that she will never marry because "I could never love anybody as much as I do Miss Hartill." When told that her little crush is not the real thing, she argues that love is love: "Where's the difference?" Though Louise speaks in the same terms as Mona in *A Sunless Heart,* her confidence has none of that character's sinister overtones. Louise thinks of herself as the protagonist in her own serious romance, but in fact her function in *Regiment of Women* is to be the victim of that mythic villainess, the lesbian teacher. Clare Hartill relishes having girls in her thrall; she wrecks Louise's health by encouraging her to study too hard, and blows hot and cold as her whims take her. Rejected by her beloved, Louise finally jumps out an attic window.

Interestingly, this minor character turns up almost twenty years later, transformed into the heroine of a German novel. Christa Winsloe's tale of a turn-of-the-century Prussian boarding school appeared in several stage and fictional forms, under a variety of different titles; the version I am looking at here is her novel, *The Child Manuela* (1933). All the schoolgirls hate the ogreish Head and adore the beautiful, kind, twenty-eight-year-old Fräulein Elizabeth von Bernburg. Strict and scrupulous, this teacher "makes no favourites," which means that just about the entire school kneels trembling for her good-night kiss, and at least one girl has scratched *E v B* into her arm. What rocks this precarious balance is the arrival of Manuela, a motherless fourteen-year-old tomboy, who is not so much more passionate than the other girls as braver and blunter. "I don't want to be a woman—I want to be a man, and to be with *you,*" she tells Bernburg. (Unlike Louise in *Regiment of Women,* she has noticed that desiring a woman is not a traditionally feminine thing to do.) The teacher gently rebukes her—then softens her words by handing over one of her own chemises on the pretext of Manuela's needing new underclothes. From private confession, Manuela makes the leap to public declaration. Drunk on punch after starring as a knight in the school play, she proposes a toast "to her we all love"—outing, as it were, the whole school—and boasts that her own passion for Fräulein von Bernburg must be reciprocated, because the gift of the chemise means "she loves me."

Fräulein von Bernburg, already dogged by unspecified "shocking" rumors about why she failed to marry her fiancé, has all the self-conscious unease that Manuela lacks.

> She dared not let one single child usurp her heart. And now that she had done so in spite of everything, from the very first moment that her eyes had encountered Manuela's, she dared not contemplate anything but self-discipline and renunciation.

The Headmistress, warning her that Manuela is "sexually abnormal," adds with audible threat, "and perhaps you know what the world thinks of such women—our world, Fräulein von Bernburg?" The change from "the world" to "our world" offers the intriguing possibility that the Head is not hinting merely at Bernburg's same-sex tastes but at her own. Bullied into promising never to be with Manuela in private again, Bernburg says goodbye to the girl, hovering on the verge of a confession of her own: "You must not love me so much, Manuela, that is not right. That's what one has to fight, what one has to conquer, what one has to kill . . . " The word anticipates the ending: Manuela, just like Louise in *Regiment of Women,* jumps out a high window to her death. The novel ends with the girls respectfully withdrawing to leave Bernburg to mourn alone over the body.

At thirteen and fourteen, Louise and Manuela are pure-hearted innocents: to them, love is simply love. But Swiss author Eveline Mahyère's *Je Jure de m'éblouir* (1958; English title, *I Will Not Serve*) is about a well-read seventeen-year-old, so it is a coming-of-age novel, tragic romance, and coming-out story in one. It begins (unusually) *after* the expulsion from Paradise: Sylvie has been thrown out of school because of her passion for her teacher (a student nun), Julienne. Sylvie has the clear conscience of Christa Winsloe's Manuela, but she writes to Julienne as a downright cocky, grown-up lover.

> There is something that you have never told me, something that I have been able to read in your look when, twenty times in a single lesson, our eyes used to meet over the little plaster statues. It is because of that look that I have left the convent, and the thought of leaving you there behind me is literally intolerable to me. If

you do not come to me, I shall carry you off by force with a silken ladder.

Here she strikes a pose as the prince to Julienne's captive Rapunzel, with the nuns as the witch who pushes him down from the tower: "They have hurled me into the void, uprooted me from life, thrown me to the wild beasts."

Sister Julienne keeps trying to pretend that the girl is simply being silly, and has had a breakdown: she writes back, "I hope that you will very quickly recover and be a healthy young rebel again." But Sylvie will not stop pushing her to take their relationship seriously. Julienne feels obliged to offer her headmistress her resignation for being "too much attached" to the girl; the pragmatic older nun refuses it, telling her "the best way to conquer sin is to surmount it, not to run away from it." Panicking, Julienne complains to Sylvie that these declarations "embarrass me like delirious raving." (Shades of Suzanne in the most famous of convent novels, Diderot's *La Religieuse*.) She insists she "saw nothing murky in my affection for you. Why have you had to distort everything so that now I am frightened of thinking of you and yet never stop thinking of you?" This reluctant admission fills Sylvie with joy; she writes back, "I love you. (And, contrary to what you suggest, this love is not in the least murky but as bright and blinding as a great fire.)" Like some medieval troubadour, she insists that her feelings are simultaneously erotic and high-minded; she declares her passion while shrugging off the "murky" meaning her culture ascribes to it. However, when Sylvie gets her chance to see her beloved in the flesh again, she messes it up: she kneels at Julienne's feet worshipfully instead of taking her in her arms. Afterward she realizes that she has missed her chance: "Because I didn't dare make her step down from her pedestal, I have lost Julienne." Sylvie goes on to drink, starve herself, and wind up in a hospital after a semiaccidental overdose. Because the author committed suicide before the novel was published, it is always assumed that Sylvie's faint on the last page is death, but it seems to me that Mahyère leaves it open, granting her eloquent, grandiose heroine at least a possibility of survival that Mahyère could not see for herself.

Like Sister Julienne, many critics have preferred not to take Sylvie at her word: because of the novel's existential debates, they often read the love story as a sort of allegory of the soul's relationship with God. Granting Mahyère's novel the rare honor of a full-page review in *Le Figaro Littéraire*, Jean Blanzart wrote loftily that "the biggest mistake would be to think that what we have here is a banal lesbian affair. It is something far more unusual, far purer and far greater." As we have seen before, it is traditional to insist that a lesbian-themed story one likes is not about lesbianism at all.

But perhaps the best fiction of schoolgirl love is Dorothy Strachey Bussy's faux memoir *Olivia*—yet another text that borrows the name of the heroine of *Twelfth Night*. Bussy wrote it in French in 1933, but when her beloved friend André Gide responded without enthusiasm, she put it aside till 1949, when it was published in English by Leonard Woolf's Hogarth Press, to great acclaim. In this loose fictionalization of Bussy's experiences at a French finishing school in the 1880s, the two headmistresses—Mlle Julie, the vivacious intellectual, and Mlle Cara, the kindly invalid—are a turbulent couple, and also rivals for the loyalties of the other teachers and girls, who are divided into "Julie-ites" and "Cara-ites." The sixteen-year-old Olivia, whose older self narrates the novel in yearning retrospect, falls for Mlle Julie all at once when watching her read Racine.

Unlike many schools in fiction, this one is charming. The power-hungry but lovable Mlle Julie visits Olivia at night for moments of tantalizing intimacy, teases her and sits her at her right hand at dinner, letting the girl drink in her witty and erudite conversation: "She communicated a Promethean fire." Less naïve than Manuela in *The Child Manuela*, and less brave than Sylvie in *Je Jure de m'éblouir*, the thoughtful Olivia gradually figures out that, even in this homoerotic atmosphere, the serious intensity of her feelings for her teacher is "something to be ashamed of, something to hide desperately," even though—perhaps all the more because—Mlle Julie loves Olivia "differently" from all the other girls in return. Realizing this brings Olivia "joy and terror," especially when she gradually deduces that the headmistresses' partnership is on the brink of collapse.

Everyone plays multiple roles (confidante, enemy, suitor) in this complex, all-female microcosm. But it is Olivia who brings on the crisis by finally declaring her passion. The tantalizing Mlle Julie laughs it off, but promises to visit her after dark and then fails to show up, leaving

Olivia to lie awake in agonizing, aroused vigil for several nights in a row. The girl perceives herself as Eve after the Fall:

> Mystery was all about me, murky suspicions, and at the bottom of my heart lay jealousy such as I had never known before, and a dreadful curiosity and a dreadful longing for wickedness. In so short a time to be cast from the glories of Paradise into this direful region!

It is Mlle Julie who breaks this terrible deadlock, by deciding to retire to Canada—whereupon the bereft Cara dies of an overdose. In her last interview with Olivia, Mlle Julie says obscurely,

> "It has been a struggle all my life—but I have always been victorious—I was proud of my victory." And then her voice changed, broke, deepened, softened, became a murmur: "I wonder now whether defeat wouldn't have been better for us all—as well as sweeter." Another long pause. She turned now and looked at me, and smiled. "You, Olivia, will never be victorious, but if you are defeated—" how she looked at me! "when you are defeated—" she looked at me in a way that made my heart stand still and the blood rush to my face, to my forehead, till I seemed to be wrapped in flame—then she suddenly broke off and brushed her hand across her eyes, as if brushing away an importunate vision.

Here, just as in the farewell scene in *The Child Manuela*, a teacher renounces not only the girl she loves but her own braver, more demanding self. "It has been a struggle all my life," says Mlle Julie (echoing Bernburg's "That's what one has to fight, what one has to conquer, what one has to kill"). The difference here is that Dorothy Strachey Bussy allows Mlle Julie a "change" of voice at this point, a brief surrender to the "sweeter" possibilities that could follow from "defeat" in the struggle to repress desire. The teacher moves from considering Olivia's life "if" she gives in to desire, to predicting what it will be "when" she does; Mlle Julie, at this moment of heightened romance, seems to be practically ordering Olivia—as a medieval lady might send out her knight—to go forth and explore all the erotic possibilities that Julie herself has renounced. So a story that in the hands of a more con-

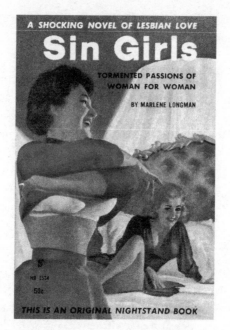

Jacket, Marlene Longman [Robert Silverberg], Sin Girls *(1960).*
    Published by William Lawrence Hamling, Nightstand Books was a best-selling series of paperback originals, often by noted young novelists. Sin Girls *was written by famous science-fiction author Robert Silverberg, four years after his first Hugo Award, during a crash in the science-fiction market; his work for Nightstand under various names bought him a twenty-room mansion. The unsigned art for this title stands out from other brooding lesbian pulp-fiction covers for its mood of jubilation.*

ventional author would probably have ended with a shuddering denunciation of girls' schools here becomes a profound drama of awakening.

Devil May Care

Colonna, by all the laws of literature, ought to have been plain, heavy, humourlessly passionate and misunderstood, pursuing in recurrent torments of jealousy the reluctant, the inexperienced and the young. She ought to have behaved like someone with a guilty secret.

The narrator's witty observation, in Mary Renault's *Purposes of Love* (1939), is hardly fair to the long tradition of writing about desire between women; it suggests that Renault was unfamiliar with the many novels and plays, over the centuries, that have broken those "laws of lit-erature" by presenting women who desire women as noble, funny, or triumphantly wicked. It also oversimplifies the type—the saturnine (but I would say rarely dull) girl-pursuer in, say, *Little Dorrit, The Bosto-nians, Regiment of Women, Marie Bonifas,* or *The Well of Loneliness.* Yet we all know what she means: in the first few decades of the twentieth century, a composite stereotype of the dogged, jealous, guilt-wracked lesbian took hold, and it has not been entirely banished in the twenty-first.

But it is often forgotten that Stephen is not the only prototype Radclyffe Hall presents in *The Well of Loneliness.* Stephen's Paris friend Valerie Seymour (based on the charismatic salon hostess Natalie Bar-ney, who inspired characters in at least eight other novels) is a confident free spirit. Womanly, but exclusively and permanently lesbian, Valerie does not explain herself in terms of gender inversion, or any of the other available discourses, whether old (sin, tragedy) or fashionable (genetics, arrested development). And she calls Stephen's grand gesture of renouncing Mary for Mary's own good absurd: "For God's sake keep the girl, and get what happiness you can out of life."

We might construct a lineage for Valerie Seymour through much older texts such as the anonymous *Travels and Adventures of Mlle de Richelieu* (1744). But unlike those premodern heroines, what I call the devil-may-care lesbian is a creature of the twentieth century—first hit-ting the page in the 1920s—who knows exactly what people say about her and finds it funny. She is a sexy, fearless sister to the gloomy stereo-type. She appears first, significantly, in some short stories. (It may well be that writers felt freer to let lesbians escape unscathed in a short piece, whereas a novel—more substantial, asking more commitment of its readers, and much more likely to be reviewed in detail—demanded a more orthodox apportioning of judgment.)

The title of Thomas Beer's startlingly relaxed story "Hallowe'en" (1927), for instance, suggests a time of riot and masquerade. It is through the calm eyes of a fat grandmother called Mrs. Egg that we see Sybil, nicknamed Bill, who is visiting the small town she left for San Francisco. Sybil/Bill mixes all her signals; she is a glamorous, chain-smoking, ex-army woman with a deep contralto voice, an Italian car, and several ex-husbands. Despite her exotic look (a long black dress, "a necklace of silver claws"), she has an unpretentious, slangy manner, so the local men call her "swell" and say things like "She's a gentleman." Mrs. Egg, deeply fond of Sybil in a motherly way, calls her the "only girl I ever saw look swell in pants."

On her brief visit, Sybil manages to stir up her hometown completely. Her dear old friend Janie has recently married a nice man called Tom but cannot seem to relax into being married. Finally Janie tells Mrs. Egg she is running away, not because of anything poor Tom has done but because "I love someone else more—more than anything. I'm running away. We can't help it." Only very slowly does Mrs. Egg realize that the dashing Sybil is the one who has won the girl. But when she does figure it out, not only does she not stop the two women from driving off to San Francisco, but she packs them a dozen sandwiches for the trip. Janie's husband is sad, but just as understanding; he even gets the suitcases down from the attic. So without spelling anything out very explicitly, this story manages to evoke a very modern world of love and tolerance. As a character tells Mrs. Egg, "There's stuff goes on you don't know nothin' like. Crazy stuff!"

Another devil-may-care lesbian woos another ingénue in the fifth chapter of Tiffany Thayer's *Thirteen Women* (1932), but this story is told much more cynically. Martha Viborg is a rich man's wife and also "just a drop in the bucket from the well of loneliness," as Thayer puts it, cheekily alluding to the novel banned four years earlier. Since Martha lives in Denver, Colorado, rather than, say, San Francisco, she has had to marry a doctor to provide a cover. Worldly and beautiful as well as "queer," Martha prides herself on the fact that "her affairs were always of the heart, and never vulgar, hurried gratifications." As the story begins, she sets out to awaken a frail, lovely innocent called Hazel Cousins. The narrator mocks all the participants in this comedy— "lady-lovers," as he calls them—but without malice. He refers to Martha's "condition" or "divergence from the norm," but refuses to give any explanations for it: "She doesn't know where she came from and your guess is as good as mine." He offers her seduction technique as a model to husbands.

It is a delight to watch Martha work. Detail! The girl is past-mistress of detail and nuance. It is a fortunate thing for the few of us men left in the metropolitan area that all dykes are not as gifted and intelligent as was Mrs Viborg. She had a different appeal for every different kind of woman she sought, and she knew exactly when the laying-on-of-hands was permissible.

The sex is so superb that Hazel—once she gets over her panic—falls madly in love, telling her mother on the phone, "I'm leaving at once for Mrs Viborg's. Goodnight." It will not be a long affair—since Hazel is wasting away from tuberculosis—but it is certainly a lively one.

Judy Gardiner's novella *Fidelia* (1967) has an equally satirical and upbeat but much more romantic tone. This cheeky tale starts with a declaration that Fidelia (Fido) and Matilda have been living as "man and wife" ever since their elopement, ten years ago, from their disapproving families. Sharing a crumbling house in the English countryside, "they worked and waltzed and made love" in complete happiness. That is, till Matilda says the fatal words, "Wouldn't it be nice if we could have a baby." Fido's surname—Denison—may hint that she will have to "deny" her "wife" a "son." When she calmly points out that "begetting" is one of the few manly skills she lacks, she upsets the sweetly delusional Matilda, who likes to think of herself as "married" and "respectable" and "like everyone else." The couple consider adoption, but find that they are disqualified because, as the form says, "No child can be placed in any form of irregular household." Fido, increasingly troubled by a craving for fatherhood, suggests that they take "a bash at this artificial insemination lark"—and they get as far as the doctor's office before Matilda loses her nerve and tells the doctor that what she's suffering from is earache.

Enter Fido's ne'er-do-well brother, Rupert, with his benevolent attitude toward the female couple's sex life. When Matilda demands—with no warning—that he service her, at first he is appalled at the notion of being used as a "rutting ram," but his big sister wins him over and persuades him to take Matilda off for the weekend to get her pregnant in a way that keeps it "in the family." Judy Gardiner has great fun with this situation: Fido suffers agonies of jealousy while the others are away, and the reader is well aware of the risk that she will have unwittingly set in motion the man-wins-woman-from-woman plot . . . but no, Matilda comes home and bursts into tears, explaining that it was so ghastly, she had to keep telling herself that she was a patient about to have an operation.

When Fido wants to know what the baby will call them, Matilda is surprised by the question, because to her the situation seems delight-fully ordinary: "I'll be mother, you'll be father." In this fairy-tale atmos-phere, they gradually allow themselves to forget that it was not their own lovemaking that conceived the baby. Waiting with the other fathers in the hospital, Fido is moved by a moment of solidarity with a bus driver who asks, "Your first?" It is not clear whether he is reading her as a man or a lesbian. The final hitch in the comedy is provided by Rupert's next visit, this time with his new wife, Vivien, who has no idea that his sister is what he flippantly calls a "practising lesbian." When she finds out about the conception, she goes into hysterics about this "unnatural vice," but her wrath has the effect of uniting Fido, Matilda, and Rupert as a happy trio who couldn't care less what anyone thinks. This hilarious novella, when it came out in 1967, anticipated the lesbian baby boom by two decades.

These carefree lesbians were outnumbered ten to one by their sui-cidal sisters in the literature of the first two-thirds of the twentieth cen-tury, but they did pave the way for the explosion of confident lesbian writing in the 1970s. Here the devil-may-care girl takes on a more politi-cized role as the "defiant lesbian hero," as Gabrielle Griffin puts it. Rita Mae Brown's *Rubyfruit Jungle* (1973), named for the female genitals, is said to be the best-selling lesbian novel ever. Cleverly combining a seri-ous quest story with comic exuberance, *Rubyfruit Jungle* follows its smart, beautiful, working-class, tomboy heroine Molly Bolt from sixth grade through an experimental adolescence.

> Me being a queer can't hurt anyone, why should it be such a terri-ble thing? Makes no sense. But I'm not gonna base my judgment on one little fuck with ole Leroy. We got to do it a lot more and maybe I'll do around twenty or thirty men and twenty or thirty women and then I'll decide. I wonder if I could get twenty people to go to bed with me?

By adulthood, Molly has decided she prefers women, but her fer-vently held preference for nonmonogamy means that this picaresque saga is never going to turn into a traditional romance. Despite her flip-pancy, her openness has many painful consequences: rejection by friends, expulsion from university, even a week locked up in a mental hospital. But what bothers her most is the sense of being narrowly defined.

> So now I wear this label "Queer" emblazoned across my chest. Or I could always carve a scarlet "L" on my forehead. Why does everyone have to put you in a box and nail the lid on it? I don't know what I am—polymorphous and perverse.

The echo of Nathaniel Hawthorne's *The Scarlet Letter* (1850)—in which the heroine is forced to wear a red A for "adulteress"—reminds us that Molly's struggle is a classic American one, a maverick's demand for life, liberty, and the pursuit of happiness. Early on, when one of her lovers is afraid they will be labeled as "lesbian," Molly reacts in a knee-jerk way: "No, we just love each other, that's all. Lesbians look like men and are ugly." But by the end of the book, living in New York, Molly has made peace with the labels issue, and come to certain lasting conclusions about herself: "I love women. I'll never marry a man and I'll never marry a woman either. That's not my way. I'm a devil-may-care lesbian." Many coming-out novels after *Rubyfruit Jungle* would adopt its lively formula of a young dyke kicking her way through society's obstacle course in pursuit of self-discovery and (maybe) love.

Sometimes the rebellion is political first (though, as the slogan goes, the personal is political). Often in women's-liberation fiction of the 1970s and '80s, feminism precedes—and opens the heroine's eyes to—desire for women. The stern mother of a newly out lesbian, in Valerie Miner's *Blood Sisters* (1982), "had known this would happen all along. Women's poetry. Women's music. It all led to women's bodies." Interestingly, these characters reach the point of loving women without necessarily renouncing men; their goal is an authentic freedom, however that is defined.

But many coming-out novels continued to follow *Rubyfruit Jungle* in narrating an individualistic quest. Jeanette Winterson's semi-autobiographical, playfully literary *Oranges Are Not the Only Fruit* (1985), written in a few weeks, won the Whitbread Award for Best First Novel. Raised as a missionary in the north of England by a fundamentalist Christian mother, the rebellious heroine Jeanette does not rebel against normality—because the way she is being raised (by a mother who

despises men and intends Jeanette to become a celibate missionary) is
anything but normal. Instead, the girl struggles to form a sense of self
that does not depend on anyone else's rules. When the elders of the
sect part her from her girlfriend and put her through a brutal two-day
exorcism of her "Unnatural Passion," Jeanette is tempted to give in. But
she figures out that if she gives up her so-called demons, she will lose
her self with them. "If I keep you, what will happen?" she asks the hal-
lucinatory "orange demon" who appears in her dark room. "You'll have
a difficult, different time," he promises her. No guaranteed happy ending, then, just an invitation to adventure that is, quite literally, devil-
may-care.

PLACES FOR US

We saw in chapter 3 that female pairs in fiction of the late nineteenth
and early twentieth centuries often long for "the beautiful house"—a
domestic haven that offers security and privacy for their love. In the
coming-out novel, this longing expands into a search for a place in
which a couple can go about their lives, and perhaps find a community
of the like-minded. "There must be others like us who can feel and love
and live together despite everything," the interracial couple tell themselves in Ann Allen Shockley's *Loving Her* (1974), the first openly lesbian novel by an African-American woman.

In Lillian Hellman's *The Children's Hour* (1934), Martha complains
fearfully that because she and Karen have been labeled as lesbians,
"There is not anywhere we can go." The reviewer from the *New York Sun*
raised an objection, very deadpan: "You immediately think of half a
dozen . . . including the city of New York." And indeed in fiction from
the 1950s on, as we saw in *Rubyfruit Jungle*, a move toward lesbian identity usually involves a flight from oppressive small-town mores to the
original queer ghetto—Greenwich Village.

Many of these novels are part of the publishing phenomenon of
lesbian pulp fiction, which reached a very broad readership in the 1950s
and '60s. Typically, their titles use code words for desire between
women (*Strange Fire, Odd Girl Out, Queer Affair*), and emphasize secrecy
and gloom (*Edge of Twilight, Love Like a Shadow, Women in the Shadows,
Shady Cloister, Women of Darkness*), taboo (*Forbidden Sex*), neurosis (*The

"*Le Sémiramis-Bar,*" *in* La Vie Parisienne *(March 27, 1909).*

This piece was the first of two that Colette published about a queer bar in 1909 in a risqué literary/humor magazine founded in 1863. "Now I will dare to inform you that while dining at Sémiramis's bar I enjoy watching the girls dancing together, they waltz well. They are not paid for this, but dance for pleasure between the cabbage soup and the beef stew . . ." The customers shown may all be women, too. The signature is not by any of the magazine's regular artists.

Strange Compulsion of Laura M.), experimentation (*Part-time Lez*), or simple wickedness (*The Mischief, Women of Evil*). Sometimes it is explained away as a matter of trauma (bad fathers, violent boyfriends) or environment (school, army, prison); often the right man can free the heroine from her trap. But the titles of certain pulp novels signal a more neutral or even upbeat coming-out narrative: *I Am a Woman, Journey to a Woman, Another Kind of Love, Love Is Where You Find It.* The first two are by Ann Bannon, the second two by Paula Christian, and this pair of authors—together with Valerie Taylor—stand out for their open-ended narratives (often in multivolume series) of young lesbians finding themselves by means of varied adventures in the liberating anonymity of New York, Los Angeles, or Paris. Gabriele Griffin makes the interesting generalization that tasteful literary writing of the 1950s and '60s often tried to win sympathy for lesbian characters by treating them as victims, whereas lowbrow pulp could be freer to assert the joys of sex and romance between women.

The city, and in particular the urban lesbian bar, often comes across as a sort of seedy haven—for lesbians, if not for lasting relationships. Maureen Duffy both celebrates and critiques a bar she calls House of Shades (based on London's famous Gateways) in her brilliantly dark and fractured novel *The Microcosm* (1966). Her central protagonist, Matt—one of several butches who go by "he" and refer to their "wives"—is a rueful Virgil, leading a *Purgatorio*-style tour of this micro-cosmic lesbian community. "He" compares it to an aquarium, with tourists ogling behind the glass, and to a rock pool where a multitude of creatures live who would be better off in the open sea. *The Microcosm* is very much of its era in its fretting over the origins of homosexuality, although by considering dozens of possibilities—biological and social as well as psychoanalytical—Duffy refuses to offer any one pat answer. But the book's lasting brilliance lies in the confidence of its narrative voice, or rather voices. This postmodernist polyphony moves among the denizens of the bar, many of whom have moved to London from small towns, and are familiar with the confinement of the closet as well as the different restrictions of the gay ghetto. At times *The Microcosm* roams even more widely, like some radio picking up transmissions of consciousness from past eras; for instance, without preamble Duffy reproduces almost thirty pages of Charlotte Cibber Charke's *Narrative of the Life* (1755), about a cross-dressed woman and her partner living from hand to mouth in a very different London. At one point, the nar-rator compares lesbians to "a lost tribe of aborigines buried deep in the heart of the social jungle" with a wall of sticks around their village, and suddenly the voice changes accordingly:

> But one full day come the lightime we stand up all together and go walk away too out of the stickwall and not sorry leave our thatches all fall down. Come to the city and man and woman, friends altogether, speak out loud along the tall houses and our young people sharp as knives put hands each on brother's shoul-der, say, "This too our people."
>
> Then we too live free among the tall houses, working our liv-ing, dancing the night of no work along the tall city peoples, unafraid, never go back to the stickwall.

At first glance this passage might seem to reinforce the lesbian myth of escape from rural misery to urban fulfillment. But once we remember that the "stickwall" is a metaphor for the urban lesbian bar scene, then the "city" in which "man and woman, friends altogether" can live freely but still "sharp as knives" in diversity reveals itself as, certainly not London circa 1966, but an imagined utopia: the city of dreams.

The cult of the city lingers in many lesbian fictions, such as Jane DeLynn's *Don Juan in the Village* (1988). But from the 1970s on, the longed-for destination was often a rural one. The lesbian-feminist movement of the '70s, influenced by hippie culture, entwined the notions of women's love and nature.

In this fiction, the rural locale is sometimes literal—the place where women fall in love—but more often a dream of female collectivity. For instance, Su in June Arnold's highly original *Sister Gin* (1975)—an alcoholic in her forties who gives up the respectability of the closet when she joins a vigilante group to punish rapists—dreams of "all women . . . in a field of brilliant green, buoyed up by unbelievable green—gathered in a giant sweep all yellow and blue and scooped it into one untouchable safe sea of women." The hope for a female haven moved into science fiction, utopia and dystopia, producing such titles as Monique Wittig's *Les Guérillères* (1969), Joanna Russ's *The Female Man* (1975), Suzy McKee Charnas's *Motherlines* (1978), and Katherine V. Forrest's *Daughters of a Coral Dawn* (1984). One of the best-known examples is Sally Miller Gearhart's *The Wanderground* (1978), in which nature has revolted against men by causing their machines to grind to a halt, and the nurturing, psychic "hillwomen" have escaped from the city to found their own idyllic settlement.

But perhaps the most fertile genre for the coming-out story in the past three decades has been historical fiction. The first lesbian historical novel is still one of the best: *Patience and Sarah*, as it is now known, was initially self-published and sold copy by copy out of a paper bag by "Isabel Miller" (Alma Routsong) under the significant title *A Place for Us*. It is also one of the best examples of the motif of a lesbian rural haven. This tough-minded romance was inspired by a real female couple, artist Miss Willson and her companion Miss Brundidge, who farmed in New York State circa 1820. Paradoxically, it was the lack of historical sources, the fact that Isabel Miller was having to invent a form of credible passion between early-nineteenth-century women, that gave the novel its clean lines and the lasting force of legend.

Sarah, a tough tomboy who wears trousers to work as her father's "boy," has a grand plan: "I figure to take up land and make me a place."

She means land acquisition by homesteading, but it is also a bolder and more symbolic project of making a place in the world, rather than merely creeping into some corner. However, Patience, her older and more womanly spinster neighbor, is the one who actually plots their escape from Connecticut and family ties. The gender difference between Sarah and Patience is the tinder spark, the thing that forces them to notice their attraction and act on it instead of sublimating it into romantic friendship. Sarah decides that it was learning to shoot a gun that did it for her: "I could take care of myself, and not be beholden, and love who my feeling went to. I suppose lots of girls loved Patience but never said. Maybe it was because I could shoot that I could say." But Patience is a rebel against some of the rules of femininity too; though she likes to sew and bake, she would rather paint pictures than sit around spinning or have babies. Gender itself must be made new in this tale of transformation: "I began to wonder if what makes men walk so lordlike and speak so masterfully is having the love of women," thinks Patience. "If that was it, Sarah and I would make lords of each other." The lovers are similar in as many ways as they are different, and throughout the book they swap roles: reckless leader and doubtful follower, greedy and cautious, seducer and resister. As an orthodox goer-to-Meeting, at one point Patience gets down on her knees to fight her desire and ends up praying for its fulfillment instead. She decides she and Sarah can be "an army of two . . . Let the world either kill us or grow accustomed to us: here we stand."

The novel's cadences are often biblical. Here is Patience on the boat:

> I held Sarah's hand and felt the ancient sea and the new wheels carry us to a life we had no pattern for, that no one we knew of had ever lived, that we must invent for ourselves on a razor's edge, and I tipped my head back and sang three hallelujahs.

Their dreams get modified; instead of going out west, which is both expensive and dangerous, they settle for the much nearer Greene County, only ninety miles from New York City—and it is indeed a "green country" to them, in the sense of the green world of Shakespearean comedy. Their real hunger is not for land but for autonomy and privacy; ultimately it is in the emotional rather than the literal sense that this is a pioneer story. Isabel Miller intended a sequel, to be called *A Time for Us,* which would have shown the women's "slow, ardent, exalted life" in detail—but writer's block got in the way. This is unsurprising, and perhaps even fortunate—because once the "place for us" is found and secured, the dramatic story is over.

Patience and Sarah was enormously influential, both on lesbian-feminist fiction in general and historical titles in particular. Many authors have followed Miller's pattern of a butch and a femme finding themselves through finding each other, and going on a quest for a place where they can settle. Interestingly, it is usually the womanly woman who is more aware and accepting of her desire, and takes the initiative in seducing the masculine one; this keeps a balance of power. One example that reached a wide mainstream audience is Fannie Flagg's *Fried Green Tomatoes at the Whistlestop Café* (1987), which presents itself disarmingly as the tale of a wonderful café, a haven from southern racism, but the real story is that of its founders in 1920s Alabama: a battered wife and the tomboy she has always loved, who go into business and raise their son with the full support of the tomboy's family. (And when the husband turns up, incidentally, they kill him and serve him as BBQ.)

The butch-femme romance is not necessarily realistic, since there is little evidence in the historical record of visibly gender-polarized lesbian couples before the late nineteenth century, and they do not seem to have been the norm except in the 1950s and '60s. Perhaps this pairing should be read as an allegory of the whole business of discovering a lesbian past; as a symbolic marriage between the femme (imagined as discreetly seeking freedom within women's roles and women's inseparable friendship) and the butch (imagined as playing the female bridegroom, or usurping male privilege in any other way she can).

These fictions, though usually conventional enough in their writing, are often highly self-conscious about their intervention in lesbian history-making. Byrony Lavery's pastiche play *Her Aching Heart* (1991), for instance, hilariously intercuts between two lovers and their nineteenth-century equivalents (booted lady of the manor and peasant girl) in a melodramatic romance the modern pair are reading. Sometimes the research process itself becomes the most thrilling plotline, as historical fiction comments on its own creation. In several novels, women are contacted by the urgent ghosts of their lesbian ancestors. One of the smartest such stories is Paula Martinac's *Out of Time* (1990), in which Harriet, a dead actress, picks Susan to help her come out posthumously, by editing and publishing a memoir of Harriet's lively, quarrelsome, early-twentieth-century "Gang." When the ghost turns seductive, Susan is reluctant to cheat on her girfriend, but Harriet gives her a tongue-in-cheek excuse: "It's for your education. Tell yourself it's for history!" The fact that Susan's girlfriend is a graduate student in women's history, who rather disapproves of Susan's amateurish interest in the Gang, may be Martinac's sly nod to the tensions between orthodox scholarship and the resurrections of fiction.

A similar self-consciousness marks Sarah Waters's 1998 first novel, *Tipping the Velvet* (named for Victorian slang for cunnilingus). While working on her PhD on lesbian and gay historical fiction, Waters decided to write a story that would reimagine the lesbian past, free from the limitations of how it probably was. Here there is no rural haven, but a range of vivid, crowded settings (from an oyster shop to music halls to the world of rent boys) through which the picaresque, sometimes cross-dressing heroine moves, finding different ways to live out her desires. Inspired more by her readings in nineteenth-century porn than by the *Patience and Sarah* mold of earnest, isolated romance, Waters presents identity as performative, and invents plausible communities ranging from a decadent Sapphist club to a network of working-class "toms."

Ultimately the quest for "a place for us" is not about geography but about cultural space: it is an attempt to make more visible the thread of desire between women that winds right through Western history, and Western literature.

Not every reader, or writer, wants that thread to stand out from the cloth. Sometimes it seems as if to identify an erotic preference is to stigmatize it, to consign it to the bargain bin of fetishes. This explains what we might call the antilabel strain in lesbian fiction. Having one's orientation identified in words is almost inevitably presented as traumatic. In Sybille Bedford's *A Compass Error* (1968), for instance, an older woman throws the "terms" at the seventeen-year-old heroine like knives.

"Is your mother aware of your . . . deviationist tastes? Don't frown. I can use other terms, there is quite a choice, classical, medical, contemporary. Let's try if you've heard of any of them." She did. "You don't like that one? Does your mother know that it applies to you? Answer me!"

"I don't think I knew myself."

Here, the words are all the more potent because Bedford does not write them down: readers will insert the labels they dread the most.

The defiant lesbian hero rarely wants to be called that . . . or anything, in fact. Molly Bolt in *Rubyfruit Jungle* (1973) is typical in being honest about her feelings for women, while itching to rip off "this label 'Queer' emblazoned across my chest." Her complaint is echoed in many lesbian novels, as well as in queer culture more generally, where the slogan "Closets Are for Clothes, Not for People" was soon followed by "Labels Are for Clothes, Not for People." In Ali Smith's clever contemporary version of Ovid's Iphis story, *Girl Meets Boy* (2007), when asked what "the proper word" for her is, Robin corrects the question: "The proper name for me . . . is me."

A similar note is often heard, too, in protests against the absurdity of dividing relationships into same-sex and opposite-sex camps. "Love is love," protests the teenage Louise in *Regiment of Women* (1917); *Either Is Love* insists the title of Elizabeth Craigin's fictionalized memoir of 1937. "What does it matter who you love?" laments the schoolteacher heroine of a Norwegian novel, Ebba Haslund's *Det hendte ingenting* (1948; in English, *Nothing Happened*), regretting how ashamed she felt of being in love with a woman who has since died. Many novelists seem to feel torn, wishing that it did not "matter" whether their protagonists fall for men or women, but trying to write truthfully about a world in which it does.

The coming-out novel is alive and well after more than a century, but it only really works in settings where coming out is still an alarming business. Lucy Jane Bledsoe's crafty *Working Parts* (1997; winner of the Stonewall Award), for instance, is about a lesbian bike mechanic in San Francisco slowly and painfully coming out as . . . illiterate. Times change, and so do stories.

But in considering the long tradition of Western literature, we can hardly escape the conclusion that whether or not it *should* matter whether you love a man or a woman, it *has* mattered very much, which is why I have written *Inseparable*.

Julie Abraham in *Are Girls Necessary? Lesbian Writing and Modern Histories* (1996) pours scorn on twentieth-century lesbian novels as mere "formula fictions based on the heterosexual plot," since they always represent a relationship between two women as either an imitation of or a deviation from a male-female relationship. At best she sees this tradition as "a history of refinements, extensions and challenges to a formula." But how else do ideas grow except by refining, extending, or challenging the old ones?

Yes, like all writing and even more than most, writing about desire between women is derivative (or, put more positively, intertextual). It reworks ancient motifs of quest, obstacle, rivalry, disguise, and fall, using and combining such genres as comedy, tragedy, romance, the crime story, the coming-of-age novel. The literature of love between women overlaps with the literature of the family, the nation, the school, the brothel, the factory, the library, the farm, the city, the car, and so on. And, of course, it overlaps with the literature of desire between men and women. If in some stories same-sex relationships stand in furious resistance to opposite-sex ones, in other works they are parallel or entwined with them, and in all these cases the connection is a tight one. The "lesbian idea" is not necessarily *non-* or *anti*heterosexual; in Western literature, these forms of love are all inseparable.

ACKNOWLEDGMENTS

I would like to thank my UK agent, Caroline Davidson, and my editor, Victoria Wilson, for their incalculable contributions to this project over the years.

NOTES

Introduction

4 "a minor subsidiary": "Angela DuMaurier's The Little Less," *New York Times*, August 17, 1941.

5 Although I occasionally say "lesbian": For brevity, I mostly use "same-sex" or "between women." The field of GLBTQ (gay/lesbian/bisexual/trans/queer) studies has been bedeviled by bickering over terminology. Some critics prefer terms that they see as more careful than "lesbian" (*lesbian-like, proto-lesbian, lesbian continuum, an early modern analogue to lesbianism as we know it*) or broader (*female intimacy, female homoeroticism, female same-sex eroticism or sexuality, female erotic friendship, practices that transgress heteronormativity, non-normative female same-sex erotics, same-sex sexual transgression, same-sex erotic affectivity, queer*). Others prefer those that seem more specific to a time and literary model (*hermaphrodite, tribade, amity/amitié, romantic friendhip, Sapphist, tommy, invert, female homosexual, lesbian-feminist,* and, again, *queer*). In the ongoing controversy known as essentialism vs. social constructionism, both extremes seem to me to verge on silliness ("Joan of Arc was a dyke" vs. "lesbianism was invented in the late nineteenth century"). In that I have found it interesting to juxtapose writings about desire between women from a period of about eight hundred years, I probably count as an essentialist, but I hope not a silly one.

5 Dating from 1977: Matthew Sweet, *Inventing the Victorians* (London: Faber, 2001), 199.

6 In writing *Inseparable:* My focus on plot means I leave out some prose classics such as Virginia Woolf's *Orlando* (1928) or Djuna Barnes's *Nightwood* (1937), as well as most poetry and almost all erotica. Nor do I include such nonfiction genres as life writing or medical or travel literature. Outside of English and French I have only been able to read what I have found in translation.

6 A hint or a glimpse: Of course, what is known as symptomatic reading or subtexting can produce some intriguing results, expecially in the case of works such as Charlotte Brontë's *Villette* (1853), in which eroticism between women is a matter of innuendo rather than plot. But like Terry Castle—see her introduction to *The Literature of Lesbianism: A Historical Anthology from Ariosto to Stonewall* (New York: Columbia University Press, 2003), 47–48—I find the still-dominant emphasis on the absence/invisibility/silence/erasure

of desire between women more than a little absurd, considering the
abundance of literature on the subject.

6 "Hermengyld loved hire": Geoffrey Chaucer, "The Man of Law's Tale" [1400],
   in *The Complete Works of Geoffrey Chaucer*, ed. F. N. Robinson (Oxford: Oxford
   University Press, 1974), 62–75 (lines 535, 625–26). This popular late medieval
   story is known as the Constance saga; Chaucer seems to have borrowed it
   from a translation of Nicholas Trivet's *Anglo-Norman Chronicle* (c. 1335), but it
   also shows up in the *Vita Offae Primi* (1100s), the *Gesta Romanorum* (c. 1350), the
   Middle English romance *Emaré*, John Gower's *Confessio Amantis* (1386–90),
   and in French, Spanish, German, Italian, Arabic, Persian, and Latin texts.

7 Because of the time frame: After Sappho, the first female author I deal with is
   Marie de France in the twelfth century; women did not enter the writing
   profession in large numbers until the eighteenth. The first American text I
   discuss is Charles Brockden Brown's novel *Ormond* (1799).

7 For the purposes of this book: Writing *by* lesbians is a whole other subject.
   Because I am focusing on the origin and development of plot motifs, I spend
   a lot more ink on, say, Renaissance plays than on the explosion of writing by
   diverse lesbian authors since the 1970s. Lesbian writing is sometimes defined
   more broadly as woman-centered writing by women, or even work by any
   writer (male or female) that disrupts the linear, patriarchal conventions of a
   form such as the novel—but to my mind, calling James Joyce a lesbian writer
   renders the term rather meaningless. Marilyn R. Farwell offers a useful
   analysis of this debate in *Heterosexual Narratives and Lesbian Plots* (New York:
   New York University Press, 1996), 4–19.

7 "On the one hand, there were Lakey-and-Maria": Mary McCarthy, *The Group*
   [1963] (New York: Avon, 1980), 392.

8 In 1921: *Parliamentary Debates* (House of Commons), Criminal Law
   Amendment Bill, August 4, 1921, para. 1799–1806.

9 If all writing is intertextual: Elaine Marks seems to have been the first to
   name the phenomenon in her groundbreaking essay on literary modes; see
   "Lesbian Intertextuality," in *Homosexuality and French Literature*, ed. Elaine
   Marks and George Stambolian (Ithaca, N.Y.: Cornell University Press, 1979),
   353–77 (356).

9 "virtually every author": Castle, introduction to *The Literature of Lesbianism*, 7.

9 "Freud envisions": Judith Roof, *Come as You Are: Sexuality and Narrative* (New
   York: Columbia University Press, 1996), xiv.

10 Also, novelists and playwrights often seem: Lesbianism is "ghosted" or
   "spectralized" and banished from the world of many fictions, but lingers to
   haunt them, Terry Castle argues in *The Apparitional Lesbian: Female
   Homosexuality and Modern Culture* (New York: Columbia University Press,
   1993), 28–65.

10 "It was perceived by the servants": Thomas Hardy, *Desperate Remedies* [1871]
   (London: Macmillan, 1912), 129.

10 "Damnit": Shirley Jackson, quoted in Judy Oppenheimer, *Private Demons: The Life of Shirley Jackson* (New York: Fawcett, 1988), 232–33.

10 "The booking troubles": Quoted in Kaier Curtin, *"We Can Always Call Them Bulgarians": The Emergence of Lesbians and Gay Men on the American Stage* (Boston: Alyson, 1987), 272.

11 "Dear, dear!": "O. Henry" (William Sydney Porter), "The Last Leaf" [1906], in *The World of O. Henry: The Furnished Room and Other Stories* (London: Hodder and Stoughton, 1974), 490–96 (495).

12 Jean-Pierre Jacques: Jean-Pierre Jacques, *Les Malheurs de Sapho* (1981), quoted by Christopher Rivers in "Inintelligibles pour une femme honnête: Sexuality, Textuality and Knowledge in Diderot's 'La Religieuse' and Gautier's 'Mademoiselle de Maupin,' " *The Romanic Review* 86:1 (January 1995): 1–29 (1).

12 "Why would playwrights": Denise Walen, *Constructions of Female Homoeroticism in Early Modern Drama* (New York: Palgrave Macmillan, 2005), 3.

13 "with an audible sigh of relief": Bonnie Zimmerman, "Is 'Chloe Likes Olivia' a Lesian Plot?," *Women's Studies International Forum* 6 (1983): 171.

13 What I hope to show: Sharon Marcus in *Between Women: Friendship, Desire and Marriage in Victorian England* (Princeton, N.J.: Princeton University Press, 2007) breaks new ground in the fine distinctions—as well as connections— she draws between various forms of Victorian voyeurism, friendship, flirtation, dominance, and unreciprocated and marital-style love between women.

13 "hungry little bird": Anon., "To C.," in Peter Dronke, *Medieval Latin and the Rise of European Love-Lyric* (Oxford: Clarendon Press, 1965), 101–2.

14 Nor do I think it particularly helpful: In an influential 1981 essay on twentieth-century fictions, Catharine R. Stimpson contrasts the "dying fall" narrative of lesbian damnation with the "ennabling escape" which brings self-acceptance; see "Zero Degree Deviancy: The Lesbian Novel in English," *Critical Inquiry* 8 (Winter 1981): 363–80. Similarly, see Terry Castle on the "euphoric" vs. the "dysphoric" plot in *The Apparitional Lesbian*, 85–86. In her introduction to *The Literature of Lesbianism* (20–27), Castle draws a more interesting distinction between what she calls the Sapphic or sublime mode of writing about desire between women, and the Roman or satiric mode.

14 The first is that it was in the sixteenth century: Castle, introduction to *The Literature of Lesbianism*, 11–13; Harriette Andreadis, *Sappho in Early Modern England: Female Same-Sex Literary Erotics, 1550–1714* (Chicago: University of Chicago Press, 2001), 15; and Valerie Traub, *The Renaissance of Lesbianism in Early Modern England* (Cambridge: Cambridge University Press, 2002).

14 As Peter Cryle comments: Peter Cryle, *The Telling of the Act: Sexuality as Narrative in Eighteenth- and Nineteenth-Century France* (Newark: University of Delaware Press, and London: Associated University Presses, 2001), 311.

15 Factors in the spread: Lillian Faderman, *Surpassing the Love of Men: Romantic Friendship and Love Between Women from the Renaissance to the Present* [1981]

(London: Women's Press, 1985), 297–99; Marcus, *Between Women*, 261; Sherrie Inness, *The Lesbian Menace: Ideology, Identity and the Representation of Lesbian Life* (Amherst: University of Massachusetts Press, 1997), 66.

15 "differing depictions": Walen, *Constructions of Female Homoeroticism*, 149.

15 "the historical search": Eve Sedgwick, *Epistemology of the Closet* (Berkeley: University of California Press, 1990), 44, 47. David Michael Robinson comes to the same conclusion about continuity; see "The Metamorphosis of Sex(uality): Ovid's 'Iphis and Ianthe' in the Seventeenth and Eighteenth Centuries," in *Presenting Gender: Changing Sex in Early-Modern Culture*, ed. Chris Mounsey (Lewisburg, Pa.: Bucknell University Press, and London: Associated University Presses, 2001), 171–201.

Chapter One: Travesties

17 "transvestite theatre": Marjorie Garber, V*ested Interests: Cross-Dressing and Cultural Anxiety* (London: Routledge, 1992), 39. See also Laurence Senelick's *The Changing Room: Sex, Drag and Theatre* (London: Routledge, 2000), which studies cross-dressing in many forms of performance across cultures and time.

17 Since all the roles: On the viewer's simultaneous awareness of all these levels, see Michael Shapiro, *Gender in Play on the Shakespearean Stage: Boy Heroines and Female Pages* (Ann Arbor: University of Michigan Press, 1994), 4–5.

17 "an ideal in which the erotic charge": Winfried Schleiner, "Le feu caché: Homosocial Bonds Between Women in a Renaissance Romance," *Renaissance Quarterly* 45:2 (Summer 1992): 293–311 (296).

18 A helpful mnemonic: In Isaac Bashevis Singer's story "Yentl the Yeshiva Boy," a girl passing as a boy marries a naïve girl and, the author tells us enigmatically, finds "a way to deflower the bride" before running away; see *Short Friday and Other Stories* (New York: Fawcett, 1978), 131–59 (149). The 1983 film *Yentl* starring Barbra Streisand replaces the deflowering with a spilled glass of wine to fool the families. In *Tootsie* (1982), Dustin Hoffman plays an actor who puts on drag to land a TV role as a prim middle-aged spinster, then falls for his female co-star.

18 Marjorie Garber has argued: Garber, *Vested Interests*, 9.

19 "Women in seventeenth-century literature": Joseph Harris, *Hidden Agendas: Cross-Dressing in 17th-Century France* (Biblio 17, 156) (Tübingen: Gunter Narr Verlag, 2005), 102.

19 Passionate attraction: Valerie Traub, *The Renaissance of Lesbianism in Early Modern England* (Cambridge: Cambridge University Press, 2002), 6.

19 In both drama and prose: For instance, in the romance that was Shakespeare's main source for *As You Like It*, Thomas Lodge's *Rosalynde* [1590], 2nd ed. [1592], facsimile reprint (Menston, U.K.: The Scholar Press, 1972), no page numbers.

19 "something in cross-dressing": Harris, *Hidden Agendas*, 125.

19 In Aelfric's *Lives of Saints:* Aelfric, "Saint Eugenia," in *Lives of Saints* [990s],
     ed. Walter W. Skeat (London: Oxford University Press, 1966), 24–50. The
     accusation of rape by a rejected woman is known as the Potiphar's Wife motif
     (see Genesis 39); it shows up in later works such as Pierre-Corneille
     Blessebois's tragedy *Eugénie* (1676).

19 For the last thousand years: Examples include Heldris de Cornuälle, *Le
     Roman de Silence* (1200s); Anon., *Le Roman de Cassidorus* (c. 1270, part of the
     cycle *Les Sept Sages de Rome*); Giovanni Fiorentino, *Il Pecorone* (1300s); Anon.,
     Miracle de Théodore (1300s); Giovanni Francesco Straparola, *Piacevoli Notte*
     (1550); Matteo Bandello, *Novelle* (1554); Jean-Pierre Camus, *L'Iphigene* (1625);
     Giambattista Basile, *Il Pentamerone* (1634).

21 "Iphis loved a girl": Ovid, *Metamorphoses*, trans. Mary M. Innes
     (Harmondsworth, U.K.: Penguin, 1955), 221–24. David Robinson offers very
     interesting readings of this and other tales by Ovid alongside seventeenth-
     and eighteenth-century texts in *Closeted Writing and Lesbian and Gay Literature:
     Classical, Early Modern, Eighteenth-Century* (Aldershot, U.K.: Ashgate
     Publishing, 2006). The story gets a charming commentary in Ali Smith's novel
     of contemporary Inverness (part of Canongate's *The Myths* series), *Girl Meets
     Boy* (Edinburgh: Canongate, 2007), 82–101.

21 Without the benefit of modern biology: Bruce Bagemihl, *Biological
     Exuberance: Animal Homosexuality and Natural Diversity* (New York: St.
     Martin's Press, 1999).

22 The Iphis story was radically reworked: Anon., *La Chanson d'Yde et Olive*
     [before 1311], trans. Lord Berners, in *The Ancient, Honorable, Famous, and
     delightfull Historie of Huon of Bordeaux* [c. 1534], 3rd ed. (London: for Edward
     White, 1601), chapters 167–70, no page numbers. This brilliant work has
     received very little attention till recently; see Anna Roberts, *Queer Love in the
     Middle Ages* (Basingstoke, U.K.: Palgrave Macmillan, 2005).

22 *Ide and Olive:* This popular fairy-tale motif is found in, for instance, Perrault's
     "Donkeyskin."

22 Interestingly, three other medieval romances: See Michele Szkilnik, "The
     Grammar of the Sexes in Medieval French Romance," in *Gender Transgressions:
     Crossing the Normative Barrier in Old French Literature*, ed. Karen J. Taylor (New
     York: Garland Publishing, 1998), 61–89 (67).

22 Joseph Harris shows: Harris, *Hidden Agendas*, 166–67.

23 "I will wed her": By contrast, the disguised heroine in *Tristan de Nanteuil* stalls
     by insisting her bride convert from Islam to Christianity.

23 She makes the traditional claim: In the anonymous fourteenth-century
     Roman d'Ysaïe le Triste, "he" explains that "he" is not "equipped as a man and
     does not perform what Nature requires and neither do his brothers"—which
     begs the question of how impotence can be hereditary. See *Roman d'Ysaïe le
     Triste*, ed. André Giacchetti (Rouen: Press of the University of Rouen, 1989),
     179. Translation by Emma Donoghue.

24 Intriguingly, their crime: Diane Watt, "Behaving Like a Man? Incest, Lesbian Desire, and Gender Play in *Yde et Olive* and Its Adaptations," *Comparative Literature*, 50:4 (Autumn 1998): 265–85.

24 *Ide and Olive* may have been shocking: Robert L. A. Clark, "A Heroine's Sexual Itinerary: Incest, Transvestism and Same-Sex Marriage in *Yde et Olive*," in *Gender Transgressions*, ed. Taylor, 89–105 (97).

25 But his basic impulse: Vergil, Eclogues X.69: *Omnia vincit amor et nos cedamus amori* (Love conquers all; let us all yield to love).

25 "too innocent": Isaac de Benserade, *Iphis et Iante* [1637], ed. Anne Verdier with Christian Biet and Lise Leibacher-Ouvrard (Vijon: Editions Lampasque/Desclée de Brouwer, 2000), 52 (I.iv.: Ils sont brulés tous deux d'un feu trop légitime, / Et sont trop innocents pour savoir faire un crime), 55 (II.i.: "Un saint hymen succède à cet amour bouffon"). All translations from *Iphis et Iante* by Emma Donoghue.

26 "do the impossible for her": Benserade, *Iphis et Iante*, 74 (II.vi., "Quoi, je m'endormirais auprès de cette belle, / Et je ne ferais pas l'impossible pour elle?"), 93 (IV.i., "Je meure de soif auprès d'une fontaine").

26 "Possessing her": Benserade, *Iphis et Iante*, 112–13 (V.iv., "Son mécontentement me donnait du souci, / Mais la possession me ravissait aussi, / Et quique mon ardeur nous fut fort inutile, / J'oubliais quelque temps que j'étais une fille. / Je ne reçus jamais tant de contentements, / Je me laissais aller à mes ravissements, / D'un baiser j'apaisais mon amoureuse fièvre, / Et mon âme venait jusqu'au bord de mes lèvres, / Dans le doux sentiment de ces biens superflus / J'oubliais celui même où j'aspirais de plus, / J'embrassais ce beau corps, dont la blancheur extreme / M'excitait à lui faire une place en moi-même, / Je touchais, je baisais, j'avais le coeur content." "Honteuse de se voir la femme d'une fille.") Another play in which the female bridegroom cannot bear to break the news until she and her bride are in bed is G. Gilbert's *Les Intrigues amoureuses* (1667; in English, *The Love Intrigues*).

27 "This marriage is sweet": Benserade, *Iphis et Iante*, 105 (V.i., "Ce marriage est doux, j'y trouve aussez d'appâts / Et si l'on n'en riait, je ne m'en plaindrais pas," "Sans offenser le ciel et la loi naturelle").

27 *Iphis et Iante* is an odd play: See Marianne Legault, "Iphis & Iante: traumatisme de l'incomplétude lesbienne au Grand Siècle," in *Representations of Trauma in French and Francophone Literature*, ed. Nicole Simek and Zahi Zalloua, *Dalhousie French Studies* 81 (Winter 2007): 83–93.

27 "I will make their paines": John Lyly, *Gallathea 1592* (Malone Society Reprints, no. 161) (Oxford: Oxford University Press, 1998), 29, 41. Theodora A. Jankowski offers a good reading of the situation in *Pure Resistance: Queer Virginity in Early Modern English Drama* (Philadelphia: University of Pennsylvania Press, 2000), 14–27.

28 "You must leave these fond affections": Lyly, *Gallathea*, 52–53.

29 Sometimes the deceived woman: Denise Walen, *Constructions of Female*

Homoeroticism in Early Modern Drama (New York: Palgrave Macmillan, 2005), 58. On punishment of the mistaken women, see Harris, *Hidden Agendas*, 168.

30 "Make me a willow cabin": William Shakespeare, *Twelfth Night* [pub. 1623], in *The Complete Works of William Shakespeare*, ed. Peter Alexander (London: Collins, 1978), 349–76 (355, I.v.252–60). Terry Castle points out that because of Shakespeare's play, "After *Sappho* and *Diana*, *Olivia* is perhaps the most 'lesbian-sounding' name one can give a female character in English literature"; see *The Literature of Lesbianism: A Historical Anthology from Ariosto to Stonewall* (New York: Columbia University Press, 2003), 100.

30 "The virtuous Oronce": Anon., *Amadis de Gaule*, XX:213v, translated in Schleiner, "Le feu caché," 301.

30 "What thriftless sighs": Shakespeare, *Twelfth Night*, 356 (II.ii.37). Similarly, the widow in Barnaby Rich's tale "Apolonius" (1581) has no hope of "recompence" for her desires; see *Rich's Farewell to Military Profession* [1581], ed. Thomas Mabry Cranfill (Austin: University of Texas Press, 1959), 75.

31 "I pitty both of you": Abraham Cowley, *Love's Riddle* (London: for Henry Seile, 1638), I.i., II.i.

31 Cowley's play: The best example is a joke about "a flat bargaine" (alluding to a slang phrase for lesbian sex, "the game of flats") in Richard Brome, *The Mad Couple Well Matched* [1653], in *The Dramatic Works* (London: John Pearson, 1873), 1:1–99 (96). See also Thomas Middleton and John Webster's *Anything for a Quiet Life* (1620–21).

31 As Joseph Harris points out: Harris, *Hidden Agendas*, 51.

31 "If sight and shape be true": William Shakespeare, *As You Like It* [pub. 1623], in *The Complete Works of William Shakespeare*, ed. Peter Alexander (London: Collins, 1978), 254–83 (III.v. and V.iv., 273, 282).

32 In the twentieth volume: Anon., *Amadis de Gaule,*, XX:211v (misnumbered 122v in the original), 319–319v, translated and discussed in Schleiner, "Le feu caché," 303: Schleiner argues that Licinie's "shudder" here has "proto-features of homophobia."

32 In some plays: John Ford, *The Lover's Melancholy* [1629], ed. R. F. Hill (Manchester, U.K.: Manchester University Press, 1985), 71, 103, 108–9, 106. See Walen, *Constructions of Female Homoeroticism*, 84–85.

32 "Madame": Anon., *Amadis de Gaule*, XXI: 148v, translated and discussed in Schleiner, "Le feu caché," 306.

33 "Blush, greeve and die": Robert Greene, *James the Fourth* [1598], in *The Plays and Poems of Robert Greene*, ed. J. Churton Collins, 2 vols. (Oxford: Clarendon, 1905), 2:79–158 (150). I have modernized the spelling here from *u* to *v* and from *i* to *j*. Another character who admits to painful difficulty in converting desire to friendship is Bellula in Cowley's *Love's Riddle* (1638).

34 "In passed times": Ludovico Ariosto, *Orlando Furioso* [1516–32], trans. John Harrington [1591], ed. Robert McNulty (Oxford: Clarendon, 1972), 279–83 (Canto 29, v.21–54). For a full and subtle reading of the Fiordispina episode,

see Mary-Michelle DeCoste, "Knots of Desire: Female Homoeroticism in *Orlando furioso* 25," in *Queer Italia: Same-Sex Desire in Italian Literature and Film*, ed. Gary P. Cestaro (New York: Palgrave Macmillan, 2004), 55–70. The English poet Edmund Spenser borrowed but rather deeroticized the episode for his epic poem *The Faerie Queene* (1589–96).

35 The substitute-brother ending: Interestingly, it is not always necessary for the bride to be tricked; sometimes, as in Barnaby Rich's tale "Apolonius" (1581), on learning that her beloved is female, she makes the best of it and accepts the cross-dresser's brother as a substitute.

35 Often, as in the case: Anon., *Gl'Ingannati* [1537], fragmentary translation by Thomas Love Peacock published as *Gl'Ingannati: The Deceived* [1862] in *The Works* [1875] (New York: AMS Press, 1967), X, 231–324.

35 "I lov'd you well": Thomas Middleton, *No Wit, No Help like a Woman's* [written c. 1611, pub. 1653], ed. Lowell E. Johnson, Regents Renaissance Drama Series (Lincoln: University of Nebraska Press, 1976), V.ii.369–70.

36 "A sister!": Shakespeare, *Twelfth Night*, V.i. 374–75.

36 But Denise Walen argues: Walen, *Constructions of Female Homoeroticism*, 60.

36 The motif of the female bridegroom: Examples I lack space to discuss include Lording Barry, *Ram Alley* (1611); John Fletcher, *Love's Pilgrimage* (1616); Peter Hausted, *The Rival Friends* (1632); Shackerly Marmion, *The Antiquary* (1634–36); James Shirley, *The Sisters* (1642); Margaret Cavendish, *Love's Adventures* (1658); Robert Stapylton, *The Slighted Maid* (1663); William Killigrew, *The Siege of Urbin* (1666); Thomas Betterton, *The Counterfeit Bridegroom* (1677); William Wycherley, *The Plain Dealer* (1677); Thomas Corneille and Jean Donneau de Visé, *La Devineresse* (1678); Thomas Shadwell, *The Woman Captain* (1680); Aphra Behn, *The Widow Ranter* (1689) and *The Younger Brother* (1696); Thomas Southerne, *Sir Anthony Love* (1690) and *Oroonoko* (1695); George Farquhar, *Love and a Bottle* (1698) and *The Recruiting Officer* (1706); William Burnaby, *The Ladies Visiting-Day* (1701); Colley Cibber, *She Would and She Wou'd Not* (1702) and *The Lady's Last Stake* (1707); Richard Steele, *The Tender Husband* (1705); William Taverner, *The Artful Husband* (1717); Eliza Haywood, *A Wife to Be Lett* (1723); George Colman the Elder, *The Female Chevalier* (1778); Alicia Sheridan, *Ambiguous Love* (1781); Baroness Craven, *The Miniature Picture* (1781); Hannah Cowley, *A Bold Stroke for a Husband* (1783); William Macready, *The Bank Note* (1795); William Mason, *Sappho* (1797).

36 "would love to be forced": "Voudroit bien se voir un peu forcée," IV.ii. quoted in Harris, *Hidden Agendas*, 51.

36 A novelty in Jacobean treatments: Examples of this delayed revelation include George Chapman, *May Day* (1601); Thomas Middleton, *No Wit, No Help Like a Woman's* (performed c. 1611) and *The Widow* (performed c. 1616); *Anything for a Quiet Life* (1620–21), by Middleton and John Webster.

36 In Margaret Cavendish's *Matrimonial Trouble*: Margaret Cavendish, *Matrimonial Trouble*, in *Playes* (London: John Martyn et al, 1662), 422–88 (428).

36 Similarly, in Antoine Jacob Montfleury's: Antoine Jacob de Montfleury, *La Femme juge et partie* [performed 1669], analyzed in Harris, *Hidden Agendas*, 163–65, 170.

37 "But shall I not expose": James Shirley, *The Doubtfull Heir*, in *Six New Playes* (London: for Humphrey Robinson and Humphrey Moseley, 1653), 36, 44, 49–51, 55.

38 "Look, the day breakes": Sir John Suckling, *Brennoralt* (London: for Humphrey Moseley, 1646), 44, 46–49. As Denise Walen points out (*Constructions of Female Homoeroticism*, 89), plays in which two women become more erotically bonded to each other than to the man they were fighting over could be considered seventeenth-century examples of what Terry Castle has identified in some twentieth-century fiction as the "lesbian counter-plot" (*The Apparitional Lesbian: Female Homosexuality and Modern Culture* [New York: Columbia University Press, 1993], 72–73).

38 The storyline spread: Examples include Penelope Aubin, *Life and Amorous Adventures of Lucinda* (1722); Sarah Scott, *A Journey Through Every Stage of Life* (1754); Mary Robinson, *Walsingham* (1797); Anon., *A General History of the Pyrates* (1724); Anon., *Life and Adventures of Mrs Christian Davies* (1741); Anon., *The Female Soldier; or, The Surprising Life and Adventures of Hannah Snell* (1750); Charlotte Cibber Charke, *Narrative of the Life of Mrs Charlotte Charke* [1755], intro. by Leonard R. N. Asheley (Gainesville, Fla.: Scholars' Facsimiles and Reprints, 1969).

38 My favorite female bridegroom story: Anon., *The Travels and Adventures of Mademoiselle de Richelieu*, 3 vols. (London: for M. Cooper, 1744). This edition claims to be translated from the French. A different version appeared as *The Entertaining Travels and Surprizing Adventures of Mademoiselle de Leurich*, 2 vols. (London: McLeish, 1751). In her essay " 'My Heart So Wrapt': Lesbian Disruptions in Eighteenth-Century British Fiction," *Signs* 18:4 (1993): 838–65, Carolyn Woodward suggests Lady Mary Wortley Montagu as a possible candidate for authorship (854–55), and argues that the travelogue material, within which the love story is inserted in installments that only amount to about a sixth of the travelogue's length, may be "camouflage" for the lesbian themes, but also gives erotic liberty a context of freedom of movement (849). Susan Lanser groups *Mademoiselle de Richelieu* with other texts from the first half of the eighteenth century (Eliza Haywood's *The British Recluse*, Mary Delariviere Manley's *The New Atalantis*, Jane Barker's "The Unaccountable Wife," and Charlotte Cibber Charke's *Narrative of the Life*) under the heading of "sapphic picaresque," since they all associate same-sex love with mobility (and sometimes with cross-dressing), and offer it as a satisfying alternative to marriage; see "Sapphic Picaresque, Sexual Difference, and the Challenges of Homo-Adventuring," *Textual Practice* 15:2 (2001): 251–68.

39 "How happy do you make me": Anon., *Richelieu*, 2:229, 245, 34, 328, 3:124, 358. One possible source may be the faux autobiography *Mémoires de la vie de*

Mademoiselle Delfosses (Amsterdam: 1696), in which two cross-dressed women—one of whom declares that she cannot stand men—end up embracing in bed (179, 186).

40   "None of the nymphs": Ovid, *Metamorphoses*, 61–63. Kathleen Wall, in *The Callisto Myth from Ovid to Atwood: Initiation and Rape in Literature* (Kingston, Ont.: McGill-Queen's University Press, 1988), sees rape as punishment for Callisto's retreat into a world of women (5), but is curiously uninterested in the homoerotic consequences of Jove's disguise. On sixteenth- and seventeenth-century versions of the Callisto story, see Harriette Andreadis, *Sappho in Early Modern England: Female Same-Sex Literary Erotics, 1550–1714* (Chicago: University of Chicago Press, 2001), 160–70, and Traub, *The Renaissance of Lesbianism*, 234–57.

42   "coupled / And twinn'd": Thomas Heywood, *The Golden Age* [1611], in *The Golden and Silver Ages*, ed. J. Payne Collier (London: Shakespeare Society, 1851), 1–87 (30, 32).

42   "He feeleth oft": William Warner, *Albion's England* (London: 1586), 51.

43   The man-in-skirts motif: For instance, James Shirley's play *The Bird in a Cage* (1633) starts with a group of women locked up together, who are already acting out a lewd play about Jove's rape of Danaë by the time the disguised hero breaks in; see Traub, *The Renaissance of Lesbianism*, 59–61, 175–77.

43   The disguised man: Traub, *The Renaissance of Lesbianism*, 1.

43   In many texts: Examples include the thirteenth-century French fable *Trubert;* Heldris de Cornuälle, *Le Roman de Silence* (1200s); Raoul Lefevre, *Recuyell of the Historyes of Troye* (1474 translation of 1454 French original); G. B. della Porta, *La Fantesca* (1592); W. Haughton, *Englishmen for My Money* (1598); John Marston, *Antonio and Mellida* (1602); Thomas Artus, *L'Isle des Hermaphrodites* (1605); James Shirley, *The School of Compliment* (1631); Anon., *The Pastoralle of Florimene* (performed 1635). There are more overtly misogynistic plays about men invading and subverting all-female Amazon societies: John Fletcher, *The Sea Voyage* (1622); Anon., *Female Rebellion* (1659); Joseph Weston, *The Amazon Queen* (1667); Edward Howard, *The Women's Conquest* and *Six Days Adventure* (both 1671); and Thomas D'Urfey's *A Commonwealth of Women* (1685). A late example of this storyline is Alfred Lord Tennyson's long poem *The Princess* (1853), 37.

43   The earliest example: Guillaume de Blois, *Alda* [c. 1170], summarized and quoted in Paul Barrette, *Robert de Blois's Floris et Lyriopé* (Berkeley: University of California Press, 1968), 60–65. This penis-as-dildo motif shows up in eighteenth-century erotica, such as Gilles Jacob (attrib.), *A Treatise of Hermaphrodites* (London: E. Curll, 1718), 40–45, and the anonymous *A Spy on Mother Midnight* (London: E. Penn, 1748), 32–34.

44   "I don't know": Robert de Blois, *Floris et Lyriopé* [1200s], ed. Paul Barrette, 106 (lines 999–1013). " 'Ne sai,' fait ele, 'que je die. / Trop amer me semble folie. / Nos nos davons bien entramer, / Mais amors me fait sospirer, / Estandre,

baillier et doloir. / Ce ne tien pas a savoir. / Ne sai se ce me vient d'amer / Que sovant m'estuet sospirer. / Si me debrise, si m'en duel, / Si t'ain mout plus que je ne suel. / Et de ce tant ne quant ne dot, / Ains sai bien que tu m'aimmes mout. / Onques mais n'an oï novales / Que s'entramassent dous puceles. / Mais n'ameroie pas, je croi, / Nul home tant con je fais toi, / Ne tant, ce cuit, ne me plairoit / Li baisier, s'uns hons me baisoit.'" I am deeply grateful to Professor Mario Longtin of the University of Western Ontario's French department for the translation.

45 Just as we saw: Two examples are Agnolo Firenzuola's *Ragionamenti* (1555) and Hans Jakob Christoffel von Grimmelshausen's 1669 *Der Abentheurliche Simplicissimus Teutsch* (in English, *The Adventurous Simplicissimus*).

45 Joseph Harris points out: Harris, *Hidden Agendas*, 103–4.

45 "cherished and caressed": Honoré D'Urfé, *L'Astrée* [1607–27], ed. Hugues Vaganay, 5 vols. (1925; Geneva: Slatkine Reprints, 1966), 3:548, 598, 605. "Chéry et caressé." "Et se la pressant contre le sein, et la sentant presque tout nue, ce fut bien alors que pour le peu de soupçon que la bergere eust eu d'elle, elle se fust pris garde que ces caresses estoient un peu plus serrées que celles que les filles ont accoustumé de se faire; mais elle qui n'y pensoit en façon quelconque, luy rendoit ses baisers, tout ainsi qu'elle les recevoit, non pas peut-estre comme à une Alexis, mais comme au portrait vivant de Céladon." All translations from *L'Astrée* are by Emma Donoghue; no complete English translation exists. Several dozen plays were adapted from the romance by the 1650s. Eric Rohmer has filmed it as *Les Amours d'Astrée et de Celadon* (2007).

46 Other texts that support: See Harris, *Hidden Agendas*, 114–16.

46 "From then on": D'Urfé, *L'Astrée*, 4:264–66. "Dé là je dirois un adieu à toute sorte de plaisir et de contentement." "Ny violence de parents, ny incommodité d'affaires, ni consideration quelconque qui puisse tomber soubs [*sic*] la pensée, ne me separeront jamais de ma chere maistresse, que j'embrasse, dit-elle, luy jettant les bras au col, et que je ne laisseray point sortir des liens de mes bras qu'elle ne m'ait fait ce serment; si pour le moins elle ne veut point que je meure a cette heure mesme de desplaisir." "Pour n'estre veues." Interestingly, women in some other texts, more focused on sex, respond with enthusiasm to the prospect of such a transformation; see Ariosto, *Orlando Furioso* (1516–32), Barnaby Rich, "Of Phylotus and Emelia" (1581), and an anonymous Scottish adaptation for the stage, *Philotus* (1603).

47 "My plan, said the Druid": D'Urfé [actually B. Baro], *L'Astrée*, 5:97, 259. "Mon dessein, di le Druide, estoit alors de vous faire epouser Astrée, et non pas cet habit." "Perfide et trompeuse Alexis, meurs pour l'expiation de ton crime." See Harris, *Hidden Agendas*, 117–23.

47 Notably, Filande: D'Urfé, *L'Astrée*, 3:72–75, 275, and 1:222–23. "N'en soyez point en doute, et n'en accusez que la nature, qui veut que chacun aime son semblable." "Vous estonnez-vous qu'estant Callirée, je vous parle avec tant d'affection? Ressouvenez-vous qu'il n'y a impuissance de condition qui m'en

fasse jamais diminuer; tant s'en faut, ce sera plustost ceste occasion, qui la
conservea, et plus violente et eternelle, puis qu'il n'y a rien qui diminue tant
l'ardeur du désir, que la jouissance de ce qu'on désire, et cela ne pouvant estre
entre nous, vous serez jusques à mon cercueil tousjours aimée, et moy
tousjours amante. Et toutesfois si Tiresias, après avoir esté fille, devint
homme, pourquoy ne puis-je espérer que les dieux me pourroient bien autant
favoriser, si vous l'aviez agréable? Croyez, ma belle Diane, puis que les dieux
ne font jamais rien en vain, qu'il n'y a pas apparence qu'ils ayent mis en moy
une si parfaite affection, pour m'en laisser vainement travailler, et que si la
nature m'a fait naistre fille, mon amour extrême me peut bien rendre telle,
que ce ne soit point inutilement." María de Zayas y Sotomayor took up this
piquant notion of a man in skirts defending lesbian love in Neoplatonic
terms; see the sixth of her set of ten gritty novellas about how men trick
women, "Love for the Sake of Conquest" in *The Disenchantments of Love*
[1647], trans. H. Patsy Boyers (Albany: State University of New York Press,
1997), 203–43 (214, 224, 227, 232, 236).

48 "For a girl to love a girl": Feliciano de Silva, *Amadis de Gaule*, XI, trans.
Jacques Gohory (Paris: for Vincent Sertenas, Libraire, 1556), 33, 59, 82, 139. "Fille
aymer fille, hélas qu'est-ce sinon estre amoureux de la lune qu'il faudroit
prendre aux dentz?" "Ne pouvoit comprendre ceste violence d'Amour de fille
a fille." Translation by Emma Donoghue. The available English translations
of *Amadis de Gaule* are incomplete, and tone down the love scenes.

49 By far the most psychologically probing: Sir Philip Sidney, *The Countess of
Pembroke's Arcadia (The New Arcadia)* [1593], ed. Victor Skretkowicz (Oxford:
Clarendon, 1987). The so-called *Old Arcadia* circulated in manuscript from
about 1577 but was not published till 1912; the much longer *New Arcadia* was
left unfinished and published posthumously in 1590. The text I am discussing
is the one that had the most influence, a patchwork of the other two known
as *The Countess of Pembroke's Arcadia* because it was edited by his sister. See
Kathryn Schwarz's *Tough Love: Amazon Encounters in the English Renaissance*
(Durham, N.C.: Duke University Press, 2000), 175–201. There were at least
three dramatic adaptations of Sidney's *Arcadia*—John Day's *The Isle of Guls*
(1606), James Shirley's *The Arcadia* (1640), and the anonymous *Love's
Changelinges Change* (1630–40)—but they all underplay the female
homoeroticism.

49 Interestingly, the narrator: Sidney, *Arcadia*, 22, 106. In a neat allusion to the
female bridegroom motif, Sidney's narrator tells us that Pyrocles chose the
name as an act of homage to a woman called Zelmane, who disguised herself
as a man and died for love of him, long ago.

49 "full of impatient desire": Sidney, *Arcadia*, 82–85, 111–13, 48, 87, 144–49.

50 "paleness": Sidney, *Arcadia*, 189, 230–33.

51 "suddenly enamoured": Jorge de Montemayor, *Diana* [1559], trans.
Bartholomew Yong [1598], in *A Critical Edition of Yong's Translation of George of*

Montemayor's Diana and Gil Polo's Enamoured Diana, ed. Judith M. Kennedy (Oxford: Clarendon Press, 1968), 93–103, 32–48 (36–39). The Selvagia storyline was borrowed by Isaac du Ryer for his play *Le Mariage d'amour* (1621), and similarly in Gilbert Saulnier Du Verdier's parodic novel *Le Chevalier hypocondriaque* (1632), a woman pretends to be "Daraïde," a man-disguised-as-a-woman from *Amadis de Gaule*.

53 Philosophically: See Winfried Schleiner, "Male Cross-Dressing and Transvestism in Renaissance Romances," *The Sixteenth Century Journal* 19:4 (Winter 1988): 605–19 (619).

53 "O my Jewell": John Fletcher, *The Loyal Subject* [1647], ed. Fredson Boyers, in *The Dramatic Works in the Beaumont and Fletcher Canon*, vol. 5, ed. Fredser Boyer, 10 vols. (Cambridge: Cambridge University Press, 1996), 5:151–288 (161, 194, 247, 250, 256).

54 Denise Walen makes: Walen, *Constructions of Female Homoeroticism*, 132.

54 "act Lovers-parts": Margaret Cavendish, *The Convent of Pleasure*, in *Plays, Never Before Printed* (London: A. Maxwell, 1668), 14–16, 22–23, 32–33, 37–38, 48. See Andreadis, *Sappho in Early Modern England*, 83–88, and Traub, *The Renaissance of Lesbianism*, 177–80.

55 But Joseph Harris makes: Harris, *Hidden Agendas*, 176.

55 It lingered: See Laurence Senelick, *The Changing Room: Sex, Drag and Theatre* (London: Routledge, 2000), 190–93. Other late examples are Elizabeth Inchbald, *The Widow's Vow* (1786, based on a French farce), L. B. Louvet de Couvray's best-selling *Les Amours du Chevalier de Faublas* (1785–87), and the anonymous novel *Anecdotes of a Convent* (1771), in which a boy raised as a girl has no idea he is male.

55 It is hard to date: See Harris, *Hidden Agendas*, 153.

56 "makes love": Anon., *The Actor* (London: R. Griffiths, 1750), 202.

56 In Elizabeth Gaskell's: It is significant that Gaskell's Amante is masculine long before she cross-dresses to pose as husband to her beloved employer; see "The Grey Woman" (1861), in *Cousin Phillis* (New York: AMS Press, 1972), 300–361 (318–19, 333, 341, 349, 354–55, 358).

57 "What she said or did": Théophile Gautier, *Mademoiselle de Maupin* [1835], trans. Helen Constantine, intro. by Patricia Duncker (London: Penguin, 2005), 220–44, 332–33.

57 Patricia Duncker points out: Gautier, *Mademoiselle de Maupin*, 270–71. Duncker, introduction, xxvii–xxviii.

58 "I am of a third, separate sex": Gautier, *Mademoiselle de Maupin*, 318, 336.

58 In the preface: Gautier, *Mademoiselle de Maupin*, 23. Duncker, introduction, xxvii.

59 In the twentieth century: Perhaps the first was Renée Vivien in "Prince Charming" (1904), in *The Woman of the Wolf*, trans. Karla Jay and Yvonne M. Klein (New York: Gay, 1983), 23–28.

59 "I went back to her house": Jeanette Winterson, *The Passion* [1987] (London:

Penguin, 1988), 59–60, 65–66, 71, 94–96, 144–46. Carolyn Allen does a thoughtful reading of *The Passion* in *Following Djuna: Women Lovers and the Erotics of Loss* (Bloomington: Indiana University Press, 1996), 52–62. Winterson gives another wink to the female bridegroom tradition in *The PowerBook* (2000), whose sixteenth-century heroine, Ali, has a tulip bulb in her codpiece that—shades of Ovid—turns to flesh as required. Her 1992 *Written on the Body* received much attention for its refusal to specify the rakish narrator's gender, but earlier experiments in this line include Brigid Brophy's *In Transit* (1969), Maureen Duffy's *Love Child* (1971), and—in French, a much trickier task— Anne Garréta's *Sphinx* (1986). June Arnold's *The Cook and the Carpenter* (1973) goes one better by using the invented pronouns "na" and "nan" for all her characters.

Chapter Two: Inseparables

60   So why is it: Denise Walen, *Constructions of Female Homoeroticism in Early Modern Drama* (New York: Palgrave Macmillan, 2005), 54.

60   Like calls to like: See Laurie Shannon, "Natures's Bias: Renaissance Homonormativity and Elizabethan Comic Likeness," *Modern Philology* 98:2 (2000): 183–210. It is significant that the newly created Eve in Book IV of John Milton's epic poem *Paradise Lost* (1667), glimpsing her own reflection in the water, is naturally drawn to this female image, and offers it her "sympathy and love"; God and Adam have to rebuke her for her "vain desire" ("vain" meaning foolish and useless, rather than conceited) before she learns to live "inseparably" with her husband instead. See *Paradise Lost* [1667], ed. John Leonard (London: Penguin, 2000), 85–86.

60   "Have no doubt about it": Honoré D'Urfé, *L'Astrée* [1607–27], ed. Hugues Vaganay, 5 vols. (Geneva: Slatkine Reprints, 1966), 3:72–75, 275. "N'en soyez point en doute, et n'en accusez que la nature, qui veut que chacun aime son semblable." All translations from *L'Astrée* are by Emma Donoghue.

61   "Equality and Sympathy": Leonard Wallen, *Astraea; or, True Love's Myrrour* (London: for Henry Cripps and Lodowick Lloyd, 1651), 67–69.

61   More than two centuries: See Walen, *Constructions of Female Homoeroticism*, 143: "Homoeroticism and heterosexuality are constituent forms of romantic love." Likewise, Elizabeth Wahl finds no sharp distinction between female same-sex and opposite-sex desires in the eighteenth century; see *Invisible Relations: Representations of Female Intimacy in the Age of Enlightenment* (Stanford, Calif.: Stanford University Press, 1999), 7–8.

61   "Intreat me not": The book of Ruth, 1:14–17, 4:15–17. The King James Version of 1611 is not the most accurate translation, but I quote it because it had the greatest influence on literature in English.

62   One of them, in a Scottish poem: Poem XLIX, *The Maitland Quarto*

Manuscript [1586], ed. W. A. Craigie (Edinburgh: Blackwood, 1920), 160–62. A modernized version is given in *The Literature of Lesbianism: A Historical Anthology from Ariosto to Stonewall*, ed. Terry Castle (New York: Columbia University Press, 2003), 82–85.

62 "as an ideal": Sharon Marcus, *Between Women: Friendship, Desire, and Marriage in Victorian England* (Princeton, N.J.: Princeton University Press, 2007), 4.

63 Whatever private views: There are exceptions, for instance in seventeenth-century drama: Thomas Dekker's *Satiro-Mastix* (1602), John Fletcher's *The Woman's Prize* (1610), Philip Massinger's *The Bondman* (1623), and Richard Brome's *The Antipodes* (1638) all include strong hints that women can have sex with one another. Denise Walen argues interestingly that Renaissance writings on relationships in general draw the line not so much between friendship and sex as between love (a generous, loyal, tender, and uplifting relationship, which can include sex) and lust (deceptive, abusive, uncontrolled, and only about sex); see *Constructions of Female Homoeroticism*, 19–20, 149–53. Similarly, Elizabeth Wahl refuses the usual classification of women's relationships as either sexual or blandly sexless; she suggests instead a "sexualized" model and and an "idealized" or "polite" one, which sometimes overlapped; see *Invisible Relations*, 9–10, 14.

63 "Precisely because": Marcus, *Between Women*, 113–14. She suggests a helpful definition: "Erotic relationships involve intensified affect and sensual pleasure, dynamics of looking and displaying, domination and submission, restraint and eruption, idolization and humiliation."

63 The fervor of the girls' love: For passionate relationships between sisters, see Germaine de Staël, *Corinne* (1807); Frances Burney, *The Wanderer* (1814); Harriet Martineau, *Deerbrook* (1839); Geraldine Jewsbury, *The Half-Sisters* (1848); Nathaniel Hawthorne, *The Blithedale Romance* (1852); Ann S. Stephens, *Mary Derwent* (1858); Wilkie Collins, *The Woman in White* (1859–60; discussed in chapter 5) and *No Name* (1862); Christina Rossetti, *Goblin Market* (1862); Elizabeth Stuart Phelps, *Hedged In* (1870); and Mary E. Wilkins Freeman, *By the Light of the Soul* (1907). To complicate the matter, one of the sisters is mixed-race in some titles: James Fenimore Cooper, *The Last of the Mohicans* (1826); Dinah Mulock Craik, *Olive* (1850); Emily C. Pearson, *Ruth's Sacrifice* (1863). See Sarah Annes Brown, *Devoted Sisters: Representations of the Sister Relationship in Nineteenth-Century British and American Literature* (Aldershot, U.K.: Ashgate, 2003). Passionate friends of different ages may also be revealed, at the last minute, as mother and daughter, as in Charlotte Brontë's *Shirley* (1849).

63 The shorthand I use: Some of my thoughts in this chapter were developed in collaboration with Chris Roulston during the writing of her paper "Separating the Inseparables: Female Friendship and Its Discontents in Eighteenth-Century France," *Eighteenth-Century Studies* 32:2 (1998–99): 215–31 (216). The term *inseparable* was so enduringly fashionable that some writers used it mockingly; see Wahl, *Invisible Relations*, 207.

64 William Shakespeare's comedy: *As You Like It* [1623], in *The Complete Works*, 254–83 (255, 259–60, 272, 275) (I.i.103; I.ii.6, 20; I.iii.35, 68–74, 92–95; III.iv.19–28; IV.i.112). Thomas Lodge, *Rosalynde* [1590], 2nd ed. [1592], facsimile reprint (Menston, U.K.: The Scholar Press, 1972), no page numbers. See Jessica Tvordi, "Female Alliance and the Construction of Homoeroticism in *As You Like It* and *Twelfth Night*," in *Maids and Mistresses, Cousins and Queens*, ed. Susan Frye and Karen Robertson (New York: Oxford University Press, 1999), 114–30 (117–18).

65 In her groundbreaking study: Valerie Traub, *The Renaissance of Lesbianism in Early Modern England* (Cambridge: Cambridge University Press, 2002), 18, 174. Traub calls this "femme-femme love," and argues that it is the orthodox femininity of the inseparables that blinds readers to the homoeroticism (80).

65 Emilia: William Shakespeare and John Fletcher, *The Two Noble Kinsmen* [1634], ed. Eugene M. Waith (Oxford: Clarendon Press, 1989), 102. Laurie Shannon offers a thorough reading of this play in *Sovereign Amity: Figures of Friendship in Shakespearean Contexts* (Chicago: University of Chicago Press, 2002), chapter 3.

66 "fond excess of love": William Davenant, *Love and Honour* [1649], in *Love and Honour and The Siege of Rhodes*, ed. James W. Tupper (Boston: D. C. Heath & Co., 1909), 63, 118, 122.

66 "My Mistresse is my husband": John Fletcher, *The Pilgrim* [1622], ed. Cyrus Hoy, in *The Dramatic Works in the Beaumont and Fletcher Canon*, vol. 4 (Cambridge: Cambridge University Press, 1985), 111–224 (V.ii., V.vi., 191, 205). Other endlessly devoted maids or governesses are found in Charlotte MacCarthy, *The Fair Moralist* (1745); Charlotte Lennox, *Henrietta* (1758) and *Euphemia* (1790); Marie-Jeanne de Riccoboni, *Miss Jenny Salisbury* (1764).

66 But perhaps the most extraordinary: Jane Barker, "The Unaccountable Wife" [1723], in *The Galesia Trilogy and Selected Manuscript Poems of Jane Barker*, ed. Carol Shiner Wilson (New York: Oxford University Press, 1997), 49–173 (144–47). See Kathryn King, "The Unaccountable Wife and Other Tales of Female Desire in Jane Barker's *A Patchwork Screen for the Ladies*," *The Eighteenth Century* 35: 2 (1994): 155–71, and Christine Roulston, "The Eighteenth-Century Ménage-à-Trois: Having It Both Ways?," *The British Journal for Eighteenth-Century Studies*, 27:2 (Autumn 2004): 257–77.

68 "inseparable Cousin": Jean-Jacques Rousseau, *Julie; or, The New Héloïse* [1761], trans. Philip Stewart and Jean Vache (Hanover, N.H.: University Press of New England, 1997), 39, 81, 94, 146, 328, 490, 507, 602. For another example of devoted women friends rearing their children together, see Percy Bysshe Shelley, "Rosalind and Helen: A Modern Eclogue," in *The Poetical Works of Shelley*, ed. Newell F. Ford (Boston: Houghton Mifflin, 1975), 136–51, 612, 146, 94, 507.

68 But as Janet Todd argues: Janet Todd, *Women's Friendship in Literature* (New York: Columbia University Press, 1980), 132–67.

68 Although St. Preux's: For other examples of the same attitude, see the

anonymous *Travels and Adventures of Mlle de Richelieu* (1744), 1:107, and
Charlotte Lennox, *Euphemia*, 4 vols. (London: for T. Cadell and J. Evans,
1790), 3:47–48.

69 "the ambiguity is preserved": Hans Wolpe, "Psychological Ambiguity in *La
Nouvelle Héloïse*," *University of Toronto Quarterly* 28:3 (April 1959): 279–90 (288).

69 "consolatory adjuncts": Susan Lanser, "Befriending the Body: Female
Intimacies as Class Acts," *Eighteenth-Century Studies* 32:2 (1998–99): 179–98 (188).

69 "marriage plots": Marcus, *Between Women*, 79; see also 3, 82.

69 'Oh, Alice': Anthony Trollope, *Can You Forgive Her?* (1864–65) (London:
Penguin, 1986), 345. See Marcus, *Between Women*, 227–55.

70 risk their own reputation: Susanna Centlivre, *The Wonder* (1714); Germaine de
Staël, *Delphine* (1802); Maria Edgeworth, *Helen* (1834); Mary Taylor, *Miss Miles*
(1890).

70 men they cannot stand: Mary Pix, *The Double Distress* (1701); Mary
Wollstonecraft, *Mary, A Fiction* (1788); Wilkie Collins, *Man and Wife* (1870).

70 Interestingly, nineteenth-century novels: This pattern was identified by
Suzanne Raitt in "Fallen Women: Charlotte Mew in Context," in *Volcanoes
and Pearl Divers: Essays in Lesbian Feminist Studies*, ed. Suzanne Raitt (London:
Onlywomen, 1995), 52–73.

70 It is no accident: See Ruth Vanita's fascinating comments on the nineteenth-
century link between Marian imagery and desire between women in *Sappho
and the Virgin Mary: Same-Sex Love and the English Literary Imagination* (New
York: Columbia University Press, 1996), 7, 18–35.

70 "I'm goin' to save you now": Rosa Mulholland [Lady Gilber], *The Tragedy of
Chris* (London: Sands & Co., 1903), 127, 293.

71 "Only one summer": Louisa May Alcott, *Work*, 2 vols. (London: Sampson
Low, 1873), 1:198.

71 Even an author: Compare Christina Rossetti's weird poem *Goblin Market*
(1862), in which Lizzie wins her spellbound sister Laura back from the goblins
in a scene of startling oral eroticism.

71 "It is not absence": Grace Aguilar, *Woman's Friendship* (London: Groombridge
& Sons, 1851), 39.

72 "female friendship": Todd, *Women's Friendship in Literature*, 132.

72 This motif of women friends: On the triangle of two male friends competing
for a woman, see Eve Sedgwick, *Between Men: English Literature and Male
Homosocial Desire* (New York: Columbia University Press, 1985).

73 "a rehearsal in girlhood": Henry Wadsworth Longfellow, *Kavanagh* [1849]
(Boston: Ticknor, Reed and Fields, 1853), 79, 84, 168. Other examples of rivalry
dividing friends include Catherine Bernard's tragedy *Laodamie reine d'Epire*
(1680); Marie-Jeanne de Riccoboni, *Histoire de Jenny Salisbury* (1764) and
Histoire du Marquis de Cressy (1758); and Jane Austen, *Emma* (1816).

73 "We, Hermia": Shakespeare, *A Midsummer Night's Dream* (1600), in *The
Complete Works*, 198–222 (211) (III.ii.198–216).

74 "give up Mankind": Nicholas Rowe, *The Tragedy of Jane Shore* [1714], facsimile of 1914 ed. (Menston, U.K.: The Scholar Press, 1973), 10–11.

75 "share my divided heart": Catherine Trotter (later Cockburn), *Agnes de Castro* [1696], facsimile reprint in *The Plays of Mary Pix and Catherine Trotter*, ed. Edna Steeves, 2 vols. (New York: Garland, 1982), 2:1–47 (6, 5, 7, 30, 34). Like Eurione in George Chapman's *Monsieur D'Olive* (1606), Agnes is reluctantly persuaded to accept the widower's proposal out of affection for his dead wife, but in this case her own death spares her at the eleventh hour. In many Victorian novels the Constantia type (a happily married woman) and the Agnes type (a sworn spinster) are joined in devoted friendship.

76 Over the eighteenth: Examples include Lady Mary Wroth, *Love's Victory* (written around 1620); Eliza Haywood, *The Surprize* (1724); Sarah Fielding, *Familiar Letters between the Principal Characters in "David Simple," and some Others* (1747) and *The Governess* (1749); Fanny Burney, *Cecilia* (1782); Helen Maria Williams, *Julia* (1790); Eliza Fenwick, *Secresy* (1795); Mary Robinson, *Walsingham* (1798); Harriet Downing, *Mary; or, Female Friendship: A Poem* (1816); Harriet Martineau, *Deerbrook* (1839); Elizabeth Barrett Browning, *Aurora Leigh* (1856); George Eliot, *The Mill on the Floss* (1860); Thomas Hardy, *The Hand of Ethelberta* (1876); Olive Schreiner, *The Story of an African Farm* (1883); and Annie E. Holdsworth, *Joanna Traill, Spinster* (1894). In one of the latest and oddest of these sacrifice stories, Mary E. Wilkins Freeman's *By the Light of the Soul* (1907), Maria fakes her own death so that her husband and the half sister she adores can marry, and is rewarded with a loving partnership with a rich dwarf woman.

76 "an altruistic exchange": Marcus, *Between Women*, 88–89.

76 "a touch of manhood": Charlotte Brontë, *Shirley* [1849], ed. Herbert Rosengarten and Margaret Smith (Oxford: Clarendon Press, 1979), 223, 224, 264, 292, 295–96. There has been speculation that Brontë meant Caroline to die, but that, having suffered through three deathbed vigils in a year, including that of her sister Anne, on whom she based Caroline, Brontë gave her heroine a last-minute reprieve.

76 It has recently been suggested: Anne Longmuir, "Anne Lister and Lesbian Desire in Charlotte Brontë's *Shirley*," *Brontë Studies* 31:2 (July 2006): 145–55.

77 The eleventh-hour appearance: Examples include Charlotte MacCarthy, *The Fair Moralist* (London: published for the author, 1745); and Sarah Fielding, *The History of David Simple* (1744) and *The Cry* (with Jane Collier, 1754).

77 The earliest example: A striking seventeenth-century drama about rivals who fall in love is Lodowick Carlell's *The Deserving Favourite* [1629], in Charles Gray, *Lodowick Carliell: His Life, a Discussion of His Plays, and "The Deserving Favourite"* (Chicago: University of Chicago Press, 1905), 126, 128, 147. Like Robert Wilson's *The Three Ladies of London* (1584), Philip Massinger's *The Picture* (1629), and Margaret Cavendish's *The Comical Hash* (1662), it contains a highly erotic kissing scene between the two women. Along with Suckling's *Brennoralt* and Shirley's *The Doubtful Heir*, Carlell's *The Deserving Favourite* is an early

example of the subordination of the third (male) term, what Terry Castle calls the lesbian counter-plot (*The Apparitional Lesbian*, 72–73).

78 From the seventeenth century: As the concept of romantic friendship came under suspicion toward the end of the nineteenth century, it became almost impossible to write stories of female inseparability which were not primarily investigations of lesbian identity (discussed in chapter 6). The nearest modern equivalent to the motif of inseparables separated may be the lesbian novel of bereavement or loss: examples include Barbara Burford, *The Threshing Floor* (1986); Barbara Wilson, *Cows and Horses* (1988); Jan Clausen, *The Prosperine Papers* (1989); Sarah Schulman, *After Delores* (1989); Jenifer Levin, *The Sea of Light* (1992); May Sarton, *The Education of Harriet Hatfield* (1993); Marion Douglas, *Bending at the Bow* (1995); Sarah Van Arsdale, *Towards Amnesia* (1995); and Carol Anshaw, *Seven Moves* (1997). The timing of this cluster suggests that AIDS (or, rather, gay men's AIDS fiction) was an influence.

78 "It was noticed": Elizabeth Stuart Phelps, *Hedged In* (Boston: Fields, Osgood & Co., 1870), 283–84.

78 "tree of knowledge": Mary E. Wilkins (later Freeman), "The Tree of Knowledge" (1899), in *The Love of Parson Lord* (New York: Harper & Bros., 1900), 85–140 (140). Compare her novels *The Portion of Labor* (1901) and *The Shoulders of Atlas* (1908), which both feature obsessive relationships between older and younger women.

79 Such painful denials: Examples include Charles Dickens, *Bleak House* (1863) and *Our Mutual Friend* (1865); Elizabeth Stuart Phelps, "At Bay" (1867); George Meredith, *Diana of the Crossways* (1885); and Isabella Ford, *On the Threshold* (1895).

Chapter Three: Rivals

80 "Blest as th'immortal": *The Works of Anacreon and Sappho*, trans. Ambrose Phillips (London: E. Curll and A. Bettesworth, 1713), 74–75. For a fascinating discussion of issues in the translation of Fragment 31, see Joan DeJean, *Fictions of Sappho, 1546–1937* (Chicago: University of Chicago Press, 1989), 57, 131–34, 321–25.

81 This lyric: "Lesbiai," female inhabitants of Lesbos, was used in 914 in a Christian commentary by Arathas to mean women who desire women; see Bernadette Brooten, *Love Between Women: Early Christian Responses to Female Homoeroticism* (Chicago: University of Chicago Press, 1996), 5. On Sappho's reputation, see Harriette Andreadis, *Sappho in Early Modern England: Female Same-Sex Literary Erotics, 1550–1714* (Chicago: University of Chicago Press, 2001), 27–53.

81 Anne Le Fèvre Dacier: Anne Le Fèvre Dacier, ed., *Les Poésies d'Anacréon et de Sapho* (Paris: D. Thierry, 1681), 403.

81 "Whatever might have been": A. Phillips, ed., *The Works of Anacreon and Sappho* (London: E. Curll and A. Bettesworth, 1713), 74–75.

81 François Gacon: François Gacon ["Le Poète sans fard"], *Les Odes d'Anacréon et de Sapho* (Rotterdam: Fritz et Böhm, 1712). Translation by Joan DeJean in *Fictions of Sappho*, 133–34. E. B. Greene, ed., *The Works of Anacreon and Sappho* (London: J. Ridley, 1768), 144–45.

81 In 1795: Abbé Jean-Marie Coupé, *Soirées litteraires*, 16 vols. (Paris: Honnert, 1795), 6:146.

82 And in 1855: See DeJean, *Fictions of Sappho*, 238.

82 But over the period: Marjorie Garber calls this the "bisexual plot" in *Vice Versa: Bisexuality and the Eroticism of Everyday Life* (New York: Simon and Schuster, 1995), 456.

82 Which means that: One early, high-minded example is Lodowick Carlell's play *The Passionate Lovers* (London: for Humphrey Moseley, 1655), in which Clorinda tries to fob off her besotted cousin Olinda by thanking her for "your love, / Rather your friendship" and suggesting she redirect it toward an unwanted male suitor of Clorinda's called Clarimant—but Olinda rejects both the glossing of "love" as "friendship" and the advice, insisting that she is a legitimate rival to Clarimant for Clorinda's love (part 2, III.i., V.i. [123–24, 149]). This is a daring notion, but Carlell does not follow through at the level of plot: later, Olinda announces that she has come to love Clarimant after all, but will be happy to see him marry the far more deserving Clorinda.

82 "so fervent a friendship": Samuel Richardson, *Clarissa* [1747–48], ed. Angus Ross (London: Penguin, 1985), 637, 40, 133, 863.

83 "If you allow of it": Richardson, *Clarissa*, 931–32,992–93, 331, 549, 1088, 1403. Lisa L. Moore argues that in eighteenth-century English fiction, "the sexual Other of the virtuous bourgeois woman is her slightly Sapphic female friend"; *Dangerous Intimacies: Towards a Sapphic History of the British Novel* (Durham, N.C.: Duke University Press, 1977), 12.

84 "the force of *female friendship*": Richardson, *Clarissa*, 1130. A rich analysis of Anna and Clarissa's relationship can be found in Janet Todd, *Women's Friendship in Literature* (New York: Columbia University Press, 1980), 46–68.

85 "a *tender Heart*": Anthony Hamilton, *Memoirs of the Life of Count Grammont*, trans. Abel Boyer (London, 1714), 234–37, 246, 251, 259–64. Excerpted in *The Literature of Lesbianism*, ed. Castle, 219–28.

85 Terry Castle points out: Terry Castle, introduction to *The Literature of Lesbianism: A Historical Anthology from Ariosto to Stonewall* (New York: Columbia University Press, 2003), 41, 44.

86 Pierre Choderlos de Laclos: Pierre Choderlos de Laclos, *Les Liaisons Dangereuses* [1782], trans. P. W. K. Stone (London: Penguin, 1961), 170–76 (170–71). See Christine Roulston, "Separating the Inseparables: Female Friendship and Its Discontents in Eighteenth-Century France," *Eighteenth-Century Studies* 32:2 (1998–99): 215–31 (220–21).

87 "inflexible purpose": Charles Brockden Brown, *Ormond; or, The Secret Witness* [1799], ed. Mary Chapman (Peterborough, Ont.: Broadview, 1999), 226, 219, 241.

88 a "competitor": Brown, *Ormond*, 242–51. Kristin M. Comment places this novel in the context of the "sex panic" of the 1790s—a widespread unease about female independence and the erotic freedoms (including same-sex ones) that might go with it; "Charles Brockden Brown's *Ormond* and Lesbian Possibility in the Early Republic," *Early American Literature* 40:1 (2005): 57–78.

89 "emotions of normal love": Harry R. Warfel, *Charles Brockden Brown: American Gothic Novelist* (Gainesville: University of Florida Press, 1949), 135.

90 "Madam, my wife": Sarah Scott, *A Description of Millenium Hall* [1762] (London: Pandora, 1986), 80.

91 "I can give you all you want": Eliza Lynn Linton, *The Rebel of the Family* [1880] (Peterborough, Ont.: Broadview, 2002), 50–52, 186–87.

91 "my little wife": Linton, *The Rebel of the Family*, 54–57, 141, 51, 175, 144, 173.

92 "She will never be one of us": Linton, *The Rebel of the Family*, 185–86, 292, 330–34.

92 The novel is marked by: On same-sex eroticism in some of Linton's other works, including a novel in which she uses a male persona to tell her own life story, see Deborah T. Meem, "Eliza Lynn Linton and the Rise of Lesbian Consciousness," *Journal of the History of Sexuality* 7:4 (April 1997): 537–60.

93 "The masculine lady": Reviews excerpted as Appendix A to Linton, *The Rebel of the Family*, 399–402.

93 It is hardly surprising: The few earlier examples—Miss Barnevelt in Richardson's *Sir Charles Grandison* (1753), Harriot Freke in Maria Edgeworth's *Belinda* (1801)—are much more tentative in drawing a link between their borrowed masculinity and same-sex desire.

94 "I wished to write": Henry James, *The Notebooks of Henry James*, ed. F. O. Matthiessen and Kenneth B. Murdock (New York: Oxford University Press, reprint ed. New York: 1961), 47.

94 "her sense that she found": Henry James, *The Bostonians* [1886] (New York: Bantam Classics, 1984), 57, 67–71.

95 "the fine web of authority": James, *The Bostonians*, 85, 154, 94–96, 116–18, 137–42, 256, 145, 189.

95 "Don't attempt the impossible": James, *The Bostonians*, 173, 268, 272–73, 216, 235, 240, 281.

96 "more wedded": James, *The Bostonians*, 263, 288, 279, 300, 304, 325, 337, 357, 342.

96 Without ever naming: See Martha Vicinus, *Intimate Friends: Women Who Loved Women, 1778–1928* (Chicago: University of Chicago Press, 2004), xxii.

97 "Olive put forward": James, *The Bostonians*, 331, 395. For brilliant readings of the novel, see Terry Castle, *The Apparitional Lesbian: Female Homosexuality and Modern Culture* (New York: Columbia University Press, 1993), 150–85; Annamarie Jagose, *Inconsequence: Lesbian Representation and the Logic of Sexual Sequence* (Ithaca, N.Y.: Cornell University Press, 2002), 57–76; Garber, *Vice Versa*, 457–67.

97   Her gloomy shadow: See, for instance, L. T. Meade's *The Cleverest Woman in England* (1898), in which Imogen passionately resents the marriage of her fellow suffragette Dagmar, and drops heavy hints about her love.

97   "We are a partnership": Florence Converse, *Diana Victrix* (Boston: Houghton Mifflin, 1897), 63, 145, 240–41. Similarly, at the end of Caroline Fothergill's saga, *Put to the Proof* (1883), Angel discards her obtuse fiancé so she can move with her beloved Margaret (and Margaret's accommodating husband) to New Zealand.

98   "Do you also be loyal": Converse, *Diana Victrix*, 345, 347, 360. See Kate McCullough, " 'But Some Times . . . I Don't Marry,—Even in Books': Boston Marriages, Creoles, and the Future of the Nation," in *Regions of Identity: The Construction of America in Women's Fiction, 1885–1914* (Stanford, Calif.: Stanford University Press, 1999), 58–92.

99   It is a laundry: Klaus Mann, *Ania and Esther* (1925), in *Lovesick: Modernist Plays of Same-Sex Love*, trans. and ed. Laurence Senelick (New York: Routledge, 1999), 161–99.

100 "in a manner fell": Catherine Wells, "The Beautiful House," in *Harper's Monthly Magazine* (March 1912): 503–11 (505, 509).

100 Catherine Wells: See Katie Roiphe, *Uncommon Arrangements: Seven Portraits of Married Life in London Literary Circles, 1910–1939* (New York: Dial Press, 2007).

101 Not that this conversion: Peter Cryle, *The Telling of the Act: Sexuality as Narrative in Eighteenth- and Nineteenth-Century France* (Newark: University of Delaware Press and London: Associated University Presses, 2001), 343–48.

101 As Terry Castle points out: Castle, introduction to *The Literature of Lesbianism*, 35.

101 "tired of one another": D. H. Lawrence, *The Fox* [1922] (London: Sphere, 1968), 7, 10–11, 43, 27.

102 "Banford looked at her": Lawrence, *The Fox*, 57, 61, 96, 99.

102 "for a beast": Lawrence, *The Fox*, 101, 112–13, 115, 122.

103 "a fine story": Quoted in introduction by David Ellis to D. H. Lawrence, *The Fox, The Captain's Doll, The Ladybird*, ed. Dieter Mehl (Cambridge: Cambridge University Press, 1992), xxii–xxiii. See also appendix 1, "The Ending of the First Version of 'The Fox,' " 223–30.

103 All these changes: Similarly, in Thomas Burke's story "The Pash," a girl's "muggy friendship" with her forty-year-old female welfare officer is vanquished and "cleansed" by the love of a good man, and the loser is burned to death in a factory fire; see *East of Mansion House* (New York: George H. Doran, 1926), 37–64 (47, 49, 57–58, 64). Reprinted in *The Literature of Lesbianism*, ed. Castle, 791–800.

103 "a hundred years": Thomas Dickinson, *Winter Bound*, quoted in a review in the *New York Times*, November 13, 1929, excerpted in Jonathan Ned Katz, *Gay/Lesbian Almanac* (New York: Harper and Row, 1983), 464.

103 "Nothing in Phillida's history": Quoted in Katz, *Gay/Lesbian Almanac*, 464.

103 Janet is a PhD student: Plagiarism here suggests that Pauline is fraudulent in her usurping of a traditionally male professorial as well as sexual role.

104 "below-stairs liaison": Dorothy Dodds Baker, *Trio* (Boston: Houghton
     Mifflin, 1943), 57, 83, 117, 129–33, 156, 162, 197, 204, 213, 227. The novel ends with
     Pauline's suicide, as does the 1944 stage version (which did not prevent
     protests so furious they shut down the production; see Curtin, *"We Can
     Always Call Them Bulgarians,"* 266–80). But Dodds Baker also published a
     psychologically subtler story called "Romance" (*Harper's Bazaar*, 1941)—
     clearly a first draft of *Trio*, but one in which the girl ends up going sadly home
     to the older woman. For another failed attempt at escape from a female
     couple, see Henry Handel Richardson's "Two Hanged Women" (1934), in
     Castle, *The Literature of Lesbianism*, 926–29.

104 "Go on, then": Ernest Hemingway, "The Sea Change" (1933), in *The Literature
     of Lesbianism*, ed. Castle, 906–10 (910).

105 Marjorie Garber: Garber, *Vice Versa*, 467–71.

105 The triangle: See Honoré de Balzac, *La Fille aux yeux d'or* (1835; in English, *The
     Girl with the Golden Eyes*); Geraldine Dix, *The Girl from the Farm* (1895); Gabrielle
     Reuter, *Aus Guter Familie* (1895; in English, *A Girl from a Nice Family*); Charles
     Rivière, *Sous le manteau de Fourvière* (1926; in English, *Under Fourviere's Mantle*);
     Lucie Marchal, *The Mesh* (1948); Françoise Mallet-Joris, *Le Rempart des beguines*
     (1951; in English *The Illusionist*); Claire Vallier Hatvany, *Solitude à trois* (1961; in
     English, *Three Alone*); Marijane Meaker, *Shockproof Sydney Skate* (1972); Ann
     Patchett, *The Magician's Assistant* (1997).

105 "She loved them": Constance Fenimore Woolson, "Felipa" (1876), reprinted in
     The Literature of Lesbianism, ed. Castle, 508–20 (520). Other examples of a
     woman involved with a male-female couple include Ernest Hemingway's *The
     Garden of Eden* (written 1946–61, published 1986) and Jonathan Franzen's *The
     Corrections* (2001).

105 "a restful diversion": Colette, *Claudine en ménage* (Paris: Ollendorf, 1902), 122.
     A similar dénouement is found in later texts: Harry Gribble, *March Hares*
     (1921); Jean Binet-Valmer, *Sur les sables couchées* (1929; in English, *Lying on the
     Sand)*; H.D., *HERmione* (written 1927, published 1981); Brigid Brophy, *The
     King of a Rainy Country* (1956); Jess Draper, *One Step More* (1963).

105 The rivalry motif: Consider the fact that four novels by Jeanette Winterson—
     The Passion (1987), *Written on the Body* (1992), *Gut Symmetries* (1997), and *The
     PowerBook* (2000)—hinge on a female or gender-unspecified narrator's affair
     with a married woman.

Chapter Four: Monsters

106 "I sole am found": Ludovico Ariosto, *Orlando Furioso* [1516–32], trans. John
     Harrington [1591], ed. Robert McNulty (Oxford: Clarendon, 1972), 280 (Canto
     29, v.27–31), 283 (Canto 29, v.54).

106 What is new: I am using "monster" here to mean both freakish and immoral,

not the way Terry Castle uses it to encapsulate the classic "first response" to homosexuality as a surprise or wonder; see her introduction to *The Literature of Lesbianism: A Historical Anthology from Ariosto to Stonewall* (New York: Columbia University Press, 2003), 19–20.

107 Drawing on references: Harriette Andreadis, *Sappho in Early Modern England: Female Same-Sex Literary Erotics, 1550–1714* (Chicago: University of Chicago Press, 2001), 28.

107 "No more": Ovid, "Sapho to Phaon" [trans. Alexander Pope, 1707], in *The Poems of Alexander Pope*, ed. John Butt (London: Methuen, 1963), 29–35 (29). "Guilty love" is a Christianized phrase; Ovid's word is *"crimine,"* which suggests being accused of something.

108 "From 1796": Jennifer Waelti-Walters, *Damned Women: Lesbians in French Novels, 1796–1996* (Montreal: McGill-Queens University Press, 2000), 6. Sharon Marcus argues that in British literature love between women was generally cast as helpful to marriage, whereas the French portrayed it as antagonistic; see *Between Women: Friendship, Desire and Marriage in Victorian England* (Princeton, N.J.: Princeton University Press, 2007), 15.

108 The bogey in these texts: Similarly, Denise Walen finds that in Renaissance drama, "playwrights use female homoerotics to address issues of social, religious, or political disorder and address all manner of moral, emotional and intellectual deficiency such as greed, arrogance, lust, infidelity, religious apostasy, and various forms of political discord"; see *Constructions of Female Homoeroticism in Early Modern Drama* (New York: Palgrave Macmillan, 2005), 4.

108 In the late eighteenth century: Two slightly earlier analogues—though hardly in the same league—are Madame Furiel and her sex slave Sapho, members of a tribades' orgy club or "anandrine [man-free] sect" in *Confessions d'une jeune fille* (1777–78; in English, *Confessions of a Young Girl*, part of *L'Espion anglois*, which has been attributed to Mathieu François Pidansat de Mairobert). In a nod to the legend of Callisto, this Sapho is seduced by a man in female disguise, gets pregnant, and is cast out by the furious Madame Furiel. See Elizabeth Susan Wahl, *Invisible Relations: Representations of Female Intimacy in the Age of Enlightenment* (Stanford, Calif.: Stanford University Press, 1999), 244–48.

108 "Frig me": Marquis de Sade, *Juliette* [1797–1801], trans. Austryn Wainhouse (New York: Grove Press, 1968), 300.

109 The libertine authors: See James Turner, *Schooling Sex: Libertine Literature and Erotic Education in Italy, France and England, 1534–1685* (Oxford: Oxford University Press, 2003), 104, 195.

110 "foolery from woman": John Cleland, *Fanny Hill or, Memoirs of a Woman of Pleasure* [1749] (London: Penguin, 1985), 71.

110 "You simply have no idea": Sade, *Juliette*, 9.

110 "We girded on": Sade, *Juliette*, 715, 12. *Bardash* or *bardache* is a sixteenth-

century English word for a man who lets himself be penetrated by another man.

111 "Mistresses of all": Sade, *Juliette*, 1027–36 (1034). On the uneven treatment of women's friendship in *Juliette*, see Janet Todd, *Women's Friendship in Literature* (New York: Columbia University Press, 1980), 168–90.

112 "a moment of consolation": Denis Diderot, *The Nun* [1796], trans. Leonard Tancock (London: Penguin, 1974), 129, 126, 133, 57, 85–86, 134, 137–38, 142, 140.

112 Suzanne fits: See Peter Cryle, *The Telling of the Act: Sexuality as Narrative in Eighteenth- and Nineteenth-Century France* (Newark: University of Delaware Press and London: Associated University Presses, 2001), 324–26, 332–34.

112 And like their heroines: David M. Robinson, "The Abominable Madame de Murat," in *Homosexuality in French History and Culture*, ed. Jeffrey Merrick and Michael Sibalis (Binghamton, N.Y.: Harrington Park Press, 2001), 53–67 (55). For good readings of this kind of "mock-unknowing" about a lesbian "Cabal" in Delarivier Manley's satire *The New Atalantis* (1709), see Andreadis, *Sappho in Early Modern England*, 91–94, and Wahl, *Invisible Relations*, 121–29.

113 " 'We' as men": Christopher Rivers, "Inintelligibles pour une femme honnête: Sexuality, Textuality and Knowledge in Diderot's 'La Religieuse' and Gautier's 'Mademoiselle de Maupin,' " *The Romanic Review* 86:1 (January 1995): 1–29 (18–21).

113 "She wriggles": Diderot, *The Nun*, 122, 147–48.

114 "I only have to": Diderot, *The Nun*, 164–65, 167, 170.

114 "trample me underfoot": Diderot, *The Nun*, 167, 172, 174, 176, 182–86.

115 "wild beast": Alfred de Musset, *Gamiani* [1833] (London: 1908), 46, 73, 76, 81, 88.

116 "philosapphic": Turner, *Schooling Sex*, 104, 195.

116 "The (supposed) inability": Cryle, *The Telling of the Act*, 316–19.

116 "martyrdom": Musset, *Gamiani*, 133–34.

117 No doubt Dickens: In a fascinating analysis of how Miss Wade's "female perversity" has come to be read as lesbianism, Annamarie Jagose pays close attention to this question of the order of narration; see *Inconsequence: Lesbian Representation and the Logic of Sexual Sequence* (Ithaca, N.Y.: Cornell University Press, 2002), 37–56.

117 "History of a Self-Tormentor": Charles Dickens, *Little Dorrit* [1857] (London: Collins, 1958), 35–36, 506, 618–19.

117 "a singular likeness": Dickens, *Little Dorrit*, 30–31, 619–25, 38, 625, 39.

118 "composure": Dickens, *Little Dorrit*, 309, 313–16.

119 "fidelity": Dickens, *Little Dorrit*, 624, 506, 616. Tattycoram reappears as the heroine of Audrey Thomas's clever metafiction *Tattycoram* (2004), in which Dickens's own maid relates her story and fiercely resents being fictionalized in *Little Dorrit;* the lesbian angle is not addressed directly, but seems included in Dickens's misrepresentation.

119 "She murmured": Thomas Hardy, *Desperate Remedies* [1871] (London: Macmillan, 1912), 61. Terry Castle points out that hair brushing stands in for sex between women in this and other texts; see her introduction to *The Literature of Lesbianism*, 44. Compare Vasco Pratolini's *Cronache dei poveri amanti* (1947; in English, *A Tale of Poor Lovers*), in which fascism is personified by the bedridden, disfigured Signora, who forces her young female attendants to submit to her caresses.

119 "her dependence": Hardy, *Desperate Remedies*, 71, 87, 90, 93–96.

120 Some of the awkwardness: Deborah T. Meem argues that it was in the 1870s that the theme of "*amour saphique*" crossed the Channel; see "Eliza Lynn Linton and the Rise of Lesbian Consciousness," *Journal of the History of Sexuality* 7:4 (April 1997): 537–60.

120 When the *Spectator*: See Geoffrey Harvey, *The Complete Critical Guide to Thomas Hardy* (London: Routledge, 2003), 19.

120 "too rank": See Thomas Hardy, *Desperate Remedies*, ed. Mary Rimmer (London: Penguin, 1998), 419.

120 "a creature of flame": Edith Johnstone, *A Sunless Heart* [1894], ed. Constance D. Harsh (Peterborough, Ont.: Broadview, 2008), 90, 101, 107, 145, 178, 134–35, 150.

121 "*be as others are*": Johnstone, *A Sunless Heart*, 178, 193–97.

121 "But why": Reviews excerpted in Johnstone, *A Sunless Heart*, 199–206.

122 Similarly, a boarding school: There were some earlier examples, such as Lawrence's *The Rainbow* (1915), charged by the crown prosecutor for "immoral representations of sexuality" in its depiction of a girl-teacher affair. But it was *Regiment of Women* that gave lasting form to the stereotype as seen in Harvey O'Higgins, *Julie Cane* (1924); Carol Denny Hill, *Wild* (1927); Warner Fabian, *Unforbidden Fruit* (1928); Ivy Compton-Burnett, *More Women Than Men* (1933); Francis Young, *White Ladies* (1935); Hugh Wheeler, *The Crippled Muse* (1952); and Violette Leduc's *Ravages* (1955).

122 "a very real tyrant": "Clemence Dane" [Winifred Ashton], *Regiment of Women* [1917] (Westport, Conn.: Greenwood Press, 1978), 92, 30, 66, 24, 71.

122 "The changing Alwynne": Dane, *Regiment of Women*, 198, 211, 221, 248, 254.

122 "sorcery": Dane, *Regiment of Women*, 287, 290, 296, 315, 329, 334–38, 344–45.

123 By the late nineteenth: Cryle, *The Telling of the Act*, 337–40.

124 "Ah!": Adrienne Saint-Agen, *L'Affolante Illusion* (aka *Charmeuses des Femmes*) (Paris: Offenstedt, 1906), 26–27.

124 "I have seen": Charles Montfort, *Le Journal d'une Saphiste* (1902), quotation translated in Catherine von Casselaer, *Lot's Wife: Lesbian Paris, 1890–1914* (Liverpool: Janus Press, 1986), 76.

125 Despite these last examples: The exceptions are a very mixed bag. Henry Fielding's fictionalized criminal biography *The Female Husband* (1746) is about a woman who passes as a man and fraudulently marries three different women "to satisfy her most monstrous and unnatural desires"; reprinted in

The Literature of Lesbianism, ed. Castle, 272–85. In Henri de Latouche's 1829 novel, *Fragoletta*, Rachilde's *Madame Adonis* (1888), and Mary Hatch's *The Strange Disappearance of Eugene Comstock* (1895), women seduce other women in disguise and die for it, but they are by no means described as fiends. Fragoletta is technically a hermaphrodite, as are the protagonists of J. Pierre Cuisin's *Clémentin orpheline et androgyne* (1819) and Honoré de Balzac's *Seraphitus-Seraphita* (1835), who are treated as fascinating and sympathetic figures, not as monsters in the moral sense.

125 Fiends can commit: Examples include Liane de Pougy's *Idylle Saphique* (1901); Adrienne Saint-Agen, *Amants féminins* (1902; in English, *Women Lovers*); Sinclair Lewis, *Ann Vickers* (1933); Angela Du Maurier, *The Little Less* (1941); Lillian Hellman, *The Children's Hour* (1934, discussed in chapter 6); Jack Woodford, *Male and Female* (1935); Dorothy Dodd Baker, *Trio* (1943); and Isaac Bashevis Singer, "Zeitl and Rickel" (1968).

125 "their bodies": Jane de la Vaudère, *Les Demi-sexes* (1897), quotation translated in Casselaer, *Lot's Wife*, 55.

125 Honoré de Balzac's: Jennifer Waelti-Walters in *Damned Women* (27, 89) makes the interesting point that *La Fille aux yeux d'or* and Théophile Gautier's *Mademoiselle de Maupin* (both published in 1835) are both really about "the struggle which takes place within a male ego when it is faced with a desired and unpossessible woman." The same argument could apply to other stories of men who are slow to understand the lesbian threat, by, for instance, Belot, Strindberg, Proust, and Bourdet.

126 "that eternally old": Honoré de Balzac, *The Girl with Golden Eyes*, trans. Carol Cosman (New York: Carroll & Graf, 1998), 51, 54, 73.

126 "Listen, I'm chained": Balzac, *The Girl*, 86–89, 101–3, 107.

127 "she was too intoxicated": Balzac, *The Girl*, 114–18.

127 "allergic to all men": Adolphe Belot, *Mademoiselle Giraud, My Wife* [1870], trans. Christopher Rivers (New York: Modern Language Association of America, 2002), 25–27, 30, 36, 51–53, 83–85, 87–91, 109, 115.

127 All she does: In this novel and Charles Montfort's *Le Journal d'une Saphiste* (1902), to name but two, a girls' school is ground zero for lesbian contagion. But other French writers treat school more blithely, as a place of undefined, flirty, or quarrelsome eroticism among girls and women; see Colette's *Claudine à l'école* (1900; in English, *Claudine at School*) and *Claudine en ménage* (1902; in English, *Claudine Married*); Suzanne Roland-Manuel, *Le Trille du diable* (1946; in English, *The Devil's Trill*); Nicole Louvier, *Qui qu'en grogne* (1954; in English, *Who Grumbles About It*); Jeanne Galzy, *Jeunes Filles en serre chaude* (1934; in English, *Girls in a Hothouse*) and *La Surprise de vivre* (1969–76, in English, *The Surprise of Living*).

128 "reptile": Belot, *Mademoiselle Giraud*, 147, 149–50, 160, 169, 178–79, 203–6. A milder Italian equivalent is Alfredo Oriani's second novel, *Al di là* (1889; in English, *Beyond*), in which an unhappy wife is seduced by an androgynous,

female-supremacist marchesa who sneers at marital affection as "a tamed tigress licking the hand of the man who kept her cage" and insists that "a tigress can only love another tigress." That the marchesa's vocabulary of captivity is not merely symbolic is suggested by the fact that she is waited on by naked, shackled black and Arab slave girls. Alfredo Oriani, *Al di là*, in *Tutte le opere*, 2 vols., ed. Benito Mussolini (Bologna: Capppelli, 1926–34), 1: 97, 103–106. See Daniela Danna, "Beauty and the Beast: Lesbians in Literature and Sexual Science from the Nineteenth to the Twentieth Centuries," in *Queer Italia: Same-Sex Desire in Italian Literature and Film*, ed. Gary P. Cestaro (New York: Palgrave Macmillan, 2004), 117–32 (120–22).

129   "In the Criminal Court": Quoted in Lisa Duggan, *Sapphic Slashers: Sex, Violence and American Modernity* (Durham, N.C.: Duke University Press, 2000), 24. Duggan analyzes the citing of these French authors in the Mitchell case, and the case's influence on later fictions by John Wesley Carhart and Mary E. Wilkins Freeman (181–86).

129   Sales of the flower: Kaier Curtin, *"We Can Always Call Them Bulgarians": The Emergence of Lesbian and Gay Men on the American Stage* (Boston: Alyson, 1987), 51.

129   "bold and strangely": Quoted in Florence Tamagne, *A History of Homosexuality in Europe: Berlin, London, Paris, 1919–1939* (New York: Algora Publishing, 2006), 213.

130   "to dwell among": Edouard Bourdet, *The Captive*, trans. Arthur Hornblow (New York: Brentano's, 1926), 148–49, 169–70, 178.

130   Everywoman: See also a German play, Hans Kaltneker's *Die Schwester* (1922; in English, *The Sister*). Sherrie Inness makes a convincing argument that the femme lesbian in texts such as *The Captive* was far more threatening to audiences/readers than the mannish invert of, say, *The Well of Loneliness* (1928), because she was not detectable at first sight—with the result that the femme type was less popular with authors and had far less literary influence; see *The Lesbian Menace: Ideology, Identity and the Representation of Lesbian Life* (Amherst: University of Massachusetts Press, 1997), 25–32.

130   Here the monster: The Galatea story is echoed in Belot's *Mademoiselle Giraud, ma femme* (1870), Catulle Mendès's *Méphistophéla* (1890), and Alfredo Oriani's *Al di là* (1889; in English, *Beyond*), when bridegrooms fail to arouse their stony—and secretly lesbian—wives. See Cryle, *The Telling of the Act*, 78–80.

130   Bourdet claimed: Curtin, *"We Can Always Call Them Bulgarians,"* 56–57, 100; *New York Times*, March 9, 1927; Jonathan Ned Katz, *Gay/Lesbian Almanac* (New York: Harper and Row, 1983), 426–28.

132   "She felt in her heart": Marcel Proust, *In Search of Lost Time*, trans. C. K. Scott Moncrieff and Terence Kilmartin, revised by D. J. Enright (London: Vintage, 1996), 687–88.

132   "We cannot say": Marcel Proust, "Before Dark" [1896], in *The Literature of Lesbianism*, ed. Castle, 581–84 (583).

132 "devil-woman": H. Rider Haggard, *Allan's Wife* [1889] (London: Hodder and Stoughton, 1914), 102, 170.

133 "I have been very fond": Haggard, *Allan's Wife*, 188–89, 194, 246.

133 "the lower one": Haggard, *Allan's Wife*, 172.

134 The link goes back: Samuel Taylor Coleridge, *Christabel* (1816), in *The Literature of Lesbianism*, ed. Castle, 360–79 (LL.168–69, 372).

134 Ghost stories: Terry Castle argues that Western literature more broadly uses spectral language to cast lesbians as ghosts and lesbianism "as absence, as chimera or *amor impossibilis*"; see *The Apparitional Lesbian: Female Homosexuality and Modern Culture* (New York: Columbia University Press, 1993), 28–65 (30).

134 "queer-looking": Elizabeth Bowen, "The Apple Tree" (1934), in *The Collected Stories* (London: Jonathan Cape, 1980), 461–70 (468–70). Other ghost stories that hinge on such unfinished business include Margaret Oliphant's "Old Lady Mary" (1885) and Rosemary Timperley's "The Mistress in Black" (1969).

135 "took a girl": Shirley Jackson, *The Haunting of Hill House* [1959] (London: Michael Joseph, 1980), 67–69, 12, 74, 99, 111, 115, 125, 133, 137.

136 "It was as if": Edith Olivier, *The Love Child* [1927] (London: Virago, 1981), 21, 23–24, 17.

136 "attraction": Olivier, *The Love Child*, 64–70, 134, 143, 149, 179–80.

136 "I belong to Agatha": Olivier, *The Love Child*, 190, 193. A later Quebecois equivalent is Louise Maheux-Forcier's *Une forêt pour Zoé* (1969; in English, *A Forest for Zoe*), in which the narrator is preoccupied by the seductive, ghostly presence of her–possibly imaginary–childhood friend.

137 The vampire, too: For similarities between the representation of lesbians and vampires, see Richard Dyer, *Now You See It* (New York: Routledge, 1990), 272.

138 "unintelligible": Joseph Sheridan Le Fanu, *Carmilla* (1872), in *Chloe Plus Olivia: An Anthology of Lesbian Literature from the Seventeenth Century to the Present*, ed. Lillian Faderman (New York: Viking, 1994), 303–62 (316, 319–20, 329, 333). See Nina Auerbach on the twinning of victim and villain in *Christabel* and *Carmilla*, in *Our Vampires, Ourselves* (Chicago: University of Chicago Press, 1995), 32–53.

138 But even if Laura's: Le Fanu, *Carmilla*, 329, 333.

138 "the Female enraged": Bertha Harris, "What We Mean to Say: Notes Toward Defining the Nature of Lesbian Literature," *Heresies* 30:3 (September 1977): 5–8 (7).

138 In her fascinating study: Paulina Palmer, *Lesbian Gothic: Transgressive Fictions* (London: Cassell, 1999), 4, 63.

139 "Your body is not my food": Katherine V. Forrest, "O Captain, My Captain," in *Dreams and Swords* (Tallahassee, Fla.: Naiad, 1987), 107–65 (125). See Palmer, *Lesbian Gothic*, 113–14. For a discussion of lesbian science fiction, see Patricia Duncker, *Sisters and Strangers: An Introduction to Contemporary Feminist Fiction* (Oxford: Blackwell, 1992), 99–120.

139 "There are only": Jewelle Gomez, *The Gilda Stories* [1991] (London: Sheba, 1992), 31, 43.

139 "I have had Miss Wade": Dickens, *Little Dorrit*, 753, 506, 618–19.

139 "fighting a losing battle": Diderot, *La Religieuse*, 174.

139 "my diseased imagination": Musset, *Gamiani*, 46.

Chapter Five: Detection

140 Lesbians kill: See George Moore, *Sappho* (1881); Francis Lepage, *Les Fausses vierges* (1902; in English, *The False Virgins*); William Hurlbut, *Sin of Sins* (1926); Hermann Sudermann, *Die Freundin* (1913–14; in English, *The Girlfriend*); Alfred Döblin, *Die beiden Freundinnen und ihr Giftmord* (1924; in English, *The Two Girlfriends and Their Murder by Poison*); Vita Sackville-West, *The Dark Island* (1934); Flora Fletcher, *Strange Sisters* (1954); and "Vin Packer" (Marijane Meaker), *The Evil Friendship* (1958), a thinly veiled version of the Parker-Hulme matricide in 1954 New Zealand, which also inspired Peter Jackson's film *Heavenly Creatures* (1994).

140 Often they murder: See, for instance, Françoise Mallet-Joris's "Jimmy" (1965) or Leda Starr's *All at Once* (1967).

140 And they can be victims: Henri de Latouche, *Fragoletta* (1829); Honoré de Balzac, *La Fille aux yeux d'or* (1835); Adolphe Belot, *Mademoiselle Giraud ma femme* (1870); Rachilde, *Madame Adonis* (1888); Adrienne Saint-Agen, *Amants féminins* (1902; in English, *Women Lovers*); Frank Wedekind, *Erdgeist* (1895; in English, *Earth Spirit*) and *Die Büsche der Pandora* (1904; in English, *Pandora's Box*); D. H. Lawrence, *The Fox* (1922); Vita Sackville-West, *The Dark Island* (1934); Lilyan Brock, *Queer Patterns* (1935); George Willis, *Little Boy Blues* (1947); Simon Eisner, *Naked Storm* (1952); and Martin Kramer, *The Hearth and the Strangeness* (1956).

141 Perhaps the earliest: Gladys Mitchell, *Speedy Death* (London: Victor Gollancz, 1929).

142 "a hieroglyph": Marjorie Garber, *Vested Interests: Cross-dressing and Cultural Anxiety* (New York: Routledge, 1992), 188–89.

142 Inspector Wexford: Ruth Rendell, *From Doon with Death* [1964] (London: Hutchinson, 1975).

143 "the creature": Josephine Tey, *To Love and Be Wise* [1950] (London: P. Davies, 1966), 37, 242–55. For a brilliant analysis of the slippery figure of Leslie, see Garber, *Vested Interests*, 196–202.

143 "*chérie*": Cynthia Asquith, "The Lovely Voice," in *This Mortal Coil: Tales* (Sauk City, Wis.: Arkham House, 1947) 203–27 (205–8). Similarly in *The House of Stairs* (1988), by Barbara Vine (the pseudonym Ruth Rendell uses for psychological thrillers), the female narrator is infatuated with the killer, and

the erotic identification between narrator and killer undermines the traditional structure of detection and punishment.

144   "repeated kisses": Asquith, "The Lovely Voice," 209, 215–16, 221.

144   "her own wonderful colouring": Asquith, "The Lovely Voice," 227.

146   "a young, fresh": L. T. Meade, *The Sorceress of the Strand* (London: Ward, Lock & Co., 1903), 15, 24, 31.

146   "I love her": Meade, *The Sorceress*, 35, 59, 70, 81, 77, 203, 212–13.

146   "Hunting her": Meade, *The Sorceress*, 272, 307. For other sapphic characters by L. T. Meade, see, for instance, *A Sweet Girl Graduate* (1886) and *The Siren* (1898).

147   This is the case: She credited J. Edgar Chamberlain as co-author, but all he seems to have done is help her shape the piece to the syndicate's specifications.

147   Her neighbors: Mary E. Wilkins (later Freeman), "The Long Arm" (1895), in *Chloe Plus Olivia: An Anthology of Lesbian Literature from the Seventeenth Century to the Present*, ed. Lillian Faderman (New York: Viking, 1994), 372–98 (375, 378, 381, 392–93).

148   Like many fictions: Valerie Rohy, " 'The Long Arm' and the Law," *South Central Review* 18:3–4 (Autumn–Winter 2001): 102–18.

148   "I stopped it": Wilkins, "The Long Arm," 394–98.

148   "I couldn't have her": Mary E. Wilkins (later Freeman), "Two Friends" (1887), in *Chloe Plus Olivia*, ed. Faderman, 77–88 (85, 88). See also Elizabeth Gaskell's *Cranford* (1851–53), in which cravat-wearing Deborah Jenkyns prevents her sister Matty from leaving her for a man.

149   Wilkins was writing: For more about this fascinating author, see Leah Blatt Glasser, *In a Closet Hidden: The Life and Work of Mary E. Wilkins Freeman* (Amherst: University of Massachusetts Press, 1996).

149   But as Lillian Faderman: Faderman, *Chloe Plus Olivia*, 372.

149   "You loved Verity": Agatha Christie, *Nemesis* (London: William Collins, 1971), 159, 229–30.

150   Interestingly: For instance, in John Flagg, *Murder in Monaco* (London: L. Miller, 1957).

150   "Does anybody": "Hilda Lawrence" [Hildegarde Kronmiller], *Death of a Doll* (London: Chapman & Hall, 1948), 39, 89, 213, 277, 284. Stella in P. D. James's *Death of an Expert Witness* (1977) gets into the dangerous game of blackmail to secure a loan to buy the swamp cottage where she lives with her beloved secretary, Angela—which suggests her death might have been prevented if the bank had had a more enlightened policy of giving mortgages to same-sex couples.

151   "A more orthodox blackmailer": P. D. James, *Shroud for a Nightingale* [1971] (London: Penguin, 1989), 305. For a similar excessive protectiveness, see Josephine Tey's *Miss Pym Disposes* (1946), in which a gym student arranges a fatal accident to secure her beloved a good job.

151 "The happiest marriages": James, *Shroud for a Nightingale*, 3.

152 "*domestic* partner": Dorothy L. Sayers, *Unnatural Death* (London: Ernest Benn, 1927), 85, 141, 138, 176–82, 184.

152 "Humiliating": Sayers, *Unnatural Death*, 252.

153 "There's nothing": Sayers, *Unnatural Death*, 274–77.

154 "almost a moustache": Wilkie Collins, *The Woman in White*, ed. Julian Symons (Harmondsworth, U.K.: Penguin, 1974), 58, 61, 148.

155 "I won't live without her": Collins, *The Woman in White*, 61. There are many other texts published in the same decade in which sisters express romantic or pseudomarital sentiments for each other: Christina Rossetti, *Goblin Market* (1862); Elizabeth Stoddard, *The Morgesons* (1862); Charlotte M. Yonge, *The Clever Woman of the Family* (1865); George Meredith, *Rhoda Fleming* (1865); Elizabeth Gaskell, *Wives and Daughters* (1866); and Louisa M. Alcott, *Little Women* (1868). See "The Double Taboo: Lesbian Incest in the Nineteenth Century," in Sara Annes Brown, *Devoted Sisters: Representations of the Sister Relationship in Nineteenth-Century British and American Literature* (Aldershot, U.K.: Ashgate, 2003), 135–54.

155 "Men!": Collins, *The Woman in White*, 148, 203, 207–8.

156 Though not, presumably: See Kirsten Huttner, *The Woman in White: Analysis, Reception and Literary Criticism of a Victorian Bestseller* (Trier, Germany: Wissenschafflicher Verlag, 1996), 67.

156 "I am all aflame": Collins, *The Woman in White*, 63, 208, 214, 216, 236, 268, 248.

156 "our endurance must end": Collins, *The Woman in White*, 340, 342, 443, 454, 225.

157 For a modern equivalent: Perhaps the first overtly lesbian police officer appears in George Baxt's homophobic *Burning Sappho* (1972), but her investigation into the radical women's movement promptly scares her straight. The first lesbian-feminist crime novel is M. F. Beal's *Angel Dance* (New York: Daughters Publishing Co., 1977), featuring a radical, bed-hopping, half-Cuban lesbian private eye. See Sally Munt, *Murder by the Book? Feminism and the Crime Novel* (London: Routledge, 1994), 121–22, and Phyllis Betz, *Lesbian Detective Fiction: Woman as Author, Subject and Reader* (Jefferson, N.C.: McFarland, 2006).

157 It is standard protocol: Barbara Wilson (now Barbara Sjoholm), *Murder in the Collective* (1984); Katherine V. Forrest, *Amateur City* (1984).

157 "You could get killed": Katherine V. Forrest, *Murder at the Nightwood Bar* [1987] (Tallahassee, Fla.: Naiad, 1995), 216, 15, 102, 206. The title alludes to Djuna Barnes's modernist fantasia of lesbians and other outcasts, *Nightwood* (1936).

158 "If people can't imagine": Peggy Sumner, *The End of April* (London: Women's Press, 1992), 18–19.

159 "lady visitor": Sarah Waters, *Affinity* (London: Virago, 1999), 341.

159 "I feel the mounting pressure": Sarah Waters, *Fingersmith* (New York: Riverhead Books, 2002), 250.

160 "make it ours": Waters, *Fingersmith*, 124–25, 263.

160 "She has made a fiction": Waters, *Fingersmith*, 279, 244, 506–9.

Chapter Six: Out

161 The term: Sylvia Plath has been credited with its first use, in an essay in the *London Magazine* of January 16, 1963.

161 "I love, and only love": Anne Lister, *I Know My Own Heart: The Diaries of Anne Lister (1791–1840)*, ed. Helen Whitbread (London: Virago, 1988), 145, 273.

161 But this storyline: The idea of coming out as a healthy and useful process has been credited to Karl-Heinrich Ulrichs, who campaigned openly as an "Urning" (his word for a man attracted to men) in Germany from the 1860s.

162 The discovery of same-six desires: Bonnie Zimmerman, *The Safe Sea of Women: Lesbian Fiction, 1969–1989* [1990] (London: Onlywomen, 1992), 35–37.

163 In the second half of the nineteenth: The idea of the invert was first suggested in 1860s Germany in the writings of sexologists including Karl Heinrich Ulrichs and Carl von Westphal, then developed by Richard von Krafft-Ebing (*Psychopathia Sexualis*, 1886) and Havelock Ellis (*Studies in the Psychology of Sex: Sexual Inversion* [1896]). Basing his theory on his woman-loving wife, Edith, Ellis specified that the female "true invert" (as opposed to her "false invert" or "passive invert" girlfriend) had to have a certain innate (though not always visible) masculinity, plus neurosis and girlhood crushes on other girls. See Lillian Faderman, *Surpassing the Love of Men: Romantic Friendship and Love Between Women from the Renaissance to the Present* [1981] (London: Women's Press, 1985), 239–49.

164 "love that was wild": George Moore, *A Drama in Muslin* [1886] (Gerrards Cross, U.K.: Colin Smythe, 1981), 3, 6, 185–86. The names Cecilia and Alice are clearly borrowed from Longfellow's novel *Kavanagh* (1849), about two friends parted by a man.

164 "misshapen body": Moore, *Drama*, 187, 226–27, 298.

165 "The monster which had always": Catulle Mendès, *Méphistophéla* (Paris: E. Dentu, 1890), 35–36, 81, 103, 118–20, 123, 134, 138, 149. "Le monstre qui, de tout temps, fut en elle, en voulait sortir et se satisfaire." All translations from *Méphistophéla* are by Emma Donoghue.

165 "stupid creature": Mendès, *Méphistophéla*, 143, 157, 180–85, 195, 212, 269. "Stupide creature, inachevée, infirme, aimant sans savoir aimer, convoitant sans savoir posséder" . . . "les mysterieux rites du culture dont elle etait l'oblaie instinctive."

166 "sullen in her terrible joys": Mendès, *Méphistophéla*, 10–13, 258, 260, 295, 308,

323. "Elle s'en orguillissait d'etre . . . detestable." "Morose dans ses affreuses joies." "Il semble qu'elle ne veut pas son vice, qu'il lui est indifférent, odieux mème, mais qu'elle y est obligée, qu'elle y est soumise comme à une insecouable loi."

166   But as Peter Cryle notes: Peter Cryle, *The Telling of the Act: Sexuality as Narrative in Eighteenth- and Nineteenth-Century France* (Newark: University of Delaware Press and London: Associated University Presses, 2001), 320–21, 332–34. Mendès, *Méphistophéla*, 392. "Le désir jamais repu."

166   "straight to her damnation": Mendès, *Méphistophéla*, 11. 'Elle réalise sa damnation, sans halte, tout droit, comme une pierre tombe."

167   "not a marrying woman": Sylvia Stevenson, *Surplus* (London: Longmans, Green, 1924), 16, 113, 106, 66. Note that Sally's surname, Wraith, links her to Terry Castle's idea of the "apparitional lesbian." The novel was reprinted by Naiad Press in 1985.

167   "abnormal": Stevenson, *Surplus*, 134, 226, 230, 207–8, 293, 294, 299, 227, 314–15.

168   "mistaken in thinking": Reviews quoted in Jonathan Ned Katz, *Gay/Lesbian Almanac* (New York: Harper and Row, 1983), 408–10.

169   It is no accident: Not that the results are always benign; in Mary Lapsley's *The Parable of the Virgins* (1931), a female college doctor breaks up a pair of "inseparable" roommates, triggering the suicide of one of them. Similarly, in *Strange Fire* (1952) by "Vin Packer" (Marijane Meaker), the dean of women and a college doctor intervene to split up a couple (who have reached the point of naming themselves as "lesbians"), saving the not-really-queer-after-all heroine from her girlfriend (revealed as insane); this cancelled coming-out story sold 1.5 million copies and launched the genre of lesbian pulp.

169   "nunnish": Kate O'Brien, *Mary Lavelle* (London: William Heinemann, 1936), 84, 97, 100, 119, 284–86, 296–98. The novel was banned for obscenity in Ireland, and filmed as *Talk of Angels* in 1998.

169   "inverted women": Aimée Duc, *Sind es Frauen?* (1903). No complete translation into English has been published; my quotes are from the excerpts in *Lesbian-Feminism in Turn-of-the-Century Germany*, ed. Lillian Faderman and Brigitte Eriksson (Tallahassee, Fla.: Naiad: 1980), 1–21. Faderman and Eriksson emphasize how completely Duc departed from the stern conventions of lesbian-themed fiction in German, such as R. von Seyditz, *Pierres Ehe: Psychologisch Probleme* (1900); Alfred Meebold, "Dr. Erna Redens Thorheit und Erkenntnis" (1900); Jacob Wassermann, *Geschichte der Junge, Renate Fuchs* (1900); George Kenan, *Unter Frauen* (1901); Heinrich Mann, *Die Gottinen* (1902); Frank Wedekind, *Mine-haha* (1905); and Maria Janitschelk, *Die Neva Eva* (1906). See Biddy Martin's fascinating chapter on *Sind es Frauen?*, "Extraordinary Homosexuals and the Fear of Being Ordinary," in her *Femininity Played Straight: The Significance of Being Lesbian* (New York: Routledge, 1996), 45–70.

171   "That would be a crime": Renée Vivien, *A Woman Appeared to Me* [1904], trans. Jeannette H. Foster (Reno, Nev.: Naiad Press, 1976), 7–8, 1. See Martha

Vicinus, *Intimate Friends: Women Who Loved Women, 1778–1928* (Chicago: University of Chicago Press, 2004), 190–98.

171 "merely female": "Christopher St. John" (Christabel Marshall), *Hungerheart: The Story of a Soul* (London: Methuen, 1915), 58, 98, 219, 88, 226. The coincidence of the name Sally, for the straying friend, may suggest that Sylvia Stephenson read this before writing *Surplus* (1924). The one critic who has paid *Hungerheart* real attention is David Trotter, who describes its plot as "serial rather than developmental," and argues that the book avoided prosecution for its lesbian content (unlike Lawrence's *The Rainbow*, published by the same publisher in the same year) because of its disavowal of lust; see "Lesbians Before Lesbianism: Sexual Identity in Early Twentieth-Century British Fiction," in *Borderlines: Genders and Identities in War and Peace, 1870–1930*, ed. Billie Melman (London: Routledge, 1998), 193–211 (206–9). For comparison, see Jean de Kellac's *A Lesbos* (1891; in English, *To Lesbos*), in which a rebellious tomboy finds herself attracted to her own sex but insists on spurning the advances of various decadent, aristocratic women.

172 "Exaggerating her actions": Jacques de Lacretelle, *Marie Bonifas* [1925] (London: Putnam's, 1927), 40, 114, 130, 146, 148–49, 164, 177, 185, 189, 193–97, 199–202. The novel was filmed for French TV as *La Boniface* in 1968.

172 But by far the most famous: For reviews and reports on the book's legal difficulties, see Katz, *Gay/Lesbian Almanac*, 444–46.

173 Her protagonist, Stephen: See Kim Emery, *The Lesbian Index: Pragmatism and Lesbian Subjectivity in the Twentieth-Century United States* (Albany: State University of New York Press, 2002), 71–72.

173 "that wilfully selfish": Radclyffe Hall, *The Well of Loneliness* [1928] (London: Virago, 1982), 13, 121, 153, 205, 275, 302–3, 324, 316, 396, 433.

174 "difference": "Jo Sinclair" [Ruth Seid], *Wasteland* [1946] (New York: Jewish Publication Society, 1987), 33, 153, 193, 5, 155–56, 211. *Wasteland* anticipates later titles such as Noretta Koertge's *Who Was That Masked Woman?* (1981) and Lisa Alther's *Other Women* (1984) in which psychotherapy shapes the coming-out process.

174 *Wasteland* won: See Monica Bachmann, " 'Someone like Debby': (De)Constructing a Lesbian Community of Readers," *GLQ: A Journal of Lesbian and Gay Studies* 6:3 (2000): 377–88.

174 "My love for Marie": John Wesley Carhart, *Norma Trist* (Austin, Texas: Eugene von Boeckmann, 1895), 228, 67, 21, 69, 7, 61–62, 244.

176 "the existence of an individual": Kim Emery offers a fascinating analysis of Carhart's rejection of both the sexological distinction between congenital and acquired homosexuality, and lesbianism's associations with degeneration; see *The Lesbian Index*, 31–56 (47, 52).

176 "I feel no condemnation": Carhart, *Norma Trist*, 53–62 (61).

176 "psychopathia-sexualis": Carhart, *Norma Trist*, 184–85, 205–6, 209, 211–12, 216–18. Mrs. LaMoreaux, on the other hand, is a mistress of denial: when she

and Norma are not in bed yielding to "the full sway of passion's convulsive joys," she talks as if they are just good friends; she refuses to take any part in the prosecution, marries her captain, and never mentions Norma's name again; see 11, 21, 36–37, 53, 189, 204.

177   "I abhor the love": Carhart, *Norma Trist*, 218, 55–57, 182, 186–87, 205–11, 248, 239–40, 251.

177   "that all this normalcy": Emery, *The Lesbian Index*, 56. The dubiousness of hypnosis is suggested by a funny tangent to the plot: Dr. Jasper falls in love with Norma's widowed mother and it turns out that she, entirely self-taught, hypnotized him into it, to motivate him to work hard on Norma (Carhart, *Norma Trist*, 250).

178   "I love you that way": Lillian Hellman, *The Children's Hour* [1934], in *The Collected Plays* (Boston: Little, Brown, 1972), 1–69 (18, 62).

178   The *New York Times*: Brooks Atkinson, "The Children's Hour," *New York Times*, November 21, 1934.

178   But I believe: Compare Maeve Binchy's economical story "Holland Park" (in *Victoria Line, Central Line*, 1980), in which the narrator—appalled when she and her friend are mistaken for a lesbian couple by ostentatiously liberal hosts of a party—then realizes that she is in love with her friend after all.

178   Because the fact is: Even with the late revelation and suicide ending, the play was banned in Britain and only allowed to be put on by a private theater club. William Wyler had to completely heterosexualize the story to film it as *These Three* (1936); only after another quarter century was he able to remake it with original plot and title (*The Children's Hour*, 1961), which led to another battle with the censors and finally the Hays Code being significantly toned down to permit "tasteful" treatments of homosexuality. See Andrea Weiss, *Vampires and Violets: Lesbians in Film* [1992] (New York: Penguin Books, 1993), 52, 67–70.

178   "physical abnormalities": Anna Elisabet Weirauch, *The Scorpion* [1919–21], abridged and trans. Whittaker Chambers (New York: Arno Press, 1975), 29, 64–67, 88–89, 77, 98, 108, 127–28. Kim Emery points out several key ways in which *The Scorpion* influenced *The Well of Loneliness*: the early guilty crush on a family servant, for instance, and the scene in the dead father's study in which the protagonist discovers herself in medical writings; see *The Lesbian Index*, 71. In several other novels, threats of exposure in court are used to try to break up a lesbian relationship—successfully in *Winter Love* (1962), a poignant novella by Chinese-Flemish "Han Suyin" (Elizabeth Comber), but unsuccessfully in Jane Rule's quietly modern *Desert of the Heart* (1964).

179   "It would be useless": "Claire Morgan" (Patricia Highsmith), *Carol* [*The Price of Salt*, 1952] (London: Penguin, 1991), 227–29.

180   "silly promises": Highsmith, *Carol*, 248, 228, 250.

181   "lesbian mother": Sheila Ortiz Taylor, *Faultline* (Tallahassee, Fla.: Naiad, 1982), 6.

181   In works about: In Michèle Roberts's *A Piece of the Night* (1978) and Norma

Klein's *Breaking Up* (1980) the threat comes from the child's father, but Jax Peters Lowell's *Mothers* (1995) has a twist: it is the non-birth mother's mother who sues for custody on the somewhat illogical basis that her (nonbiological) grandson is being raised in an unhealthy atmosphere. Sometimes what results is more of a thriller than a courtroom drama, because mothers often go on the run from a legal system that is biased against them. Examples include Marge Piercy, *Small Changes* (1973); Sarah Daniels, *Neaptide* (1986); Cristina Salat, *Living in Secret* (1993); and Jan Clausen, *Sinking, Stealing* (1985). For comparison, narratives about mothers getting involved with women that do *not* focus on the legal angle include Iréne Monési, *Althia* (1957); Jeanne Galzy's *La Surprise de vivre* (in English, *Surprise of Life*) series (1969–76); Marijane Meaker, *Shockproof Sydney Skate* (1972); Marianne Hauser, *The Talking Room* (1976); Sheila Ortiz Taylor's trilogy *Faultline* (1982), *Spring Forward, Fall Back* (1985), and *Southbound* (1990); Gillian Hanscombe, *Between Friends* (1982); Ruth Geller, *Triangles* (1984); Ellen Frye, *Look Under the Hawthorn* (1987); Hélène de Monferrand's *Les Amies d'Héloïse* trilogy (1990–1997); Barbara Wilson (later Barbara Sjoholm), *Gaudi Afternoon* (1990); Edith Forbes, *Alma Rose* (1993) and *Navigating the Darwin Straits* (2001); Ruthann Robson, *Another Mother* (1995); Cherríe Moraga, *Mexican Medea* (1995); Mary Dorcey, *Biography of Desire* (1997); Carol Anshaw, *Lucky in the Corner* (2002); and Caroline Williams, *Pretending* (2006).

181 As Terry Castle: Terry Castle, introduction to *The Literature of Lesbianism: A Historical Anthology from Ariosto to Stonewall* (New York: Columbia University Press, 2003), 35.

181 "the love of human beings": Charlotte Brontë, *Jane Eyre* [1847] (London: Collins, 1950), 42, 59, 61, 65.

181 In schoolgirl fiction: Notably in "L. T. Meade" (Elizabeth Thomasina Meade Smith), *A Sweet Girl Graduate* (1886) and *The School Favourite* (1908); Caroline Fuller, *Across the Campus* (1899); Ellen Thorneycroft Fowler, *The Farringdons* (1900); Josephine Dodge Daskam Bacon, *Smith College Stories* (1900); Amy Blanchard, *Janet's College Career* (1904); Julia Schwartz, *Elinor's College Career* (1906); and Christina Catrevas, *That Freshman* (1910). Innocence about same-sex love within the cozy confines of the girls' school story lasted well into the second decade of the twentieth century; a striking late example is Jennette Lee's "The Cat and the King" (*Ladies' Home Journal*, 1919). See Sherrie Inness, *Intimate Communities: Representation and Social Transformation in Women's College Fiction, 1895–1910* (Bowling Green, Ohio: Bowling Green State University Popular Press, 1995), 47, 53, and her *The Lesbian Menace: Ideology, Identity and the Representation of Lesbian Life* (Amherst: University of Massachusetts Press, 1997), 33–51, as well as Rosemary Auchmuty, *A World of Girls* (London: Women's Press, 1992), 107–80. Passionate and jealous connections between schoolgirls and/or teachers are also central to texts in other genres, such as Alfred Lord Tennyson's poem *The Princess* (1853); Gabrielle Reuter, *Aus Guter*

Familie (1895; in English, *A Girl from a Nice Family*); and "Henry Handel Richardson" (Ethel Richardson), *The Getting of Wisdom* (1910).

181　Some critics dismiss: Mary Cadogan and Patricia Craig, *You're a Brick, Angela! The Girls' Story, 1839–1985* (London: V. Gollancz, 1986), 122: "The girls were at an age when they had to fall in love with someone; to pick on members of their own sex may have been just a matter of expediency." This "situational lesbianism" argument also gets applied to prisons and convents.

183　"I could never love": "Clemence Dane" (Winifred Ashton), *Regiment of Women* [1917] (Westport, Conn.: Greenwood Press, 1978), 45, 53, 124, 105, 150, 164, 175.

183　Christa Winsloe's: The play was produced in Leipzig in 1930 as *Ritter Nérestan*, then in Berlin as *Gestern und heute*. The novel was published as *Gestern und heute* in 1932, as *Das Mädchen Manuela* in Amsterdam in 1933, and translated into English as *The Child Manuela* the same year.

183　"makes no favourites": Christa Winsloe, *The Child Manuela*, trans. Agnes Neill Scott, intro. Alison Hennegan (London: Virago, 1994), 173, 183, 198, 228, 257- 59.

184　"shocking": Winsloe, *The Child Manuela*, 188, 191, 270, 290. In the famous early sound film, *Mädchen in Uniform* (1931), the suicide is averted by the last-minute intervention of the other girls, prompted by Bernburg. In Germany the film was suppressed by the Nazis. In America, censors would not let the film be shown until cuts were made and subtitles were deleted, to obscure the relationship between Bernburg and Manuela; see Vito Russo, *The Celluloid Closet: Homosexuality in the Movies* (London: Harper & Row, 1981), 56–58. There was a color film released in 1950.

184　"There is something": Eveline Mahyère, *I Will Not Serve* [1958], trans. Antonia White, intro. Georgina Hammick (London: Virago, 1984), 14, 25.

185　"I hope that you will": Mahyère, *I Will Not Serve*, 21, 27, 34, 56–59, 126, 128, 146. For another interesting, literary coming-of-age/coming-out novel, see Rosamond Lehmann's *Dusty Answer* (1927).

186　"the biggest mistake": Quoted by Georgina Hammick, introduction to Mahyère, *I Will Not Serve*, xviii.

186　Bussy wrote it: Filmed by Jacqueline Audry in 1951, with a script by Colette, it was released after considerable cutting with the lurid title of *The Pit of Loneliness*.

186　"Julie-ites": "Olivia" (Dorothy Strachey Bussy), *Olivia* [1949] (London: The Reader's Union–The Hogarth Press, 1950), 39, 24.

186　"She communicated": Bussy, *Olivia*, 30, 9, 21, 42–48, 55–57.

187　"Mystery was all": Bussy, *Olivia*, 56, 58, 63–64, 70–72, 75–76, 91, 95, 100, 105–6. The tradition of sublimated schoolgirl yearning came to a sharp end with Violette Leduc's short, explicit novel about her affair with another schoolgirl, *Thérèse et Isabelle* (written by 1954, published 1966). Brigid Brophy's *The Finishing School* (1963) hilariously reprises elements of both *Olivia* and *The*

Children's Hour: when rumors of lesbianism at a Riviera boarding school hit the papers, some pupils are withdrawn from the school, but new ones make a point of applying.

188   "Colonna": Mary Renault, *Purposes of Love* [1939] (Harmondsworth, U.K.: Penguin, 1986), 41.

189   Stephen's Paris friend: Vicinus, *Intimate Friends,* 181.

189   "For God's sake": Hall, *The Well of Loneliness,* 443.

189   Sybil/Bill mixes all her signals: Thomas Beer, "Hallowe'en," in *Mrs. Egg and Other Barbarians* [1927] (London: Cassell, 1934), 36–59.

190   "just a drop in the bucket": Tiffany Thayer, *Thirteen Women* (New York: Claude Kendall, 1932), 151–83 (159–62, 174, 183).

191   Judy Gardiner's novella: Judy Gardiner, "Fidelia" in *The Power of Sergeant Mettleship* [1967], reprinted as *Waltzing Matilda* (London: Sphere, 1972), 9–56 (9, 12–13, 15–18, 21, 25–29, 34, 38–40, 42, 44, 54.

192   This hilarious novella: There were a few earlier texts that showed two women raising children together, rather than a lesbian couple deliberately bringing a child into their relationship: a Polish novel by Paulina Kuczalska-Reinschmit, *Siostry* (1908; in English, *Sisters*); and a Danish one, Agnete Holk's *Strange Friends* (1941). In Ann Bannon's *Journey to a Woman* (1960), a lesbian and a gay man marry to have a baby. For some reason, the more recent lesbian baby boom (including birth and adoption) has not produced a great deal of fiction or drama yet. Notable exceptions are the *Dykes to Watch Out For* graphic novels (from 1986), by that Dickens of lesbian life, Alison Bechdel. See also Patricia Grossman, *Unexpected Child* (2000); Mark Ravenhill, *Handbag* (2000); Brendan Halpin, *Donorboy* (2004); and Stacey D'Erasmo's *A Seahorse Year* (2004).

192   "defiant lesbian hero": Gabriele Griffin, *Heavenly Love? Lesbian Images in Twentieth-Century Women's Writing* (Manchester, U.K.: Manchester University Press, 1993), 62.

192   "Me being a queer": Rita Mae Brown, *Rubyfruit Jungle* [1977] (New York: Bantam, 1977), 203, 44, 70.

193   "So now I wear": Brown, *Rubyfruit,* 159, 128–31, 107, 220. For a story of a sixteen-year-old lesbian runaway locked up as "incorrigible" in a mental hospital in the early 1960s, see Madelyn Arnold's *Bird-Eyes* (1998). Kim Emery points out (*The Lesbian Index,* 110) that although Brown's novel is often hailed as the complete rebuttal of *The Well of Loneliness,* its story of a brilliant tomboy who finds freedom in the big city is actually "rife with resemblance to its infamous predecessor."

193   But many coming-out novels: Persecution can lead to emigration: in Elizabeth Riley's *All That False Instruction* (1975) and Fiona Cooper's *Not the Swiss Family Robinson* (1991), an Australian and an American respectively decide to try their luck in England. Audre Lorde's *Zami: A New Spelling of My Name—A Biomythography* (1982) was very influential, with its semifictional

musings on an African-American lesbian's woman-centered Grenadan heritage. Jacqueline Woodson and Shay Youngblood mull over queer African-American childhoods (urban and rural respectively) in *Autobiography of a Family Photo* (1995) and *Soul Kiss* (1997). Judith Katz's *Running Fiercely Toward a High Thin Sound* (1992) uses magic realist techniques to illuminate the cultural complexity of two Jewish lesbian sisters at college in the 1960s, Judy Doenges's *The Most Beautiful Girl in the World* (2006) is about coming out on the wrong side of the tracks, Michelle Cliff's *Abeng* (1984) takes as its protagonist a biracial girl in Jamaica, Achy Obejas's *Memory Mambo* (1996) weighs the ups and downs and ethics of coming out in a Cuban family in Chicago, and Mary Dorcey's lyrical *A Noise from the Woodshed* (1989) does the same for rural Ireland.

193   "had known this would happen": Valerie Miner, *Blood Sisters* (London: Women's Press, 1982), 126.

193   Interestingly, these characters: Classic examples include Marge Piercy, *Small Changes* (1973); Verena Stefan, *Häutungen* (1975; in English, *Shedding*); Nancy Toder, *Choices* (1980); Joanna Russ, *On Strike Against God* (1980); and Carol Anne Douglas, *To the Cleveland Station* (1982).

194   "Unnatural Passion": Jeanette Winterson, *Oranges Are Not the Only Fruit* (London: Pandora, 1985), 89, 102, 109.

194   "There must be others": Ann Allen Shockley, *Loving Her* [1974] (Boston: Northeastern University Press, 1997), 64.

194   "There is not anywhere": Richard Lockridge, "The New Play," *New York Sun*, November 21, 1934.

194   And indeed in fiction: See Linnea A. Stenson, "From Isolation to Diversity: Self and Communities in Twentieth-Century Lesbian Novels," in *Sexual Practice, Textual Theory: Lesbian Cultural Criticism*, ed. Susan J. Wolfe and Julia Penelope (Cambridge, Mass.: Blackwell, 1993), 208–25 (215–19).

195   The first two are by Ann Bannon: Lesbian pulp was often written by and aimed at men, but Yvonne Heller proposes a useful subcategory of "pro-lesbian pulp," often written by lesbians, in "Pulp Politics: Strategies of Vision in Pro-Lesbian Pulp Novels, 1955–65," in *The Queer Sixties*, ed. Patricia Juliana Smith (New York: Routledge, 1999), 1–25. See also *Lesbian Pulp Fiction: The Sexually Intrepid World of Lesbian Paperback Novels, 1950–1965*, ed. Katherine V. Forrest (San Francisco: Cleis, 2006).

195   Gabriele Griffin: Griffin, *Heavenly Love?*, 48.

196   House of Shades: Maureen Duffy, *The Microcosm* [1966] (London: Virago, 1988), 14, 286, 70–98, 21–22. Two other bar-centered novels are Marie-Claire Blais, *Les Nuits de l'Underground* (1978; in English, *Nights in the Underground*), and Nisa Donnelly, *The Bar Stories: A Novel After All* (1989).

197   But from the 1970s: Of course, this harked back to much older fantasies about, say, Sappho's Lesbos. And the idea does come up in some earlier titles, even pulp ones. One example is Randy Salem's trashy *Man Among Women*

(1960), in which Alison and her aunt/lover Maxine have planned but not yet built their all-lesbian resort on a tiny Bahamanian island . . . when Maxine has to sacrifice herself to a barracuda so the hero can carry the wounded Alison to safety.

197   "all women": June Arnold, *Sister Gin* (London: Women's Press, 1975), 92.

197   "hillwomen": See Diane Griffin Crowder, "Separatism and Feminist Utopian Fiction," in *Sexual Practice, Textual Theory: Lesbian Cultural Criticism*, ed. Susan J. Wolfe and Julia Penelope (Cambridge, Mass.: Blackwell, 1993), 237–50.

197   The first lesbian historical: There are some earlier examples of lesbian-themed fiction set in past eras: Hope Mirrlees, *Madeleine: One of Love's Jansenists* (1919); Naomi Mitchison, "The Delicate Fire" (1933); Maude Meagher, *The Green Scamander* (1933); Sylvia Townsend Warner, *Summer Will Show* (1936); and Kate O'Brien, *As Music and Splendour* (1958). But it was only in the late 1960s that openly lesbian novelists began to consciously invent a past for their community.

197   Paradoxically: "Any stone from their hill is a crystal ball," Miller wrote in the afterword, and this was not just a metaphor: she and her partner Elizabeth Deran, in a fascinatingly collaborative and intuitive process, used a Ouija board to call up Brundidge and Willson and interview them. "Isabel Miller" (Alma Routsong), *Patience and Sarah* [titled *A Place for Us* in 1969], intro. by Emma Donoghue (Vancouver: Arsenal Pulp Press, 2005), 202, 211–14.

197   "I figure to take up land": Miller, *Patience and Sarah*, 47–48, 72, 128, 116.

198   "I held Sarah's hand": Miller, *Patience and Sarah*, 146, 183–84, 33–34, 38–39.

199   Isabel Miller intended: Miller, in a note on the fragment of it she did publish, "A Dooryard Full of Flowers," in *A Dooryard Full of Flowers* (Tallahassee, Fla.: Naiad, 1993).

199   One example: Other examples include Ellen Galford, *Moll Cutpurse, Her True History* (1984), Doris Grumbach, *The Ladies* (1984), and Morgan Graham, *These Lovers Fled Away* (1988), all of which are about the eighteenth-century Ladies of Llangollen. The following titles are about lesbians who pass as men in settings that range from 1730s Germany to 1940s America: Jeannine Allard, *Légende* (1984); Caeia March, *The Hide and Seek Files* (1988); Ingrid MacDonald, "The Catherine Trilogy" (1991); Caro Clarke, *The Wolf Ticket* (1998); Judith Katz, *The Escape Artist* (1997); and Jackie Kay, *Trumpet* (2000). Some novels (by, for instance, Fiona Cooper, Anne Cameron, and Elana Dykewomon) situate a butch-femme couple within a community of kindred spirits.

199   Sometimes the research: Two examples that stand out are Jan Clausen, *The Prosperine Papers* (1988) and Stevie Davies, *Impassioned Clay* (1999).

200   In several novels: Jane Chambers, *Burning* (1978); Caeia March, *Fire! Fire!* (1992); Molleen Zanger, *Gardenias Where There Are None* (1994).

200   "It's for your education": Paula Martinac, *Out of Time* (Seattle, Wash.: Seal Press, 1990), 55.

200   "terms": Sybille Bedford, *A Compass Error* [1968] (London: Virago, 1984), 179.

201   The defiant lesbian hero: Griffin, *Heavenly Love?*, 69.

201   "this label": Brown, *Rubyfruit*, 107.

201   "the proper word": Ali Smith, *Girl Meets Boy* (Edinburgh: Canongate, 2007), 77. Compare the famous coming-out episode of *Ellen* ("The Puppy Episode," Series 4, April 1997): When her friend asks whether they should now call her gay or lesbian, she says, "Call me Ellen."

201   "What does it matter": Ebba Haslund, *Nothing Happened* [1948], trans. Barbara Wilson (Seattle, Wash.: Seal Press, 1987), 108–9, 133.

202   "formula fictions": Julie Abraham, *Are Girls Necessary? Lesbian Writing and Modern Histories* (New York: Routledge, 1996), xix, 3–6.

SELECT BIBLIOGRAPHY

Primary Sources

I have included all the texts I discuss in any detail, but not those I only refer to once (unless they are extremely important for some reason). I have taken the unusual step of listing these not alphabetically by author, but roughly in order of composition, so as to provide a timeline of desire between women in literature.

The Book of Ruth. King James Version. 1611.

Barnard, Mary, trans. *Sappho: A Translation*. Boston and London: Shambhala, 1994.

Plato. *The Symposium*. In *The Collected Dialogues of Plato*, ed. Edith Hamilton and Huntingdon Ciarns, 526–74. Princeton, N.J.: Princeton University Press, 1961.

Ovid. *Metamorphoses*. Trans. Mary M. Innes. Harmondsworth, U.K.: Penguin, 1955.

Ovid. "Sappho to Phaon" (Epistle XV). In *Heroides*, trans. Harold Isbell, 131–45. London: Penguin, 1990.

Guillaume de Blois, *Alda* [c. 1170], summarized and quoted in Paul Barrette, *Robert de Blois's Floris et Lyriopé*, 60–65. (Berkeley: University of California Press, 1968).

Marie de France. *Eliduc* [before 1189]. In *The Lais of Marie de France*, trans. Glyn S. Burgess and Keith Busby, 111–26. Harmondsworth, U.K.: Penguin, 1986.

Blois, Robert de. *Floris et Lyriopé* [1200s]. Ed. Paul Barrette. Berkeley: University of California Press, 1968.

Anon. *Roman d'Ysaïe le Triste* [1300s]. Ed. André Giacchetti. Rouen: Press of the University of Rouen, 1989.

Anon. *La Chanson d'Yde et Olive* [before 1311]. In *The Ancient, Honorable, Famous, and delightfull Historie of Huon of Bordeaux*, trans. Lord Berners [c. 1534], 3rd ed., chapters 167–70 [n.p.]. London: for Edward White, 1601.

Chaucer, Geoffrey. "The Man of Law's Tale" [1400]. In *The Complete Works of Geoffrey Chaucer*, ed. F. N. Robinson, 62–75. Oxford: Oxford University Press, 1974.

Ariosto, Ludovico. *Orlando Furioso* [1516–32]. Trans. John Harrington [1591]. Edited by Robert McNulty. Oxford: Clarendon, 1972.

Amadis de Gaule (1540 to after 1594), 24 vols. by various hands.

Montemayor, Jorge de. *Diana* [1559]. Trans. Bartholomew Yong [1598]. In *A Critical Edition of Yong's Translation of George of Montemayor's Diana and Gil Polo's Enamoured Diana*. Ed. Judith M. Kennedy. Oxford: Clarendon Press, 1968.

Warner, William. *Albion's England*. London: 1586.

Lodge, Thomas. *Rosalynde* [1590], 2nd ed. [1592], facsimile reprint. Menston, U.K.:
    The Scholar Press, 1972.

Lyly, John. *Gallathea 1592*. Malone Society Reprints. Oxford: Oxford University
    Press, 1998.

Sidney, Sir Philip. *The Countess of Pembroke's Arcadia (The New Arcadia)* [1593]. Edited
    by Victor Skretkowicz. Oxford: Clarendon, 1987.

Greene, Robert. *James the Fourth* (1598). In *The Plays and Poems of Robert Greene*, ed.
    J. Churton Collins, 2 vols., 2:79–158. Oxford: Clarendon, 1905.

Shakespeare, William. *A Midsummer Night's Dream* (1600). In *The Complete Works of
    William Shakespeare*, ed. Peter Alexander, 198–222. London: Collins, 1978.

———. *As You Like It* (1623). In *The Complete Works of William Shakespeare*, ed. Peter
    Alexander, 254–83. London: Collins, 1978.

———. *Twelfth Night* (1623). In *The Complete Works of William Shakespeare*, ed. Peter
    Alexander, 349–76. London: Collins, 1978.

Chapman, George. *Monsieur D'Olive* (1606). In *The Plays of George Chapman: The
    Comedies: A Critical Edition*, ed. Allan Holaday, assisted by Michael Kiernan,
    397–471. Urbana: University of Illinois Press, 1970.

D'Urfé, Honoré. *L'Astrée* (1607–27). Ed. Hugues Vaganay, 5 vols. Geneva: Slatkine
    Reprints, 1966.

Heywood, Thomas. *The Golden Age* [1611]. In *The Golden and Silver Ages*, ed. J. Payne
    Collier, 1–87. London: Shakespeare Society, 1851.

Middleton, Thomas. *No Wit, No Help Like a Woman's* [written c. 1611, published
    1653]. Ed. Lowell E. Johnson. Regents Renaissance Drama Series. Lincoln:
    University of Nebraska Press, 1976.

Carlell, Lodowick. *The Deserving Favourite* [1629]. In Charles Gray, *Lodowick Carlell:
    His Life, a Discussion of His Plays, and "The Deserving Favourite."* Chicago:
    University of Chicago Press, 1905.

Fletcher, John. *The Pilgrim* [1622], ed. Cyrus Hoy. In *The Dramatic Works in the
    Beaumont and Fletcher Canon*, 10 vols., ed. Fredson Boyers, 6:111–224. Cambridge:
    Cambridge University Press, 1985.

Ford, John. *The Lover's Melancholy* [1629]. Ed. R. F. Hill. Manchester, U.K.:
    Manchester University Press, 1985.

Shirley, James. *The Bird in a Cage* [1633]. Ed. Frances Frazier Senescu. New York:
    Garland, 1980.

Shakespeare, William, and John Fletcher. *The Two Noble Kinsmen* [1634]. Ed. Eugene
    M. Waith. Oxford: Clarendon Press, 1989.

Benserade, Isaac de. *Iphis et Iante* [1637]. Ed. Anne Verdier with Christian Biet and
    Lise Leibacher-Ouvrard. Vijon: Editions Lampasque/Desclée de Brouwer, 2000.

Suckling, Sir John. *Brennoralt*. London: for Humphrey Moseley, 1646.

Shirley, James. *The Doubtfull Heir*. In *Six New Playes*. London: for Humphrey
    Robinson and Humphrey Moseley, 1653.

Cowley, Abraham. *Love's Riddle*. London: for Henry Seile, 1638.

Fletcher, John. *The Loyal Subject* (1647). In *The Dramatic Works in the Beaumont and*

Fletcher Canon, ed. Fredson Boyers, 5:151–288. Cambridge: Cambridge University Press, 1996.

Zayas y Sotomayor, María de. "Love for the Sake of Conquest." In *The Disenchantments of Love* [1647], trans. H. Patsy Boyers, 203–43 Albany: State University of New York Press, 1997.

Davenant, Sir William. *Love and Honour* [1649]. In *Love and Honour* and *The Siege of Rhodes*, ed. James W. Tupper. Boston: D. C. Heath & Co., 1909.

Wallen, Leonard. *Astraea; or, True Love's Myrrour*. London: for Henry Cripps and Lodowick Lloyd, 1651.

Carlell, Lodowick. *The Passionate Lovers*. London: for Humphrey Moseley, 1655.

Cavendish, Margaret (Duchess of Newcastle). *Matrimonial Trouble*. In *Playes*. London: John Martyn et al., 1662.

———. *The Convent of Pleasure* and *The Presence*. In *Plays, Never Before Printed*. London: A. Maxwell, 1668.

Trotter (later Cockburn), Catherine. *Agnes de Castro* (1696). Facsimile reprint in *The Plays of Mary Pix and Catherine Trotter*, ed. Edna Steeves, 2 vols., 2:1–47. New York: Garland, 1982.

Pix, Mary. *Queen Catharine* (1698). Facsimile reprint in *The Plays of Mary Pix and Catherine Trotter*, ed. Edna Steeves, 1:1–52.

Hamilton, Anthony. *Memoirs of the Life of Count Grammont*. Trans. Abel Boyer. London: n.p., 1714.

Rowe, Nicholas. *The Tragedy of Jane Shore* [1714]. Facsimile of 1914 edition. Menston, U.K.: Scholar Press, 1973.

Barker, Jane. "The Unaccountable Wife" (1723). In *The Galesia Trilogy and Selected Manuscript Poems of Jane Barker*, ed. Carol Shiner Wilson, 49–173. New York: Oxford University Press, 1997.

Haywood, Eliza. *The Rash Resolve*. London: n.p., 1724.

Anon. *The Travels and Adventures of Mlle de Richelieu*, 3 vols. London: for M. Cooper, 1744.

MacCarthy, Charlotte. *The Fair Moralist*. London: the author, 1745.

Fielding, Henry. *The Female Husband* (1746). In *Chloe Plus Olivia: An Anthology of Lesbian Literature from the Seventeenth Century to the Present*, ed. Lillian Faderman, 143–57. New York: Viking, 1994. Also in *The Literature of Lesbianism*, ed. Terry Castle, 272–85.

Fielding, Sarah. *Letters between the Principal Characters in "David Simple," and some Others*. London: the author, 1747.

———. *The Governess* [1749]. London: Pandora, 1987.

Charke, Charlotte. *A Narrative of the Life of Mrs. Charlotte Charke* [1755]. Gainesville, Fla.: Scholars' Facsimiles and Reprints, 1969.

Johnson, Samuel. *The History of Rasselas, Prince of Abyssinia* [1759]. Ed. D. J. Enright. Harmondsworth, U.K.: Penguin, 1976.

Diderot, Denis. *The Nun* [1796]. Trans. Leonard Tancock. London: Penguin, 1974.

Rousseau, Jean-Jacques. *Julie; or, The New Héloïse* [1761]. Trans. Philip Stewart and

Jean Vache. Hanover, N.H.: University Press of New England (Dartmouth College), 1997.

Scott, Sarah. *A Description of Millenium Hall* [1762]. London: Pandora, 1986.

Laclos, Pierre Choderlos de. *Les Liaisons Dangereuses* [1782]. Trans. P. W. K. Stone. London: Penguin, 1961.

Lennox, Charlotte. *Euphemia*, 4 vols. London: for T. Cadell and J. Evans, 1790.

Sade, Marquis de, *Juliette* [1797–1801]. Trans. Austryn Wainhouse. New York: Grove Press, 1968.

Coleridge, Samuel Taylor. *Christabel* (1816). In *The Literature of Lesbianism*, ed. Terry Castle, 360–79. New York: Columbia University Press, 2003.

Brown, Charles Brockden. *Ormond; or, The Secret Witness* [1799]. Ed. Mary Chapman. Peterborough, Ont.: Broadview, 1999.

Edgeworth, Maria. *Belinda* [1801]. London: Pandora, 1986.

Musset, Alfred de. *Gamiani* [1833]. London: n.p., 1908.

Balzac, Honoré de. *The Girl with Golden Eyes* [1835]. Trans. Carol Cosman. New York: Carroll & Graf, 1998.

Gautier, Théophile. *Mademoiselle de Maupin* [1835]. Trans. Helen Constantine. London: Penguin, 2005.

Brontë, Charlotte. *Jane Eyre* [1847]. London: Collins, 1950.

———. *Shirley* [1849]. Ed. Herbert Rosengarten and Margaret Smith. Oxford: Clarendon Press, 1979.

Longfellow, Henry Wadsworth. *Kavanagh* [1849]. Boston: Ticknor, Reed and Fields, 1853.

Dickens, Charles. *Little Dorrit* [1857]. London: Collins, 1958.

Collins, Wilkie. *The Woman in White* [1859–60]. Ed. Julian Symons. Harmondsworth, U.K.: Penguin, 1974.

Gaskell, Elizabeth, "The Grey Woman" (1861). In *Cousin Phillis*, 300–61. New York: AMS Press, 1972.

Trollope, Anthony. *Can You Forgive Her?* (1864–65). London: Penguin, 1986.

Phelps, Elizabeth Stuart. *Hedged In*. Boston: Fields, Osgood & Co., 1870.

Belot, Adolphe. *Mademoiselle Giraud, My Wife* [1870]. Trans. Christopher Rivers. New York: Modern Language Association of America, 2002.

Hardy, Thomas. *Desperate Remedies* [1871]. London: Macmillan, 1912.

Le Fanu, Joseph Sheridan. *Carmilla* (1872). In *Chloe Plus Olivia: An Anthology of Lesbian Literature from the Seventeenth Century to the Present*, ed. Lillian Faderman, 303–62. New York: Viking, 1994.

Alcott, Louisa May. *Work*, 2 vols. London: Sampson Low, 1873.

Linton, Eliza Lynn. *The Rebel of the Family* [1880]. Peterborough, Ont.: Broadview, 2002.

Zola, Emile. *Nana* [1880]. Trans. Douglas Parmée. Oxford: Oxford University Press, 1998.

Moore, George. *A Drama in Muslin* [1886]. Gerrards Cross, U.K.: Colin Smythe, 1981.

James, Henry. *The Bostonians* [1886]. New York: Bantam Classic, 1984.

Wilkins (later Freeman), Mary E. "Two Friends" (1887). In *Chloe Plus Olivia*, ed. Lillian Faderman, 77–87.

Haggard, H. Rider. *Allan's Wife* [1889]. London: Hodder and Stoughton, 1914.

Mendès, Catulle. *Méphistophéla*. Paris: E. Dentu, 1890.

Holdsworth, Annie E. *Joanna Traill, Spinster*. London: William Heinemann, 1894.

Johnstone, Edith. *A Sunless Heart*. Ed. Constance D. Harsh. Peterborough, Ont.: Broadview Editions, 2008.

Wilkins (later Freeman), Mary E. "The Long Arm" (1895). In *Chloe Plus Olivia*, ed. Lillian Faderman, 373–97.

Proust, Marcel. "Before Dark" (1896). In *The Literature of Lesbianism*, ed. Terry Castle, 581–84.

Carhart, John Wesley. *Norma Trist; or, Pure Carbon: A Story of the Inversion of the Sexes*. Austin, Texas: Eugene von Boeckmann, 1895.

Converse, Florence. *Diana Victrix*. Boston: Houghton Mifflin, 1897.

Vaudère, Jane de la. *Les Demi-sexes*. Paris: Paul Ollendorff, 1897.

Wilkins (later Freeman), Mary E. "The Tree of Knowledge" (1899). In *The Love of Parson Lord*, 85–140. New York: Harper & Bros., 1900.

Colette. *Claudine at School* [1900]. London: Penguin, 1963.

———. *Claudine en ménage*. Paris: Ollendorf, 1902.

Montfort, Charles. *Le Journal d'une saphiste*. Paris: Offenstadt, 1902.

Duc, Aimée. *Sind es Frauen?* Berlin: Eckstein, 1903.

Mulholland, Rosa (Lady Gilbert). *The Tragedy of Chris*. London: Sands & Co., 1903.

Meade, L. T. *The Sorceress of the Strand*. London: Ward, Lock & Co., 1903.

Vivien, Renée. "Prince Charming" (1904). In *The Woman of the Wolf*, trans. Karla Jay and Yvonne M. Klein, 23–28. New York: Gay, 1983.

Vivien, Renée. *A Woman Appeared to Me* [1904], trans. Jeannette H. Foster. Reno, Nev.: Naiad, 1976.

Henry, O. [William Sydney Porter]. "The Last Leaf" (1906). In *The World of O. Henry: The Furnished Room and Other Stories*. London: Hodder and Stoughton, 1974.

Freeman, Mary E. Wilkins. *By the Light of the Soul*. New York: Harper's, 1907.

Wells, Catherine, "The Beautiful House." In *Harper's Monthly Magazine* (March 1912): 503–11 (505, 509).

St. John, Christopher [Christabel Marshall]. *Hungerheart: The Story of a Soul*. London: Methuen, 1915.

Dane, Clemence [Winifred Ashton]. *Regiment of Women* [1917]. Westport, Conn.: Greenwood Press, 1978.

Weirauch, Anna Elisabet. *The Scorpion* [1932, rev. 1948]. Abridged and translated by Whittaker Chambers. New York: Arno Press, 1975.

———. *The Outcast* [1933, rev. 1948]. Abridged and translated by Guy Endore. New York: Arno Press, 1975.

Lawrence, D. H. *The Fox* [1922]. London: Sphere, 1968.

Stevenson, Sylvia. *Surplus.* London: Longmans, Green & Co., 1924.

Bourdet, Edouard. *The Captive* [1925]. Trans. Arthur Hornblow. New York: Brentano's, 1926.

Burke, Thomas. "The Pash." In *East of Mansion House*, 37–64. New York: George H. Doran, 1926. Reprinted in *The Literature of Lesbianism*, ed. Terry Castle, 791–800.

Lacretelle, Jacques de. *Marie Bonifas* [1925]. London: Putnam's, 1927.

Olivier, Edith. *The Love Child* [1927]. London: Virago, 1981.

Sayers, Dorothy L. *Unnatural Death.* London: Ernest Benn, 1927.

Beer, Thomas. "Hallowe'en." In *Mrs. Egg and Other Barbarians* [1927]. London: Cassell, 1934.

Hall, Radclyffe. *The Well of Loneliness* [1928]. London: Virago, 1982.

Mitchell, Gladys. *Speedy Death.* London: Victor Gollancz, 1929.

Thayer, Tiffany. *Thirteen Women.* New York: Claude Kendall, 1932.

Winsloe, Christa. *The Child Manuela* [1934]. Trans. Agnes Neill Scott. London: Virago, 1994.

Hellman, Lillian. *The Children's Hour* [1934]. In *The Collected Plays*, 1–69. Boston: Little, Brown, 1972.

O'Brien, Kate. *Mary Lavelle.* London: William Heinemann, Ltd., 1936.

Bates, H. E. "Breeze Anstey" (1937). In *Country Tales: Collected Short Stories.* London: Readers' Union, 1938.

Baker, Dorothy Dodds. *Trio.* Boston: Houghton Mifflin, 1943.

Sinclair, Jo [Ruth Seid]. *Wasteland* [1946]. New York: Jewish Publication Society, 1987.

Asquith, Cynthia. "The Lovely Voice." In *This Mortal Coil: Tales* [aka *What Dreams May Come*], 203–27. Sauk City, Wis.: Arkham House, 1947.

Lawrence, Hilda [Hildegarde Kronmiller]. *Death of a Doll.* London: Chapman & Hall, 1948.

Haslund, Ebba. *Nothing Happened* [1948]. Trans. Barbara Wilson. Seattle, Wash.: Seal Press, 1987.

Olivia [Dorothy Strachey Bussy]. *Olivia* [1949]. London: The Reader's Union–The Hogarth Press, 1950.

Tey, Josephine [Elizabeth Mackintosh]. *To Love and Be Wise* [1950]. London: P. Davies, 1966.

Morgan, Claire [Patricia Highsmith]. *The Price of Salt* [1952]. Reprinted as *Carol.* London: Penguin, 1991.

Packer, Vin [Marijane Meaker]. *Strange Fire* [1952]. San Francisco: Cleis, 2004.

Mahyère, Eveline. *I Will Not Serve* [1958]. Trans. Antonia White. London: Virago, 1984.

Jackson, Shirley. *The Haunting of Hill House* [1959]. London: Michael Joseph, 1980.

McCarthy, Mary. *The Group* [1963]. New York: Avon, 1980.

Rendell, Ruth. *From Doon with Death* [1964]. London: Hutchinson, 1975.

Duffy, Maureen. *The Microcosm* [1966]. London: Virago, 1988.

Gardiner, Judy. *Fidelia.* In *The Power of Sergeant Mettleship* [1967], reprinted as *Waltzing Matilda*, 9–56. London: Sphere, 1972.

Select Bibliography

Bedford, Sybille. *A Compass Error* [1968]. London: Virago, 1984.

Miller, Isabel [Alma Routsong]. *A Place for Us* [1969]. Reprinted as *Patience and Sarah* [1972]. Vancouver: Arsenal Pulp Press, 2005.

Christie, Agatha. *Nemesis*. London: William Collins, 1971.

James, P. D. *Shroud for a Nightingale* [1971]. London: Penguin, 1989.

Brown, Rita Mae. *Rubyfruit Jungle* [1973]. New York: Bantam, 1977.

Arnold, June. *Sister Gin*. London: Women's Press, 1975.

Beal, M. F. *Angel Dance*. New York: Daughters Publishing Co., 1977.

Rendell, Ruth. *A Sleeping Life*. New York: Doubleday, 1978.

Winterson, Jeanette. *Oranges Are Not the Only Fruit*. London: Pandora, 1985.

Forrest, Katherine V. *Murder at the Nightwood Bar* [1987]. Tallahassee, Fla.: Naiad, 1995.

———. "O Captain, My Captain." In *Dreams and Swords*, 107–65. Tallahassee, Fla.: Naiad, 1987.

Winterson, Jeanette. *The Passion* [1987]. London: Penguin, 1988.

Flagg, Fannie. *Fried Green Tomoatoes at the Whistlestop Café* [1987]. London: Vintage, 1992.

Martinac, Paula. *Out of Time*. Seattle, Wash.: Seal Press, 1990.

Lavery, Bryony. *Her Aching Heart, Two Marias* and *Wicked*. London: Methuen, 1991.

Gomez, Jewelle. *The Gilda Stories* [1991]. London: Sheba, 1992.

Waters, Sarah. *Tipping the Velvet*. London: Virago, 1998.

———. *Affinity*. London: Virago, 1999.

———. *Fingersmith*. London: Virago, 2002.

Smith, Ali. *Girl Meets Boy*. Edinburgh: Canongate, 2007.

Secondary Sources

Andreadis, Harriette. *Sappho in Early Modern England: Female Same-Sex Literary Erotics, 1550–1714*. Chicago: University of Chicago Press, 2001.

Auchmuty, Rosemary. *A World of Girls*. London: Women's Press, 1992.

Brooten, Bernadette. *Love Between Women: Early Christian Responses to Female Homoeroticism*. Chicago: University of Chicago Press, 1996.

Casselaer, Catherine von. *Lot's Wife: Lesbian Paris, 1890–1914*. Liverpool: Janus Press, 1986.

Castle, Terry. *The Apparitional Lesbian: Female Homosexuality and Modern Culture*. New York: Columbia University Press, 1993.

Castle, Terry, ed. *The Literature of Lesbianism: A Historical Anthology from Ariosto to Stonewall*. New York: Columbia University Press, 2003.

Cestaro, Gary P., ed. *Queer Italia: Same-Sex Desire in Italian Literature and Film*. New York: Palgrave Macmillan, 2004.

Curtin, Kaier. *"We Can Always Call Them Bulgarians": The Emergence of Lesbians and Gay Men on the American Stage*. Boston: Alyson, 1987.

Cryle, Peter. *The Telling of the Act: Sexuality as Narrative in Eighteenth- and Nineteenth-Century France.* Newark: University of Delaware Press, and London: Associated University Presses, 2001.

DeJean, Joan. *Fictions of Sappho, 1546–1937.* Chicago: University of Chicago Press, 1989.

Donoghue, Emma. *Passions Between Women: British Lesbian Culture, 1668–1801* [1993]. New York: HarperCollins, 1996.

Duncker, Patricia. *Sisters and Strangers: An Introduction to Contemporary Feminist Fiction.* Oxford: Blackwell, 1992.

Emery, Kim. *The Lesbian Index: Pragmatism and Lesbian Subjectivity in the Twentieth-Century United States.* Albany: State University of New York Press, 2002.

Faderman, Lillian. *Surpassing the Love of Men: Romantic Friendship and Love Between Women from the Renaissance to the Present* [1981]. London: Women's Press, 1985.

Faderman, Lillian, ed. *Chloe Plus Olivia: An Anthology of Lesbian Literature from the Seventeenth Century to the Present.* New York: Viking, 1994.

Faderman, Lillian, and Brigitte Eriksson, eds. *Lesbian-Feminism in Turn-of-the-Century Germany.* Tallahassee, Fla.: Naiad, 1980.

Farwell, Marilyn R. *Heterosexual Plots and Lesbian Narratives.* New York: New York University Press, 1996.

Foster, Jeannette H. *Sex Variant Women in Literature* [1956], 4th ed. Tallahassee, Fla.: Naiad, 1985.

Garber, Marjorie. *Vested Interests: Cross-dressing and Cultural Anxiety.* New York: Routledge, 1992.

———. *Vice Versa: Bisexuality and the Eroticism of Everyday Life.* New York: Simon and Schuster, 1995.

Griffin, Gabriele. *Heavenly Love? Lesbian Images in Twentieth-Century Women's Writing.* Manchester, U.K.: Manchester University Press, 1993.

Harris, Joseph. *Hidden Agendas: Cross-dressing in 17th-Century France.* Biblio 17, 156. Tübingen: Gunter Narr Verlag, 2005.

Inness, Sherrie A. *The Lesbian Menace: Ideology, Identity and the Representation of Lesbian Life.* Amherst: University of Massachusetts Press, 1997.

Jagose, Annamarie. *Inconsequence: Lesbian Representation and the Logic of Sexual Sequence.* Ithaca, N.Y.: Cornell University Press, 2002.

Katz, Jonathan Ned. *Gay/Lesbian Almanac.* New York: Harper and Row, 1983.

Kent, Kathryn A. *Making Girls into Women: American Writing and the Rise of Lesbian Identity.* Durham, N.C.: Duke University Press, 2003.

Koppelman, Susan, ed. *Women's Friendship: A Collection of Short Stories.* Norman: University of Oklahoma Press, 1991.

Lanser, Susan. "Befriending the Body: Female Intimacies as Class Acts." *Eighteenth-Century Studies* 32:2 (1998–99): 179–98.

———. "Sapphic Picaresque, Sexual Difference, and the Challenges of Homo-Adventuring." *Textual Practice* 15:2 (2001): 251–68.

Marcus, Sharon. *Between Women: Friendship, Desire and Marriage in Victorian England.*
Princeton, N.J.: Princeton University Press, 2007.

Marks, Elaine, and George Stambolian, eds. *Homosexualities and French Literature.*
Ithaca, N.Y.: Cornell University Press, 1979.

Merrick, Jeffrey, and Michael Sibalis, eds. *Homosexuality in French History and Culture.*
Binghamton, N.Y.: Harrington Park Press, 2001.

Moore, Lisa L. *Dangerous Intimacies: Towards a Sapphic History of the British Novel.*
Durham, N.C.: Duke University Press, 1997.

Munt, Sally. *Murder by the Book? Feminism and the Crime Novel.* London: Routledge,
1994.

Palmer, Paulina. *Contemporary Lesbian Writing: Dreams, Desire, Difference.*
Buckingham, U.K.: Open University Press, 1993.

———. *Lesbian Gothic: Transgressive Fictions.* London and New York: Cassell, 1999.

Palumbo-DeSimone, Christine. *Sharing Secrets: Nineteenth-Century Women's Relations
in the Short Story.* London: Associated University Presses, 2000.

Rivers, Christopher. "*Inintelligibles pour une femme honnête:* Sexuality, Textuality and
Knowledge in Diderot's 'La Religieuse' and Gautier's 'Mademoiselle de
Maupin,' " *The Romanic Review* 86:1 (January 1995): 1–29.

Roberts, Anna. *Queer Love in the Middle Ages.* Basingstoke, U.K.: Palgrave Macmillan,
2005.

Robinson, Christopher. *Scandal in the Ink: Male and Female Homosexuality in Twentieth-
Century French Literature.* London: Cassell, 1995.

Robinson, David M. *Closeted Writing and Lesbian and Gay Literature: Classical, Early
Modern, Eighteenth-Century.* Aldershot, U.K.: Ashgate Publishing, 2006.

Rohy, Valerie. *Impossible Women: Lesbian Figures and American Literature.* Ithaca, N.Y.:
Cornell University Press, 2000.

Rule, Jane. *Lesbian Images* [1975]. London: Pluto Press, 1989.

Schwarz, Kathryn. *Tough Love: Amazon Encounters in the English Renaissance.* Durham,
N.C.: Duke University Press, 2000.

Schleiner, Winfried. "Male Cross-Dressing and Transvestism in Renaissance
Romances." *The Sixteenth Century Journal* 19:4 (Winter 1988): 605–19.

———. "Le feu caché: Homosocial Bonds Between Women in a Renaissance
Romance." *Renaissance Quarterly* 45:2 (Summer 1992): 293–311.

Sedgwick, Eve. *Epistemology of the Closet.* Berkeley: University of California Press, 1990.

Shannon, Laurie. *Sovereign Amity: Figures of Friendship in Shakespearean Contexts.*
Chicago: University of Chicago Press, 2002.

Smith, Patricia Juliana. *Lesbian Panic: Homoeroticism in Modern British Women's
Fiction.* New York: Columbia University Press, 1997.

Taylor, Karen J., ed. *Gender Transgressions: Crossing the Normative Barrier in Old French
Literature.* New York: Garland Publishing, 1998.

Todd, Janet. *Women's Friendship in Literature.* New York: Columbia University Press,
1980.

Traub, Valerie. *The Renaissance of Lesbianism in Early Modern England*. Cambridge: Cambridge University Press, 2002.

Trotter, David. "Lesbians Before Lesbianism: Sexual Identity in Early Twentieth-Century British Fiction." In *Borderlines: Genders and Identities in War and Peace, 1870–1930*, ed. Billie Melman, 193–211. New York: Routledge, 1998.

Turner, James. *Schooling Sex: Libertine Literature and Erotic Education in Italy, France and England, 1534–1685*. Oxford: Oxford University Press, 2003.

Vanita, Ruth. *Sappho and the Virgin Mary: Same-Sex Love and the English Literary Imagination*. New York: Columbia University Press, 1996.

Vicinus, Martha. *Intimate Friends: Women Who Loved Women, 1778–1928*. Chicago: University of Chicago Press, 2004.

Waelti-Walters, Jennifer. *Damned Women: Lesbians in French Novels, 1796–1996*. Montreal: McGill-Queens University Press, 2000.

Wahl, Elizabeth Susan. *Invisible Relations: Representations of Female Intimacy in the Age of Enlightenment*. Stanford, Calif.: Stanford University Press, 1999.

Walen, Denise A. *Constructions of Female Homoeroticism in Early Modern Drama*. New York: Palgrave Macmillan, 2005.

Wolfe, Susan J., and Julia Penelope, eds. *Sexual Practice, Textual Theory: Lesbian Cultural Criticism*. Cambridge, Mass.: Blackwell, 1993.

Zimmerman, Bonnie. *The Safe Sea of Women: Lesbian Fiction 1969–1989* [1990]. London: Onlywomen, 1992.

SUGGESTIONS FOR FURTHER READING

I warmly recommend the following titles (given in order of composition), because they are available and highly enjoyable.

Philip Sidney, *The Countess of Pembroke's Arcadia* (1593). In print from Oxford World's Classics.

William Shakespeare, *As You Like It* (c. 1600). Widely available.

Samuel Richardson, *Clarissa* (1748–49). In print from Penguin Classics.

Jean-Jacques Rousseau, *Julie; or, The Nouvelle Héloïse* (1761). Full English translation in print from Dartmouth College Press.

Denis Diderot, *The Nun* (1796). In print from Penguin Classics and Everyman.

Honoré Balzac, *The Girl with the Golden Eyes* (1835). Widely available. Download free at http://www.gutenberg.org/etext/1659.

Wilkie Collins, *The Woman in White* (1859–60). Widely available.

Elizabeth Gaskell, "The Grey Woman" (1861). Full text at http://www.lang.nagoya-u.ac.jp/~matsuoka/EG-Grey.html.

Adolphe Belot, *Mademoiselle Giraud, My Wife* (1870). In print from the Modern Language Association.

Joseph Sheridan Le Fanu, *Carmilla* (1872). Widely available. Download free at http://www.gutenberg.org/etext/10007.

Henry James, *The Bostonians* (1886). Widely available.

H. Rider Haggard, *Allan's Wife* (1889). Widely available. Download free at http://www.gutenberg.org/etext/2727.

Mary E. Wilkins (later Freeman), "The Long Arm" (1895). Download free at http://home.comcast.net/~WilkinsFreeman/Short/LongArmD.htm.

D. H. Lawrence, *The Fox* (1922). Widely available.

Dorothy L. Sayers, *Unnatural Death* (1927). In print from HarperTorch and New English Library.

Radclyffe Hall, *The Well of Loneliness* (1928). In print from Virago and Wordsworth Classics.

Lillian Hellman, *The Children's Hour* (1934). Widely available.

Kate O'Brien, *Mary Lavelle* (1936). In print from Virago.

Dorothy Dodds Baker, *Trio* (1943). In print from Greenwood Press.

"Olivia" [Dorothy Strachey Bussy], *Olivia* (1949). In print from Cleis Press.

Hilda Lawrence, *Death of a Doll* (1948). In print from Pan Classic Crime.

Josephine Tey, *To Love and Be Wise* (1950). Widely available.

Patricia Highsmith (as "Claire Morgan"), *The Price of Salt,* aka *Carol* (1952). In print from Norton.

Shirley Jackson, *The Haunting of Hill House* (1959). Widely available.

"Isabel Miller" (Alma Routsong), *Patience and Sarah,* aka *A Place for Us* (1969). In print from Arsenal Pulp Press.

Rita Mae Brown, *Rubyfruit Jungle* (1973). In print from Bantam.

Jeanette Winterson, *The Passion* (1987). Widely available.

Katherine V. Forrest, *Murder at the Nightwood Bar* (1987). In print from Alyson.

Jewelle Gomez, *The Gilda Stories* (1991). In print from Firebrand.

Sarah Waters, *Affinity* (1999) and *Fingersmith* (2002). In print from Virago and Riverhead.

Finally, two invaluable anthologies, which include or excerpt many of the texts above:

Lillian Faderman, ed., *Chloe Plus Olivia: An Anthology of Lesbian Literature from the Seventeenth Century to the Present.* In print from Penguin.

Terry Castle, ed., *The Literature of Lesbianism.* In print from Columbia University Press.

INDEX

Page numbers in *italics* refer to illustrations.

picador.com

blog
videos
interviews
extracts